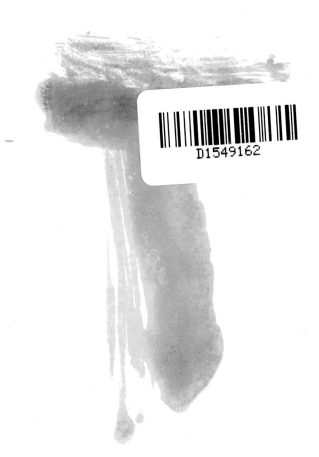

Goodbye Piccadilly'

Books by W. Macqueen-Pope

CARRIAGES AT ELEVEN

THEATRE ROYAL: THE BIOGRAPHY OF DRURY LANE

AN INDISCREET GUIDE TO THE THEATRE

HAYMARKET: THEATRE OF PERFECTION

TWENTY SHILLINGS IN THE POUND

IVOR: THE STORY OF AN ACHIEVEMENT

THE MELODIES LINGER ON

LADIES FIRST

GHOSTS AND GREASE PAINT

SHIRTFRONTS AND SABLES

FORTUNE'S FAVOURITE
(with D. L. Murray)

GAIETY: THEATRE OF ENCHANTMENT

PILLARS OF DRURY LANE

NIGHTS OF GLADNESS

BACK NUMBERS

GIVE ME YESTERDAY

MARIE LLOYD

THE FOOTLIGHTS FLICKERED

THE LIFE OF EDMUND KEAN

A CHILDREN'S BOOK OF THE THEATRE

W. Macqueen-Pope

'*Goodbye Piccadilly*'

DAVID & CHARLES : NEWTON ABBOT

ISBN 0 7153 5544 9

First published 1960
This second impression published 1972

B60 20774

Reproduced and printed in Great Britain
by Lowe & Brydone (Printers) Limited, London
for David & Charles (Publishers) Limited
South Devon House Newton Abbot Devon

To My Old and Valued Friend

SYDNEY W. WALTON

*who does so much good and asks no
thanks and to whose encouragement
and counsel I owe so much and
consequently make this humble
tribute in gratitude and affection*

Contents

Illustrations

A*

Illustrations (continued)

Explanation

First of all, why is this book called 'Goodbye Piccadilly'? Well, that is part of a song which our soldiers—and the whole nation—sang during the First World War. And what they sang was true—for that war altered not only Piccadilly but the whole of life. For many of the singers it was goodbye for ever. They never returned from the deadly mud of Flanders and France, the graveyard of Gallipoli, the bloodstained deserts of Mesopotamia and the Near East, the grey wastes of the Seven Seas, to see Piccadilly—or Piccadilly Circus, which is what most of them meant—again. Yet, in their lifetime, Piccadilly and its neighbourhood had changed and changed again—but somehow to them it had seemed the same. That is a national characteristic. Even Londoners who, by and large, show so little interest in their own city, somehow respond to Piccadilly. It means something to them—something they cannot explain—but it is there. To those who are not Londoners it means a lot more.

Every city in the world has its acknowledged centre, its summit, as it were, which it is absolutely essential for every visitor to see, for without a sight of it and actual presence on that spot, no tourist can claim to have really been in that city at all. Most of those spots are self-explanatory. Paris proudly proclaims the Champs Elysées, the Arc de Triomphe, the Eiffel Tower; Berlin boasts, or did in days gone by—its Unter den Linden; New York proffers the rival claims of Times Square and Broadway as its essence, and Venice relies on St Mark's Square and the Grand Canal. Vienna has its Prater, Rome its Corso and its ancient ruins like the Colosseum—Tsarist St Petersburg had the Nevski Prospect, and modern Moscow has its Kremlin and Red Square. Every city in the world has such places but none of them equals the marvel of Piccadilly Circus—for lure and magnetism.

Why this should be so is, at first glance, difficult to understand. Piccadilly Circus is very young as London goes. My great-grandfather, whom I both saw and knew, had seen it built. It has no great beauty of architecture, no important historical event has ever taken place there, such as occurred in the Place de la Bastille for instance—nobody of much fame has ever lived in Piccadilly Circus, indeed very few people have lived there at all. Yet it is the place which everybody simply has to visit, which it is imperative for them to see. Directly they reach London, they make for it. Its lure is irresistible and once they get there, it holds them tight. It is the last place to which they say goodbye when leaving London and they turn away with a sigh and lingering backward glances.

If you ask them why they fall under this spell, they will tell you that it is because they feel that this is the very centre of the world—not only of London or Britain—but that this is where they can hear the heart of the world beat as it can be heard nowhere else. They all say the same, all races, colours, creeds, speaking all sorts of languages and coming from the four corners of the earth. It is clear that to millions this place is the Third Magnetic Pole and naturally it is far more frequented than its two more inaccessible rivals to the North and South.

Piccadilly Circus has only one outstanding feature. That is the statue of Eros which stands in its centre and is therefore the very centre of the centre of the world. It is one of the best known statues of the whole world and certainly the most photographed. All day long the cameras click—nightfall does not stop them nowadays—and at last the operators turn away with a sigh of satisfaction. They have got pictures of Eros. They have got London on record, for that is what he means to them. Maybe they think he is an ancient monument. I know a very charming and highly cultured American lady who now lives most of her time in London, who was quite convinced, until I broke the spell, that Piccadilly Circus was so called because, in the distant past, a

Roman circus or amphitheatre had stood there and Eros had been part of it. That of course had no foundation. The Circus is modern, in the terms of London's age—and Eros is even more modern than the Circus. He only arrived there in 1893; I was a small boy starting school at the time. Though a handsome piece of work, he is no outstanding masterpiece, no rival to the art of Praxiteles. He is not made of marble but of aluminium. There he stands, this God of Love, poised on his pedestal, He has just loosed an arrow from his bow, as did that 'Cupid all arm'd, Flying twixt heaven and earth' of whom Oberon tells us in *A Midsummer Night's Dream*. According to the King of the Fairies, that Cupid 'loosed his loveshaft smartly from his bow as if to pierce a hundred thousand hearts'. Maybe that discharged and invisible arrow of the Piccadilly Eros has done the same, only his has pierced millions of hearts and does not seem to have come to earth yet. For the fascination which Eros works continues.

What is the real reason for it! That is one of the things which this book will endeavour to show, for it will try and explain this remarkable portion of London and to take you behind the scenes and below the surface. Let it be understood that it does not set out to be a guidebook, in the ordinary sense. It is merely an attempt to put on record a segment of that part of London known as the West End, from its beginning down to the present time, but to stress chiefly three periods: the Victorian, the Edwardian and Today.

It will pay very little attention to architecture and other guidebook matters but a good deal of attention to Humanity. The story of a place, whatever and wherever it may be, is largely the story of the people who lived there, worked there, played there and frequented it. Buildings decay or are destroyed, the faces of cities change—destruction under the camouflage of Progress is always going on, the Old Order must change and give place to New, as Alfred, Lord Tennyson told us. But the people who inhabit those places change very little basically. They pull down the old buildings, they have a feverish urge to eradicate all that a previous generation has built and substitute their own ideals—and they never stop to think that their work will meet with the same destruction so soon that many of them will live to see it.

London, so old in centuries, has so very little of its past left to go on show—a handful of notable landmarks which by their very glory defy the vandals, but so much of vital interest is swept away every year. That is a serious thing in many ways, and it is absurdly uneconomic in these days when there is an attempt to foster a tourist industry. More and more, as the modern years pass, London presents itself to visiting eyes as a city which looks just like any other modern city in the world—like Moose Jaw, Seattle, Medicine Hat, Rio de Janeiro, and even the cities in the Orient, save for the surroundings. That characteristic which made it London is being relentlessly erased, as buildings resembling flatirons, or the fragile houses we used to build of cards when children, tower above the remnants of Victorian and Edwardian London, marked for destruction as soon as possible—a London which was the centre of an Empire which exists no more. So does the day of mass production, the day of the machine, wipe out the day of individuality.

But it is not quite the same with the people. They alter in some respects, it is true. They have altered in the years since the Second World War more than in several centuries—but they still retain some basic resemblance to their forefathers. This chronicle will endeavour to throw the limelight on the men and women who have passed along Piccadilly and its neighbouring streets and who have circumnavigated Piccadilly Circus down the years. They are the actors, the streets and buildings are merely the scenery before which they perform. No play succeeds merely because of its scenery, what matters is the human drama which the actors provide. And there is plenty of that in this part of London—and before appropriate backcloths too.

Naturally there is no plot or consecutive story in this book but there is plenty of variety, tragedy, comedy and broad farce. We shall not linger unduly in the distant past, but it must take its

place because then the Londoners were making this portion of
their city and leaving their records imperishably in the place-
names. One cannot ignore the past, as so many people try to do
today. The past is the foundation of the present, you cannot have
one without the other. We know the past, we can see the present;
so far, only the future defeats us. Maybe science will alter all that.
That old simile which likens life to a road, along which we travel,
the past being behind us, the present the stretch we see before us,
and the future that which lies around the bend ahead, is already
out of date. For the man in the aeroplane can see beyond that
bend—to him the route is clear. . . .

But the past of London, save where preserved in the written
word or in pictures, is being swept away rapidly. All that remain
are certain blue plaques on walls—drawing not very clamant
attention to what once stood there or someone who lived there.
That is not very satisfying to visiting tourists but it is all they get.
It may well be that when the buildings which bear those plaques
are destroyed in their turn, even those tokens will vanish, as useless relics of something best forgotten, which has no place in the
restless nuclear age of speed which seeks, and succeeds, to time
itself.

But it is very important to know what manner of men and
women made the places through which one walks. Piccadilly and
all about it has changed since its birthday and is changing all the
time. I shall try and show what kind of people used that region,
especially in what were its greatest days—the latter part of the
reign of Queen Victoria, the Edwardian era and the years down
to the Great World Change, in 1914. I shall try and contrast them
with today and, believe me, the contrast is immense. I shall try
and show you what manner of people they were, how they
dressed, how they travelled, how they ate, drank, revelled and
died—and even what they carried in their pockets. I shall try and
describe their tastes and habits, their outlook on life, their morality
—how they made merry and how they mourned. I shall do my
best to make their background live before you; I have known

these places and these people and indeed have been one of them
for some sixty years and longer. Much of this book will be written
before a window which looks across Piccadilly Circus and down
Piccadilly itself. It will, I hope, be an intimate story of the people
of this land—a microcosm of social history—marking more
changes in those sixty years than Piccadilly had known in the
three preceding centuries.

It will present an ever changing scene—it is changing as the
book is being written—some of the last vestiges of the past are
falling before modernity. I want to leave a record of it as it has
been down some momentous years, to awaken the memories of
those who knew it in former days—to supply a view in retrospect
for those who come after. So I invite you to come with me for a
loiter through this part of London, when we shall see it as it is and,
more important still, as it used to be. I don't think you will find it
dull. I am in great request as an unofficial amateur guide by overseas visitors and take much pleasure in showing them round.
They give my name and address—which they mostly call
ADDress—to their friends, who when they come to this city
ring me up and ask me if I will do for them what I did for their
friends. I hasten to repeat that I do this for pleasure, not for gain.
It gives me pride and joy to take these visitors around and introduce them to nooks and corners of London which otherwise
they would not have seen, which, although not specified in guide
books, are the true essence of London. These people take the
keenest interest in being told why Bond Street is so-called, also
Coventry Street, the Haymarket, Shaftesbury Avenue—there is
always a reason. It is not much use visiting this great exhibition
known as London without a catalogue of the exhibits and one of
the smaller functions of this book is to provide for that want—not
in a dry-as-dust manner but in a chatty informal way, to give you
a sight of the British people as well as the city in which they live.

London is still the most romantic city in the world. You can still
turn a corner and step back a couple of centuries—not quite so
easily as before the Second World War—but it is still possible.

That is something I do for those who come walking with me and something I want to achieve in this book too. I did it with an American friend recently. I call him a friend although our acquaintance lasted for only a week or so. He is a professor in an American provincial university. He got into touch with me through a mutual friend, also an American, because primarily he wanted to be taken round Theatre Royal, Drury Lane—of which I am official historian. He did that trip and he seemed to be in love with London. It was his first visit. So I took him for some little walks on a few afternoons in what was a lovely summer. We went down St James's Street and I swung him round a corner and asked him to look at a wall there. To the ordinary passerby it is just a wall, but to those who know, it is the actual wall, still standing, of the dairy which supplied King Henry VIII with his butter, eggs and milk. Not far away from that corner we went round another.

We were suddenly right back in Regency Days. Nobody would have been surprised if Beau Brummell himself had stepped up and offered his snuff box. And only a few yards further on, we went under an archway—and there was an ancient coaching yard, with tiers of stabling and inclined ramps up which the horses walked. At any moment a stage coach, with its four steaming horses, might have rattled through the arch, hooves clinking on cobble stones and the guard blowing lustily on his 'yard o' tin'.

I took him down to the city and showed him some of the old by-ways and corners—I showed him Aldgate Pump and London Stone—and many other things. He was hypnotised and enchanted. 'This is just what we want to see', he said, 'but nobody tells us. We know all about the Changing of the Guard, Buckingham Palace, The Tower, The Abbey, St Paul's and the rest of the big show. But this—this is real London—behind the scenes.'

That is what I want this book to show you—the real London which has passed and is still passing round this way. For although London destroys so much of its past, there are little pockets and corners which hold on, defiant of progress, and believing in the beauty and dignity of their own times. Somehow even Londoners who have all the indifference of proximity to their own city, feel the magic of Piccadilly and Piccadilly Circus. Maybe, if they read this book, it will open their eyes to what those places mean in their heritage. Over a decade ago I wrote a book called *Twenty Shillings in the Pound*—which still sells merrily—and that put on record a vanishing section of English life—The Middle Classes. People of that class—and not only of that class—read it and had their memories revived. Tens of thousands of them have written to me about it from all parts of the world—from what had once been their Empire. They write to me still. Not only the aged and the middle aged found pleasure in it and still do so, but younger people who read it tell me it has enabled them to understand their parents, their elders, better than they had done before. That book had no plot or consecutive story, any more than this present volume has—but it gave great pleasure to British people and to a great number of Americans who were proud to have British blood in their veins and to learn what manner of people their grandfathers and grandmothers had been at home.

I am now trying to do for a certain district of London what *Twenty Shillings in the Pound* did for a certain class of people. I knew those people because I am one of them—I know that district because I have spent nearly all my life in it. But whereas *Twenty Shillings* has a mainly British appeal, this one is for all those who come to see Eros on his pedestal on his island in the centre of the world. They come from every strata of society and their name is legion. They are the unwitting slaves of Eros, and some of them realise that fact. I know a very eminent American lady who occupies a high position at home and who is always to the fore in good works of international scope. Naturally she often visits London. And the first thing she does on arrival is to make a beeline for Piccadilly Circus and sit at the feet of Eros, feeling the pulse of the world beat, feeling the world revolve and watching it pass by. That is what she says herself—also, that it puts her in tune with life and humanity in a way that nothing else can do. She is one of very, very many. . . . That is one of London's great attractions, something of immense value, and something which one fears may be in danger of destruction, if not now, then in the near future—for commercialism may beat imagination—it usually does. It is something which should be saved at all costs—but one fears the worst.

Why are Piccadilly and its circus so strangely alluring? Largely, I think, because of its curious name—such a foreign-sounding name to find in the heart of the greatest English city—which is still the greatest city in the world. Anyway, that is one of the many things which this book will seek to tell you as it draws a picture of London and the Londoners of that oddly named place. So will you come for a little voyage of exploration in and around this important corner of the West End? We shall not be hurried, that way we should see little and learn less. We shall proceed in a leisurely manner, chatting as we go and, I hope, getting to know each other. We shall have time to read, mark, learn and inwardly digest. The beauty of books is that there is no hurry—you are not bound by time—unlike television, the programme has not got to end at a certain moment and on the dot. So we can take a loiter, in book form, through this magical district—for magical it is to those who know it and to those who discover it anew. Those whose one desire is to get from one place to another at breakneck speed have nothing to do with us. We should suit them as little as they suit us. We want, not only to see London as it is today, but as it was yesterday and many yesterdays ago—to watch its crowds and have time to distinguish the ghosts which mingle with them—who once walked this way in the full flush of life and who have left their mark on the ether of its tapestry of remembrance. Also we want to hear what this section of London has to say to us, for it has seen so much, contained so much, changed so much and yet still retains its strange individuality. It speaks a universal language which anyone can understand, for it is the language of life and humanity itself. It speaks of romance, achievement and failure, success and disaster, laughter and tears, happiness and sorrow—things common to all races and tongues. And to those who have understanding and who feel akin to it, it speaks very clearly indeed.

If you will take me for your guide, we will pass along Piccadilly itself first and leave that magnetic pole of Piccadilly Circus to be our journey's end. But before we reach it we shall have passed through a pageant of strange places and things, odd characters of all kinds. Kings and Queens, great nobles, aristocrats and humble folk, great architects, men of the arts and professions, shopkeepers and their shops, the men and women who worked in them, and we shall glimpse the conditions under which they worked. We shall see carts, carriages, cars and vehicles of all kinds—the playhouses and music halls from whence came the songs inspired by this portion of London. We shall see great palaces, meet prostitutes, crooks, prizefighters, restaurateurs, wits, writers, authors, poets—observe brothels, banks and banquets, encounter young bloods, lovely ladies and flower girls—barmaids—the flotsam and jetsam of the streets—the buses, cabs and tubes and all that goes to make Piccadilly Circus and its tributary streets into the Hub of the World—the centre of that amazing, always wonderful palimpsest which is London Town. . . .

1

The Ghosts of Piccadilly

The most magical mile in London is that which is called Piccadilly. It is almost precisely a mile in length and every yard of it teems with stories—with steps in the progress of our nation. It takes a firm hold on the imagination of all people from overseas and also on the people from the provinces of this country. There is not the slightest doubt that the spring from which this romantic fascination bubbles is the curious name—Piccadilly. What does it mean? And an added bit of fascination is that nobody really knows, exactly. There is what seems to be a reasonable source—at any rate nobody is able to deny that it is incorrect.

Piccadilly, as a thoroughfare, is of no antiquity when viewed in the perspective of the age of London itself. It was not there at all when the Armada threatened our shores, at least, it was not there as Piccadilly. The district then was open country, fields, meadows, apple orchards, ditches and hedgerows and little streams. In the delightful old English way, those fields had names—such as 'The Great Field of St James's', 'St Martin's Field', Mewes Close, Scavenger's Close, St Giles' Field, Cunditt Meadow, Windmill Fields—and many of these names are preserved by the streets of today. There was actually a windmill in Windmill Fields—and a street called after it is there today—also a theatre. And it so happens that what is now Great Windmill Street was the actual birthplace of Piccadilly—or at any rate, its godfather who gave it its name.

There was a rough trackway which trickled along what is now Piccadilly, and was known as 'The Way from Colbroke (now Colnbrook) to London' and alternatively 'The Way from London to Reading'. Nobody called it Piccadilly. The district did not have a very good reputation. In the reign of James I, the local authorities were concerned about it, and from old registers and rate books one finds that round about 1606, they were clearing out the ditches and lopping the hedges because 'Thieves and harlots sheltered there to the destruction of the King's subjects in winter time—and in summer time all the harlots continue to lie there.' Although recent legislation has swept the harlots under cover, those old parish fathers did not conquer them. They continued to frequent Piccadilly for centuries. In Victorian and Edwardian days, if one wished to describe the calling of a 'Lady of the Town' one said she was 'On the Dilly'. As regards the thieves, they can still be found in and around Piccadilly. In the highly civilised atomic age of violence and sudden death in which we live, it is perfectly easy to be robbed, knocked on the head and even murdered in Piccadilly, although the hedges and ditches have long since gone.

The first mention of Piccadilly—only it is spelt 'Pickadilly'—occurs in the will of one Robert Baker, who departed this life in 1623. He had been a tailor and had done well. He bought land in and around what is now Great Windmill Street, for there he lived. He was charitable and gave money to his Parish Church, which was St Martin's. In legal documents he is described for a time as 'Tailor'. Then he retired and at once became described as 'Gentleman'. It was not possible in those days to be a tailor and a gentleman at the same time. In his will he is said to be of 'Pickadilly Hall'. That is the first we hear about Piccadilly. Why did he call his house 'Pickadilly Hall'? It is not absolutely certain that he did so—that name might have been applied to the whole of the property which he owned around Windmill Fields—and the houses there were the extreme western edge of London. They stood amongst fields with only scattered farmhouses and a few taverns near or beyond them.

But house or property, from Robert Baker comes the reason for the name of Piccadilly. He had made what were called Pickadils. They have been described by one Thomas Blount in his 'Glossographia' in 1656 as follows: 'A Pickadil is that round hem or the several divisions set together about the skirt of a garment or other thing; also a kind of stiff collar, made in fashion of a band. Hence perhaps the famous Ordinary near St James's called Pickadilly took denomination, because it was then the utmost or skirt house of the suburbs that way. Others say it took its name from this: that one Higgins, a tailor, who built it, got most of his estate by Pickadillies, which in the last age were much worn in England.'

Mr Blount is not very accurate. The 'ordinary' named Pickadilly came after Baker's Piccadilly Hall and took its name therefrom. Research shows that there never was a tailor named Higgins mixed up in this affair. He is a myth arising from wrong information or references improperly understood. But there most certainly was Robert Baker—godfather and part owner of Piccadilly. The 'ordinary' named Pickadilly will be met with again later. Geographically its site no longer belongs to Piccadilly as we know it now.

There was a good deal of litigation, one way and another, concerning Mr Baker's Piccadilly property which he left to his wife. At one time her houses were said to be contaminating the water supply to Westminster which came through a conduit—and there was Cunditt Meadows, it will be remembered, and there is Conduit Street today. At any rate by 1663 the name of Pickadilly—in various forms of spelling—had become attached to the district, although the main thoroughfare had not taken shape. In Gerarde's famous 'Herbal' there is an entry concerning 'the wild buglosse which grows about the drie ditches about Pickadilla'. The district was still almost entirely open country as the maps show.

But the probability of London spreading westward had not escaped the eye of certain far-seeing men. A family named Pulteney had already speculated in real estate in the district. Thomas Pulteney held land there in the days of Elizabeth I: he owned St James's Farm and his annual rent was £7.1.od. —a pretty good sum then. It looks as if he was given to the good old game of 'land grabbing' by enclosure for he threatened publicly 'death to anyone who should presume to open up what I have enclosed'. He gained power and money and passed them on to his family. His descendant, Sir William Pulteney or Poulteney, got grants of leasehold land from Charles II and succeeding monarchs. That land became very valuable. The family name is enshrined in Great and Little Pulteney Street. Sir William also built Brewer Street—where two brewhouses stood. The original windmill stood at the junction of Brewer Street and what is now Gt Windmill Street. But the originator of the name of Piccadilly was Baker, the tailor, and there is every reason to believe that it was the pickadils which gave rise to the name. Probably the only man today who knows how to make a pickadil is Archie Nathan, the famous theatrical costumier, whose firm originated nearly two centuries ago in Titchfield Street, near Piccadilly Circus, then moved to Coventry Street and then to Panton Street—all around Piccadilly. London began to move outward and westward, quite seriously, in the 17th Century. Like everything else, it followed the sun. Great men, nobles, men of substance and wealth wanted to move out of the noise and smell of Town. The constantly recurring Plague provided another urgent reason, and the tremendous visitation which preceded the Great Fire speeded this and the Fire itself destroyed many homes. The out of London movement had always of course been to the west; the Strand had seen the first development of this kind. But now so fast was the growth of London that the Strand was populous and anything but quiet and rural. So the eyes turned further west.

In 1663 what had been called 'The way to Reading' became

known as Portugal Street in honour of Catherine of Braganza, wife of Charles II. But that only applied to a portion of it—from what is now Coventry Street, Lower Regent Street and the Haymarket—down about as far as the Green Park. The Circus did not then exist and what we now call Coventry Street was regarded as being in the district of Piccadilly.

The beginning of Piccadilly itself was noble. The first great house arose there—and we must call it Piccadilly from now on—in 1667. Its builder and owner was no less a personage than Edward Hyde, Earl of Clarendon, Keeper of the Great Seal of England and Keeper of the King's Conscience. He was a man of tremendous power but little or no integrity or morality. He was firmly believed to have sold Dunkirk to the French and to have made much money out it. Few people had a good word to say about him, but he brought the beginnings of greatness to Piccadilly—his was the first noble name to be associated with it and he may be said to be its Father and Founder. There is no trace of that first Piccadilly mansion left today, indeed, it was very short lived, but it was the beginning, and where Clarendon led others followed.

He got possession of a large tract of Piccadilly by Letters Patent in 1664. He did not want all the land he acquired for himself, so he sold off a lot of it and made money thereby. He built himself a mansion on what was left and it was a house which, in its day, struck beholders with wonder. Clarendon was the equivalent of what is now Prime Minister. And he was the man whom the country held responsible for any trouble which arose. He was most unpopular and there was justification for it. He was evidently an expert grafter and although it is not known how he handled the King's Conscience, it is certain that his own troubled him not at all. With him, the end justified the means. Previously he had lived in a mansion in the Strand and the manner in which he had built that was open to question. The public was quite sure, it appeared, that when he built Clarendon House in Piccadilly he diverted much of the brick and stonework intended for the building of St Paul's to his own use. He employed Sir Roger Pratt as architect, and both Pepys and Evelyn vie in their praise of the nobility of the structure, which cost between £40,000 and £50,000 to build.

But the general public did not hold this new London palace in regard or veneration. They disliked its builder and considered this place an outward and visible sign of his dishonesty. Andrew Marvell summed up popular feeling when he wrote:

> 'Behold, in the depth of our Plague and our Wars
> He built him a Palace which outbraves the stars
> Which house (*we* Dunkirk, *he* Clarendon names)
> It looks down with shame upon St James.
> But 'tis not his golden globe will save him
> Being less than the Custom House farmers gave him
> His chapel for consecration calls
> Whose sacrilege plundered the stones of St Pauls.'

Pretty bad poetry but it caught the public taste. The golden globe was a gilded dome which stood on a central cupola. But there was an even graver charge against Clarendon than the suspicion of diversion of materials. He was said to have furnished the house with goods sent as peace offerings to him—in other words to appease official blackmail. Indeed, the contemporary Lord Paulett humbly craved Clarendon's permission to have copies made of the Vandyke portraits of his own ancestors, which Clarendon had 'acquired'. The interior of that house was a kind of National Portrait Gallery, so many ancestral portraits by great painters had Clarendon 'collected' to grace his walls. He had what was doubtless the finest art collection of his day—and had paid for none of it.

He moved in as soon as the great house was completed. It stood actually facing the top of St James's Street, and its grounds were parklike. It was the beginning of Piccadilly but the house was as ill fated as its occupant. He had wealth, with which he could not buy pleasure; power, which he felt slipping away, and his health was terrible. He took up residence in his magnificent abode in 1667. In the June of that year there was considerable trouble with the Dutch, who sailed up the Medway. The public laid this achievement on the part of their enemies at the door of Clarendon. They cut down the trees outside his walls, they smashed every window they could reach, they erected a gallows before his gates and on it was an inscription 'Three sights to be seen; Dunkirk, Tangier and a barren Queen'. However much Clarendon had been involved over Dunkirk and Tangier, it was hardly fair to blame him for the sterility of Catherine of Braganza.

The Earl had no pleasure out of his Piccadilly home. The gout got firm hold and all he could do was to sit in a wheeled chair and watch his garden growing round him. He never saw it come to fruition. He fell from power in that same year and fled the country, never to return alive. His corpse was brought home and for two hundred years his bones lay under an unmarked stone in the North Ambulatory of Westminster Abbey—until 1867, when Dean Stanley caused an inscription to be placed on the grave. Clarendon House brought no luck to anyone. The Duke of Ormonde took it and whilst he was living there the infamous Colonel Blood—the stealer of the Crown Jewels—made a violent but unsuccessful attack on his life. In 1675 the second Duke of Albemarle bought the house for £25,000—a real bargain—but only lived there for two years. He got into financial difficulties and sold the freehold to Sir Thomas Bond and some other speculators in real estate, for £35,000.

This Duke of Albemarle was the son of General Monk, created Duke because he restored Charles II to the throne. He was a curious character—a confirmed and hardened drinker in an age of drinkers—he was said to be 'burnt to a coal with liquor'. He managed to get himself appointed to the Governorship of Jamaica. He believed he knew where there lay a galleon filled with treasure. He took some partners with capital for this treasure hunt and he did actually find the galleon, and the treasure. But he died as soon as he had discovered it. His wife cheated the partners and returned home, very rich. She went mad and announced that she would marry nobody except The Grand Turk. Naturally, needy suitors pressed round her. Ralph, first Duke of Montague, pretended to be The Grand Turk and paid her court in full splendour and state. She believed him and married him. He promptly put her under control as a lunatic and with her money he built Montagu House—not in Piccadilly but where the British Museum now stands. Out of what had been Clarendon House, Piccadilly began to take shape. Those speculators led by Sir Thomas Bond, demolished the great mansion and got more from the sale of the material than they had paid for the whole property. They were off to a fine start. On the land they built a whole nest of streets, and perpetuated their names thereby. Sir Thomas Bond began to build a street to which he gave his name —Bond Street—which he declared was to be the smartest street in London. He never lived to see it finished. He had an estate in Peckham—then of course in the country—where he lived. He had lent money to Charles II when the king was in exile and had been Controller to Queen Henrietta Maria, Charles II's mother. So it was easy to get favours. His partners stamped their names into the ground and into Piccadilly too. There was Dover Street, called after Henry Jermyn, Earl of Dover; Stafford Street, after Thomas Wentworth, Earl of Stafford, and Albemarle Street after the ex-landlord, the second Duke of Albemarle. Thus did the members of the British aristocracy dig their memories firmly into the soil of what was to be the most aristocratic and celebrated street in the metropolis. Piccadilly is a sort of Debrett of noble names. Whatever the position of the aristocracy today and what may be its fate to-morrow, old family names are part of London and one hopes that will never be altered—for it is part of our history, too.

Another pioneer of Piccadilly was Lord Berkeley of Stratton, who had served the Royalist cause with distinction in the Civil War. He was related to that Henry Jermyn who, as Earl of Dover, had already got his name into Piccadilly. Berkeley was most popular with the Royal Family and Charles had ennobled him whilst in exile. He did not build quite such a wonderful house as Clarendon but it was grand enough. It cost him £30,000. Hugh May was the architect. There were most extensive grounds in which Evelyn the diarist advised him to plant holly hedges but they did not thrive. It was a fine building surmounted by a figure of Britannia in white marble which cost £3,500. Inside, a great feature was a very lovely staircase made entirely of cedar wood. Lord Berkeley moved in in 1672, on his return from Ireland where he had been Lord Lieutenant. He died in 1678 and his widow let the house to Princess Anne—afterwards Queen Anne—and her husband-consort, Prince Georg of Denmark—the fat somnolent man who so often fell asleep and snored loudly when escorting his Queenly wife to public functions.

Lady Berkeley, the widow, was a very good business woman. She had no use for the immense grounds which surrounded the house—she considered that far too much valuable property was thus going to waste. Therefore she built Stratton Street and Berkeley Street, thus perpetuating the family names firmly in Piccadilly and London, and also adding about £1,000 a year to her income. That was a lot of money then. In 1698, just before she died, she sold the freehold of the land on which Berkeley House stood, to the first Duke of Devonshire, and the Cavendish family began a very long association with Piccadilly. But Lady Berkeley, although the house and grounds were sold, still had more land and on this was built Bruton Street and the greater portion of Berkeley Square—all built on what had been the gardens and grounds of a Piccadilly mansion.

The Duke of Devonshire had been living at the previously mentioned Montagu House, but it was burnt down. He moved to a house in Whitehall which was also burnt down; he appears to have been a bad risk for fire insurance. He moved once again, into St James's Square and then set about negotiating for Berkeley House. He had a rival bidder—Lord Normanby who became Duke of Buckingham. Both claimed that they had purchased this wonderful property and there was a law suit which the Duke of Devonshire won. His rival bought Arlington House, on the site of which Buckingham Palace now stands. It then belonged to the Duchess of Grafton. The first Duke of Devonshire moved into Piccadilly and died there in 1707. His successor, living in the same house, died in 1773, but a very long association between this great family and Piccadilly had begun and ended only a few years ago. . .

In October 1773 fire again smote the Cavendish family and Berkeley House was entirely destroyed. The white marble statue of Britannia crashed into the flames and the cedar wood staircase scented the air for a long distance round as fire consumed it. All that was left of this proud mansion was a heap of smoking ruins— but the garden wall of the original house stood there for many years, right up to 1924. It was the last link with the original Piccadilly. Of course, the Devonshire family built a new house of which William Kent was the architect. It was not a building of great exterior beauty; it was, if anything homely and plain and as the years went on it got very grimy. But it was a real ducal mansion in the very heart of London and made magnificent by size. It was a relic of very different days. Inside, it was a place of beauty and contained a vast number of treasures. The cedar staircase had been replaced by a marble one which was a great feature and was trodden by the feet of the famous people of the world. There were family portraits in profusion and naturally they included one of a lady who can be reckoned as one of the greatest ghosts of Picca- dilly—Georgiana, Duchess of Devonshire—often called 'The Piccadilly Beauty'. Born a Spencer of Althorp, she married the fifth Duke of Devonshire shortly before her seventeenth birthday. She was a most ardent politician and she made Devonshire House —for so the new mansion was named—the headquarters of the Whigs. She supported Charles James Fox and she will always be remembered for her active canvassing on his behalf during the celebrated Westminster Election of 1784. This was one of the bitterest political duels in the history of our democracy. Mighty forces were arraigned against Fox—the King himself was in open

30

opposition. It is doubtful if any candidate ever faced a stiffer battle. But Fox had the Duchess—the Piccadilly Beauty—on his side. The campaign lasted for six weeks, and everything happened except loss of life: there was rioting, running fighting, ceaseless speechmaking and mud-throwing to a degree undreamt of today, whilst bribery and corruption went on all the while. The Duchess was a canvasser who left nothing to chance. She went herself into the shocking corners and alleys around Covent Garden, entering houses which looked as if they held as much evil and crime as they undoubtedly harboured dirt and filth. She was here, there and everywhere—shining like a sudden sunbeam in a slum. She persuaded a butcher named Steel to vote for Fox, by the simple expedient of giving him a kiss. And during the campaign she received, from an Irishman, what must have been the prettiest compliment which even she had ever been paid. 'I could light my pipe at your eyes, he exclaimed. That puts her charm, liveliness and beauty into a nutshell. She was of course victorious. Fox was elected, in company with Lord Hood, the popular Admiral.

Duchess Georgiana must have brought sunshine to Devonshire House, to the Cavendish family, to Piccadilly and indeed to all who knew her. She was completely democratic, she would go anywhere and do anything. There was a member of the Cavendish family who 'did not mix'. He was Henry Cavendish, a shy retiring man who only emerged to meet his relatives when important family events compelled him to do so. He lived like a hermit and had his meals at The Crown and Anchor Tavern in the Strand, because it was there that The Royal Society, of which he was a member, had its meetings. He was a scientist in a day when such things were not understood. Duchess Georgiana liked him and went often to visit him, on the quiet. Her husband, the Duke, did not approve. 'You cannot visit him,' he said, 'why—he works!' Which was the way in which the aristocracy and nobility of the 18th century regarded the arts and sciences. But the Duchess went all the same. She is a jewel in the history of Piccadilly, this lovely vivacious woman with the sparkling eyes, the gay smile and even gayer laugh, this woman who moved so well and with so much grace—and who had more than a tint of red in her hair. She also had a strong will and knew exactly what she wanted—traits no doubt inherited from her direct ancestress, Sarah, Duchess of Marlborough. Maybe she still flits in shadowy form over what was once her home, though no vestige of it stands today. The extent of the area which held that mansion and grounds can be gauged by the fact that The Mayfair Hotel stands within what was once the Devonshire House gardens. During its last years the ducal mansion had lovely wrought iron gates, brought up from another mansion at Chiswick, but they were not there for very long. They remain in Piccadilly, leading into the Green Park and adding a touch of ancient grace and craftsmanship to the modernity which surrounds them. Devonshire House will be met with again.

There is another great Piccadilly mansion which must be put on record, because although it has altered its form, it stands there still and bears its old name. It is Burlington House. The first house on that historic site was a red brick, private residence built for Richard Boyle, 2nd Earl of Cork and 1st Earl of Burlington. Sir John Denham is said to have been the architect. This house was altered almost entirely in 1718 by the third Earl of Burlington, himself an amateur architect of considerable talent. He faced it with stone, in the Palladian style and erected a colonnade which aroused the admiration of Horace Walpole. That worthy and observant man had been in Italy when this new house was being built and it rather burst upon him. He wrote, 'At daybreak, looking out of the window to see the sun rise I was surprised with the vision of the colonnade that fronted me. It seemed one of those edifices in fairy tales that are raised by genii in a night time.' It must indeed have been part of the magic of Piccadilly. But the man in the street could not see it for a long wall, said to be the 'most expensive wall in England' masked it from view. But it can hardly have been the guardian of greater treasures than the wall of Devonshire House. It is all gone now, pulled down in 1866.

Burlington House, from its earliest days, was a great Piccadilly rendezvous devoted largely to all forms of art. It still lives up to its reputation. Kent, the architect, lived there for thirty years, under the patronage of the noble family. Gay, of 'The Beggar's Opera' fame, was a frequent and welcome guest.

The Burlingtons intermarried with the Devonshires who were their neighbours in Piccadilly. The fourth Duke of Devonshire married Lady Charlotte Elizabeth Boyle (of the Burlington family) and she brought him the entire Burlington estates. The Duke of Portland, who also married into the family, was another notable resident of Burlington House. In 1815, the sixth Duke of Devonshire sold Burlington House to his uncle, Lord George Cavendish, for £75,000, and for him the Burlington title was revived. He kept himself to himself and bloodhounds roamed the grounds at night to protect the property. He was extremely taciturn and never said an unnecessary word, nor did his brother, the fifth Duke of Devonshire. Both also were men of unruffled calm and sangfroid. Once, whilst travelling together, they halted at an inn for the night. They were shown into a room which contained three beds, all four posters with their curtains drawn. Both, in turn, looked into one of the beds, turned away and chose another. Not a word was spoken. They passed a peaceful night and in the morning breakfasted in silence and then continued the journey. When they had travelled some distance without a word, the Duke said, 'Did you see what was in that other bed last night?' 'I did, brother,' replied Lord George. Nothing else was said about the matter. In fact, that third bed had held a corpse. No wonder the English had a reputation for phlegm.

It was Lord George who created The Burlington Arcade. He did it to prevent people living on the other side of his wall from throwing rubbish into his grounds. The reason published at the time stated that he built it for the 'gratification of the publick and to give employment to industrious females'. What the employment was is not stated. Presumably, sales ladies in the shops.

There are many ghosts in Piccadilly but there is room in this chronicle for very few. That London oasis, known as Albany, must not be overlooked. The ghosts gather thickly there. And it should be noted that it is not THE Albany—just plain Albany. Originally there were three houses on that site, one of which belonged to Lord Sunderland, who was as good a schemer against kings and constitutions as could be desired and was in all the best plots of his day. He bought the other two houses and made them into one. Stephen Fox, the second Lord Holland, lived there, a genial good living ghost, and sold it to Lord Melbourne, who rebuilt the whole place and added a ceiling by Cipriani to the ballroom. Then he swopped houses with the Duke of York and Albany—son of George II—and from that royal personage came the present name. In 1804 it was converted into chambers and had its garden built over. To walk through the covered way across its centre is to feel as if one were in the quadrangle of the college of an ancient university. Time and Life stand still, and the noise of London, so loud without the walls, is stilled to the faintest murmur. But the ghosts are a large company, so many famous people lived there. One of them was Lord Macaulay. One of the most curious ghosts is Mat Lewis, who was a literary 'lion' of his day. He wrote a tremendous amount of stuff, none of which has survived. He had been well educated and his father was very wealthy. He held a kind of literary court and young authors considered it a great honour to be presented to him. One such, who was patronised by him and given a dinner, left it on record that he 'had never felt such elation before'. That young man's name was Walter Scott. Somehow there came a revulsion against Lewis and he was attacked on the score that his books were indecent and blasphemous. But he kept on doing what he considered good work and living in Albany. The panels of his book cases were mirrors, for he was very vain, and he kept a black servant. He was also a snob. Byron was a friend of his and Mat Lewis told him with tears of pleasure in his eyes that the Duchess of York had said something so kind to him. 'Never mind, Lewis,' replied Byron, 'don't cry. She did not mean it.'

Lewis did many good and generous things whilst he lived. His parents were estranged but he championed his mother and shared all he had with her. He went to Jamaica in 1817 to try and improve the lot of the slaves. He died on his return journey and was buried at sea, but one thinks his ghost made straight for K1 Albany, where he loved to live. Byron resided there, and Bulwer Lytton. William Ewart Gladstone lived there for some time before he married. Albany holds all sorts of ghosts of all sorts of people, nobles, poets, authors, wits, politicians—there is no end to them. One of the chief is naturally Lord Byron, who is an English immortal. He had boxing lessons there, for an hour each day, from Gentleman Jackson, the Champion of England himself, and Angelo taught him fencing. Canning too is an Albany ghost. It has always had a literary flavour and it retains it now, for authors still live there. J. B. Priestley was there for some time. But maybe there was a little flutter amongst the respectable Albany dovecots when an author created one of the greatest criminals in modern literature—the so-called amateur but highly successful cracksman known as 'A. J. Raffles' and gave him chambers in Albany. 'A.J.' as his friends called him, was the forerunner of many similar characters.

He was presumably a gentleman, he was Public School, University and a first class cricketer, yet he robbed his hosts and double crossed hardworking professional crooks. He put his best friend 'on the spot' by confessing his crimes to him, thereby sealing his lips for ever, for no Edwardian gentleman could 'split' on a friend. 'A.J.' moaned 'Bunny', the best friend, 'the whitest man I ever knew'. That tradition of silence was the same as that which prevented a woman's name ever being mentioned in the Mess. E. W. Hornung, the creator of 'Raffles', was so fortunate as to get him on the stage in the person of Gerald Du Maurier, who made a tremendous and overwhelming success. The villain became the hero—it was topsy-turveydom with a vengeance. But an American detective had his suspicions about 'A.J.'—maybe the English gloss of good breeding did not baffle him. This detective, named 'Curtis Bedford', pursued Raffles relentlessly. The last scene—a most exciting one, took place in Raffles's chambers in Albany. There was a thick London Particular fog outside, the devil was looking after his own. Raffles, with justice and the law battering on the door, dived through a trick clock which led to a private way of escape and so evaded his just punishment. The detective and the police burst in and found their bird had flown. The sleuth said 'Gone—disappeared—fog outside—he'll get clear away. Good, I'm glad. He's bully. . . .' It was probably one of the most immoral plays ever staged but intensely thrilling.

The Stage had had a good many representatives in Albany. When Byron lived there he was serving on the Committee which ran the newly-rebuilt Theatre Royal, Drury Lane. Mr Priestley is of course a distinguished dramatist as well as novelist; Prince Littler, who now controls Drury Lane, lived there too and so did 'Bill' Linnit, a well known theatrical manager who died recently. There have been and there are others. Albany keeps its distinction, its aloofness, its exclusiveness and its air of cloistral calm. It is still a stronghold of Yesterday where the spirit of Piccadilly lives well. Every inch of Piccadilly whispers of the social, artistic, political and military might of this country.

So many ghosts—and so little space to accommodate even immaterial shades. All that one can do is to pick out some of the most famous—just to show what Piccadilly meant to London— and indeed to the whole realm—why it remains as it does today. For just as a building accumulates atmosphere from things which have happened in it and people who have lived there—so does a street do the same thing, derived from those who lived and worked there, too. King George IV, although he never resided in Piccadilly, altered the surroundings a good deal in his time, and was actually the cause of founding a very celebrated Piccadilly Club—in fact, the first. Some of his friends complained about the monotony of the food at their own clubs—describing what they called 'the eternal joints or beef steaks, the boiled fowl with oyster sauce and an apple tart'. That appeared to be unchangeable. The

Prince sympathised, sent for his own chef, Watier, and asked him if he could organise a dinner club with better and more varied fare. Watier agreed at once; named Madison, who was the Prince's Page, as manager, and Labourie, from the Royal kitchens, as chef. So, in 1807, Watier's Club began at what was then 81 Piccadilly. It soon became famous, and Beau Brummell was made Perpetual President. The food was magnificent—but play became so high that many people were ruined there. Watier's only lasted for twelve years. A great and outstanding feature of Piccadilly is still the Naval and Military Club, better known as 'The In and Out' on account of the traffic signs at its entrance. This place began its life in 1760, being built for the Earl of Egremont (George O'Brien Wyndham)—whose charities were magnificent, who was a patron of the arts and who encouraged Turner. He was a curious man; he never married, but he had children, and they lived with him too, in happiness, peace and comfort. He was followed in his Piccadilly home by the Duke of Cambridge, brother of George IV. This Royal Duke did little of note but had some rather endearing habits. Not the least of these was his custom of speaking his thoughts aloud—especially in church, where he kept up a little running commentary on the sermon, quite oblivious of doing so, and when the clergyman said 'Let Us Pray,' His Royal Highness would chime in with 'By all means, by all means.'

But a greater than he came to live in that mansion, which had taken the title of Cambridge House. Lord Palmerston was ageing when he came to live in Piccadilly, but he was still that same Palmerston who left such a mark upon the history of his country. He would stand for hours at the top of the staircase in his Picca-dilly mansion, at the almost endless receptions, with a smile and a kindly handshake for the guests who filed before him in seemingly never ceasing procession. He was never discourteous or off-hand—a great Englishman resident in a great street—Piccadilly. He stood so often for England at its very best; he was beloved of cartoonists because of the short piece of straw in the corner of his mouth which made him so human, and upon him the public bestowed that accolade of public favour and affection, a nickname—for they called him 'Pam'.

By way of contrast to the Englishness of Palmerston, there was a Frenchman at what was then No 106, in 1860. He was the comte de Flahault, and he had been aide-de-camp to Napoleon. He married a Scotswoman, named Margaret Mercer, who besides the French title she gained by marriage had already two in her own right, for she was Baroness Keith and Baroness Nairne. She loved living in Piccadilly. Before she married de Flahault, there seemed a likelihood that Lord Byron would wed her and she would not have objected to that. When the scandal of his parting from the woman he had married caused him almost complete social ostracism, Margaret told him 'You ought to have married me.' When he left the country to go into voluntary exile, he sent her a little present and a message saying 'Tell her that if I had been fortunate enough to marry a woman like her, I should not now be obliged to exile myself from my own country.' Margaret Mercer, comtesse de Flahault, Baroness Keith, Baroness Nairne, was a great lady of Piccadilly. And in the house which stood next door to her, No. 107, there were memories of Lord Rosebery and of the family of Rothschild into which he married. Nathan Rothschild had lived at 107 up to his death—a son of the founder of the great banking family. It was said of him that he told Spohr that the only music he cared about was the rattle of money— (he would not be able to hear that today but maybe the papery lisp would have served) and another dictum of his was that he could not afford to know an unlucky man. But he had a sense of humour because when a very important personage called upon him, he said 'Oh, if you please—take two chairs.'

One of the most delightful ghosts of Piccadilly is that of Harriot Mellon, the Drury Lane actress of obscure origin, who married Coutts the famous banker, made him very happy and later became the Duchess of St Albans. The house in which she lived with her husband Coutts, was actually No. 1, Stratton Street, but it abutted on to Piccadilly and more of it stood therein than in Stratton Street. She loved that house very much, and grieved deeply when her husband died in it. When her own time came to leave the world, as Duchess of St Albans, she had herself carried to that partly Piccadilly mansion and breathed her last in the same room and in the same bed from which her beloved first husband had slipped out of life. She told Lady Guilford, one of Mr Coutts's daughters by his first marriage, that he had come back to her in the shape of a little bird and was then singing outside the window. It was established that the old man, when dying, had promised her that he would do this and she firmly believed it. Indeed, she always became very happy when a bird fluttered by her window. That may be only a sentimental memory but it brings a touch of romance into the magical mile. The Mellon-Coutts marriage, despite the disparity in ages, had been supremely happy. For many years that house became one of the best known in Piccadilly, because of a bird. In a window thereof hung a china cockatoo and millions glanced at it when passing by. Many of them believed it was a real bird. It became a feature of London life, the Piccadilly Cockatoo. Once indeed it stopped a riot. A mob was marching down Piccadilly, with a view to holding a meeting in Hyde Park, there to preach and probably practise violence. The sight of that bird in the window brought them to a stop. They argued amongst themselves as to whether this was a real bird or not. The argument began with the leaders and spread rapidly through all ranks. So interested did they become that they forgot their original intention and the police had no trouble in dispersing them—but before they broke up they gave three hearty cheers for the lady who owned the bird.

She was the Baroness Burdett-Coutts, a very great philanthropist who did so much for the poor, and especially the poor of London. She had been left that house and a fortune by Harriot Mellon—Mrs Thomas Coutts—the Duchess of St Albans—who herself had adorned Piccadilly and the world and had done so many good deeds. Alas, both house and china bird have gone now—but across the road, in the Green Park, blackbirds still sing. . .

There is another stage representative who, if he did not actually live in Piccadilly, often passed down it. Edmund Kean, the greatest tragedian that ever lived and whose greatest tragedy was his own life, would come galloping along Piccadilly to his house just off it, in Clarges Street—inflamed by the applause of the multitude and by brandy. Clarges Street perpetuates the memory of Sir Thomas Clarges, who fought a duel in the Green Park.

A tragic ghost of Piccadilly is that of Emma Hamilton. She lived with her husband, Sir William Hamilton, at what was 23 Piccadilly. They were some of her happy days. There Nelson would call—and to her in that house came the news of Copenhagen in 1801—and there too little Horatia was born. Later she moved into Clarges Street and there the days were not so gay. But for a time that lovely Hamilton—the ex-domestic servant who ruled the heart of the greatest sailor the world has ever known—had her home in Piccadilly.

But one of the greatest of all the great ghosts of Piccadilly is Old Q—the Duke of Queensberry. He lived in what became Nos. 138 and 139—down at the Hyde Park Corner end. He merits a book to himself and indeed many such have been written. He was a great profligate and a great sportsman. He was considered a very bad man, yet he did many kind and generous actions. He had within himself all the good and evil of the great city in which he lived and maybe he is himself the epitome of Piccadilly. He carried on his profligate ways into an age when such things were a crying scandal but he did not care. Almost up to the day of his death—and he lived to be 86—he would sit on a balcony before his house—under a sunshade on fine days, and watch the ladies driving by in their carriages. If one took his fancy, and one or more always did, he would send his groom, Jack Radford, who stood by ready for the purpose, to find out who she was. Despite his rackety life of open depravity, he was active right up to his death in 1810 and was buried under the altar in St James's,

THE GHOSTS OF PICCADILLY

Piccadilly's own church. His will caused a tremendous sensation for he left so many bequests to so many favourites. They called him 'The Star of Piccadilly' and so he was. It is well worth while reading his full life story, for such people do not exist today.

Perhaps the mightiest ghost of Piccadilly lived at Apsley House —known as No 1, London, and if that does not show the importance of Piccadilly, nothing does. That ghost was of course the Duke of Wellington, the conqueror of Napoleon at Waterloo and the saviour of the freedom of the world at that time. Strangely enough the site had been linked with war long before the Iron Duke went there. Part of the site of that house was given by George II to an old soldier named Allen whom the king recognised as a veteran of Dettingen, at which the King himself had also fought, he being the last British sovereign to lead his men into battle. Allen's wife erected a stall there and got a living. In 1771, Apsley, the Lord Chancellor, began a building on the site which would wipe out the stall. Mrs Allen protested vigorously and brought an action against him, Lord Chancellor or no. She won it, too, and got handsome compensation. And then came the great Duke. This is no place in which to write his story except to remind readers of how this country is apt to treat its leaders and heroes, especially if they go into politics as the Duke did. In 1815 Wellington was the hero, not only of his own country but of the world. In 1831, when his wife lay dying in Apsley House, the mob of London rioted outside and smashed his windows because they considered that he had opposed reform. He had iron shutters fixed after that and kept them until his dying day. He said little about that manifestation of dislike but he never forgot it. Later when another mob cheered him to the echo outside his house, he made no direct reply to the reception: he just pointed to the shutters and left it at that. Apsley House, one of the most beautifully sited houses in London, still stands and is a Wellington Museum.

There is one more Shade—of recent passing from this world— who joins the throng which makes Piccadilly a metropolis of ghostland. It is that of a man quite young, who came to live a few doors from Apsley House when he was a Royal Duke bringing his beloved Scots bride to Piccadilly. The turn of the wheel of fate made him King of England, to be an example to his people and to all the world, of steadfast courage and loyalty of purpose throughout the greatest war the world had ever known. For King George VI, when Duke of York, lived in Piccadilly and to him the other ghosts give loyal respect and right of way.

Few streets anywhere in the world have a richer or more varied background in accordance with their age than this great artery of the west, called after a tailor's residence and a specimen of his craft—in the true haphazard and odd way of London.

2

Trade Comes to Piccadilly

Piccadilly really began when the British Empire was first being established and grew with it to greatness. For many years it was a thoroughfare of nobility, composed of houses as noble as those who lived in them. Then, true to the character of this race, trade began to infiltrate, quietly and unobtrusively at first but with a tempo which quickened as the 18th Century merged into the 19th. When Napoleon called us a nation of shopkeepers, he was not far wrong.

The first evidence of commercialism in Piccadilly had to do with cakes, confectionary and later, tea. This pioneer of commerce stood at the corner of Bond Street and Piccadilly. It was known as Stewart's Corner and in due course it became famous all over the world. It opened its doors in 1688. There is no doubt that this original building was built by Sir Thomas Bond on ground once covered by Clarendon House. When it was rebuilt in 1907 the original massive foundations were laid bare. In its new form it became the smartest teashop and confectioner's in London. Originally the shop had resembled Fribourg and Treyer's, still to be seen in The Haymarket. It was discreet and it served the nobility with efficiency and devotion. Until it left Piccadilly so recently it must have been the oldest baker's and confectioner's business in

London—making old established firms like Gunters and Birch's look like juveniles. It became to London what Florian's was to Venice, Delmonico's to New York and Rumpelmeyer's to Paris. All the great people dropped in there for over a couple of centuries. It is said that it was the only place in which you could buy a special form of confectionery called Piccadilly Cakes. Stewarts no longer stands in Piccadilly. Its site is occupied by QANTAS, the Australian Airline—typical of the changing world and changing Piccadilly.

But the second oldest inhabitant of Piccadilly, from the trading point of view, still flourishes and is also concerned with the sale of food in all forms—and nowadays with a great many other things too. It is one of the two great giants of Piccadilly, from the point of view of antiquity, of years spent in that thoroughfare and from prestige as well. To think of it is to think immediately of Piccadilly—the two seem synonymous—for the senior firm in Piccadilly today, and the second oldest in all time, is the House of Fortnum and Mason. Stewarts started in 1688—Fortnum and Mason has its roots in the year 1705. It has served Piccadilly—London—the Monarchy—the whole world during twelve reigns. This establishment and its next in seniority, its near and famous neighbour, which has been rooted in Piccadilly since 1797, seem to have absorbed into themselves and taken into their very fabric some of that nobility which founded Piccadilly. For the second giant of Piccadilly is the world famous booksellers, Hatchards—a place unique and steeped in atmosphere and richness.

It is impossible to tell the story of Piccadilly without embroidering upon it the fascinating history, even if only in outline, of these two firms which still embellish the Magic Mile today. For although both have moved with the times and are abreast of modernity in every way, there still remains that tradition of quality and service and there still linger the memories and ghosts of all the famous people, from crowned heads downwards, who were customers of and visitors to those princely establishments. They are well matched, for cakes and confectionery came first to

Piccadilly, with literature and bookshops well on their tails. Let us take Fortnum and Mason's first. It is now such an established part of London and especially Piccadilly, that even its customers take it for granted, as Londoners accept the Tower, Westminster Abbey and St. Paul's. They do not think about how it began or who created it. But the story is so worth while and so typical of the emergence of Piccadilly itself from a mere trackway to a world famous thoroughfare, that it must be given space in any account which devotes itself more to life and personalities than to mere bricks and mortar, stocks and stones.

Fortnum and Mason is a delightful combination of names, well balanced and pleasant to say and hear. There are so many such— and they have mostly risen to greatness—Swan and Edgar, near neighbours of Fortnum and Mason, Dickens and Jones, Crosse and Blackwell, Bryant and May, Bourne and Hollingsworth. Swears and Wells, Lincoln and Bennett, Debenham and Freebody, Waring and Gillow, Lilley and Skinner, Anderson and Sheppard, Burkinshaw and Knights—so many more, all of which sound so completely matched that it would be impossible to part them. But who worries about the origin of these people? Sometimes a comedian cracks a gag about them or a humorist turns his pen that way, yet they were all very real people. And Mr Fortnum and Mr Mason, the original founders, were very real indeed. They even had a royal angle from the beginning and they were entirely bound up with Piccadilly.

The name of Fortnum has gone through many changes in spelling down the years, as indeed have most names, for time was when one spelt one's name as one liked—as witness the several forms of the name of Shakespeare. The first trace of this now so thoroughly Piccadilly name is Nicholas Fortanon—a yeoman farmer in Oxfordshire in 1273—and he probably did not spell his name at all. But the family spread and crop up from time to time—they had become Fortynhams in the reign of Henry VIII. They were still country folk. The first of them to be lured to London was attracted thereto by a disaster—nothing less than the Fire of

London. So one William Fortnam—the name had undergone another change—who had given up farming to become a builder, rightly surmised there would be plenty for him to do in building up London again. He displayed that foresight and opportunism which always marked the firm. He established himself in Stepney and despite one or two setbacks did pretty well; well enough to encourage a cousin of his, also named William, but spelling his name Fortnum, to venture into London as well. This William Fortnum matters a great deal, for he brings the 'u' into the name and, in the parlance of today, Fortnum and Mason's certainly run their business on a 'U' basis.

Mr William Fortnum decided—like Herbert Pocket in *Great Expectations*—to look about him. He did not choose the East End or the City; he chose the West End as his place of survey, and to that end he lodged with a Mr Hugh Mason, who had a small grocer's shop in St James's Market, adjacent to Piccadilly and the Haymarket. Little did either of them think what was to become of this first association as lodger and landlord.

William Fortnum soon found a good job. He became a footman in the Household of Queen Anne. Thereby he established a connection with royalty which Fortnum and Mason's carry on today. He was an energetic man and saw opportunities besides his occupation as footman. Those were the days of perquisites— and one of William's perquisites was the candle ends and candles left unconsumed in the royal candlesticks. There were plenty of them and they had a distinct value—for candles were the only form of lighting. Actors often accepted the candle ends from the footlights and stage lighting if business had been bad and their salaries were not forthcoming. No doubt Mr William contracted out for all the candle ends in the Palace—and they were wax candles too. He did a good trade in them in the Palace itself and did not see why he should not branch out. He did so, as tallow chandler and grocer—the two trades were complementary then. When he had made quite a bit of money he decided to give up being a footman, even a royal footman, and go into business on his own account. He had made himself popular in the Palace and built up quite a connection. His preference was for grocery, which was perfectly natural for there was his landlord and now friend, Mr Mason, skilled in the trade and ready to help. They went into partnership. They took what was probably a stall—it appears to have been located in a doorway only a stone's throw from the present premises—and so in 1707, the firm of Fortnum and Mason was born, in Piccadilly.

It was a period of boom. The might of Great Britain was increasing all the world over. The real British Empire was being forged. Fortnum and Mason's stood in the very middle of an area which was being developed. The Court was at St James's and was always busy and vital with much coming and going. Mansions were springing up around the Court. They wanted groceries and Fortnum and Mason could and did supply them. And they branched out again. There were not only human beings for whom to cater but horses as well. Coaches, carriages, wagons, wains and riding horses thronged the district. So Mr Mason, of Fortnum and Mason, opened stabling in Mason's Yard, just off Duke Street— and Mason's Yard is there today. Thus early did this firm show the adaptability, that very British character of improvising to meet the situation, which it has shown ever since.

But the firm did not rocket to success: it grew steadily by giving the best of goods and service. It took two generations to get the shop into the top or luxury class. And then once more that Royal Connexion was resumed.

In 1761, Charles Fortnum, grandson of the founder of the firm went into Royal Service—that of good Queen Charlotte. He was twenty-three years of age, and his wages from his royal job amounted to £10.5.5d per quarter. That did not worry him. He also had his 'perks' and these had grown from the candle ends of his grandfather to such things as food, coal, house linen and wine. All this went into the firm and Charles was able to persuade his fellow servants—of all grades—that if they wanted the right stuff at the right price, Fortnum and Mason's was the place for them.

The Royal Household then was a very complicated piece of domestic machinery with hundreds of servants and scores of departments, each of which had its own chiefs, who had titles such as Clerk to the Spicery, Yeoman and Groom of the Pastry, etc. Charles had the ear of them all and business boomed to such an extent that in 1788 he begged leave to retire on the score of ill health, but one is more inclined to believe that he wished to pay close attention to the business because the Mason of that period was only eighteen. Charles Fortnum ran the business for another eighteen years and then sold his interest to his son Richard and to John Mason, in proportions of 75 % to the former and 25 % to the latter.

But Charles had become a personage at Court. Despite his advancing years he was recalled. He became Page of the Presence (the equivalent today would be Equerry or Private Secretary) and three years later became Groom of the Chamber, deep in the confidence of his Queen and a person of the utmost importance to all those desiring an audience. None of which did any harm to the flourishing business. He died whilst still in the Royal service and was the last of the Fortnums to work directly with their monarchs. From now on the family were very busy running their own little kingdom and encouraging it to expand as the British Empire was doing. As new things came into circulation, so Fortnum and Mason's marketed them. John Company, which became the East India Company, laid the foundation of what was to be the Indian Empire. Oriental spices, new brands of tea and all sorts of novelties came into the warehouse of Fortnum and Mason. For there were Fortnums in John Company although they spelt the name Fortnom and were regarded by the Piccadilly Branch as 'The Indians'. By 1788 Fortnum and Mason's were supplying delicacies never before thought of: poultry and game in aspic, 'decorated' lobsters and prawns, potted meats, hardboiled eggs in forcemeat (called Scottish eggs), eggs in cake soaked in brandy with whipped cream added, mince pies, savoury patties and fruits both fresh and dried,'all decorated and prepared so as to require no cutting'.

The people on their books who were also their neighbours

were of the utmost distinction. In Pall Mall there were the Dowager Princess of Wales, the Duke of Cumberland (a Royal Duke), the Earls of Orford, Egmont and Temple, the Countess of Waldegrave and the Lords Sandwich and Godolphin. The former must have had a fellow feeling for the firm. In St James's Square they served three dukes—Norfolk, Cleveland and Leeds. In Cleveland Row their customers included the Duke of Bridgewater, General Harvey, Sir William Musgrave and the offices of the Secretary of State.

The Napoleonic Wars brought Fortnum and Mason's more trade. There was no proper system of rationing in the Army then and although the private soldier did not deal with Fortnum and Mason's, the officers did. To be an officer in those days, when commissions were bought, demanded private income. The young men lived well. When they found themselves on active service in the Peninsula their accustomed fare could not be come by locally so they put their faith in Fortnum and Mason's of Piccadilly. There are many letters in possession of the firm which read like heart cries: 'I beg you to send me out hams, tongues, butter and cheese' ... one even appeals for candles, thereby going back to the origin of the firm. And Fortnums coped with it all. And at this time too they extended their trade in preserves and the like—honey, dried fruits, spices, cereals, all were in demand to lighten the rigours of the campaign.

On 30 December 1817, Fortnum and Mason's advertised in *The Times*: 'New Portugal Plums, Tours Plums, and French Dried Pears. Fortnum and Mason take the earliest opportunity of informing their friends that these fruits have been landed, are in great perfection and may be had at their warehouse, 185 Piccadilly; the Portugals in the usual round boxes, and the Tours Plums dried apples and pears in small square baskets, together with a very choice variety of Foreign Fruits. Owing to the handsome packages, the above are particularly adapted for Presents.' One likes the way in which the firm appeals to its friends. . .

In 1819, Sir William Edward Parry took a couple of hundredweight of their unsweetened cocoa-powder with him on his expedition to discover the North West Passage.

The prosperous Victorian Age arrived. Fortnum and Mason's prospered with the rest and were always leading the way. They had a special branch to deal with clubs and supplied the very best and most exclusive of them. They created a startling novelty which, if it did not succeed very well at the time—may yet be the basis of the diet of tomorrow. They introduced 'Concentrated Luncheons of Savoury Lozenges' which—they said—had the virtue of 'forming a desirable and portable Refreshment in travelling, hunting, shooting, and other sports'; the lozenges were also recommended to 'Members of Parliament, Gentlemen detained on Juries and when long abstinence from meals is indispensable.' There is no record that this innovation was a success, but their tinned goods began to boom. Instructions went with every tin 'To open the canister first stab a hole with the butt-end of a knife, near the upper rim. Then insert the blade as far as it will go. Draw the handle towards you and the blade will be found to cut through the tin with perfect ease' . . . one hopes. The chief lines were Scotch salmon and beef stews. Ready to eat food gained great favour especially during the activity and excitement of the Great Exhibition of 1851. Swarms of foreign visitors came to London and met the Fortnum and Mason delicacies for the first time. Many became regular customers. At that time Fortnums were providing ready roasted duck and green peas at 5/-; partridges at 2/6d; real West Indian turtle at 10/- a pound; a whole truffled pheasant at 15/-. And you could buy excellent port at 115 gallons for £70.

Fortnum and Mason's went to the front in the Crimean War too, as they had done in the Napoleonic Wars. Their fame was such that they had to discontinue having their names displayed on the cases of goods—because it caused so much 'leakage'. Queen Victoria sent the firm an order for a large consignment of concentrated beef tea, which was to be sent to Miss Florence Nightingale. This was done at once and a letter came from Miss

Nightingale's mother which said 'I am requested by my daughter to thank you for your letter announcing 250lbs of Concentrated Beef Tea, a present from Her Majesty. It is particularly acceptable, as the state of exhaustion in which the sick are now arriving at Scutari renders it very difficult to find adequate support for them.' Thus in concentrated form Piccadilly went to the Crimea.

Fortnum and Mason now received many forms of recognition with which they were granted Warrants of Appointment: in 1863 as Grocers to H.R.H. the Prince of Wales; in 1867 came appointments as Grocers and Tea Dealers to H.R.H. The Duke of Cumberland; Oilmen to Their Royal Highnesses Prince and Princess Christian of Schleswig-Holstein; Furnishers to the Establishment of H.R.H. The Crown Princess of Prussia, and The Princess Royal of Great Britain and Ireland; and Confectioners and Foreign warehousemen to H.R.H. the Princess of Wales. In 1887 they became Foreign Warehousemen to H.R.H. the Prince of Wales (Edward VII) and in 1898 Purveyors of Oilery to H.M. The Queen.

But perhaps the picture which stands out most vividly and with the greatest charm in the saga of Fortnum and Mason's, is Derby Day in the time of Victoria and of Edward VII! This great institution was served faithfully by the Piccadilly institution. Derby Day in the Victorian Age and Edwardian Era was a test not only of the speed and stamina of the picked three-year-old thoroughbred racehorses but of the speed and stamina of the staff of Fortnum and Mason's. Every man jack of them was on duty and standing by ready at 4 a.m. And very shortly afterwards a long unbroken line of coaches, and carriages of all kinds, queued up and were duly loaded with the hampers ordered—containing the luncheon to withstand the fatigues of race-going and the champagne wherewith to salute the winnings or drown the memory of the losses on the Turf.

That is a sight which nobody will ever see again, that almost endless line of coaches and carriages, their bodies shining like the skin of their horses, the metal work gleaming in the sun; an outward and visible sign of the richness and prosperity of the

British Empire and the sportsmanship of its people, a sight which could be seen nowhere else in the world except Piccadilly.

Charles Dickens, a regular customer of Fortnum's, put the whole thing into words: 'Well, to be sure, there never was such a Derby Day as this present Derby Day! Never, to be sure, were there so many carriages, so many fours, so many twos, so many ones, so many horsemen, so many people who have "come down by rail", so many fine ladies in so many broughams, so many Fortnum and Mason hampers, so much ice and champagne. If I were on the Turf and had a horse to enter for the Derby, I would call it Fortnum and Mason, convinced that with that name he would beat the field. Public opinion would bring him in some-how. Look where I will—in some connection with the carriages, made fast upon the top, or occupying the box or peeping out of a window I see Fortnum and Mason. And now, Heavens! All the hampers fly wide open and the green Downs burst into a blossom of lobster salad... And if one recalls that famous picture by Frith—"Derby Day", the figure of the child acrobat in the fore-ground is delaying rushing into his father's arms to do his trick—because he is gazing at a footman who is laying out the contents of a hamper—doubtless by Fortnum and Mason...' Statesmen were not above consulting this Piccadilly firm—The Grand Old Man, Mr Gladstone himself wrote to them for information:
'Dear Sirs,

I have often heard that it is the custom of grocers and all who deal in sugar to sell that article on rather bare profits as compared with the usual and what may be called regular profits of traders. Would you kindly give me the advantage of hearing on authority whether this is so. There would be no necessity of my naming you in any reference I might make in Parliament to this subject.

I remain, dear Sirs,
Your faithful servant,
W. E. Gladstone.'

All through the Victorian era Fortnum and Mason's grew, flourished and decked Piccadilly. They supplied goods to the officers in all those wars which then seemed so important and now seem so insignificant. Indeed food boxes specially made and bearing their name were carried on the heads of the porters who followed the victorious Sir Garnet Wolseley into Coomassie when he captured that capital in the Ashanti War. One wonders if the advertisement meant much to the local inhabitants.

In the Boer War the firm went into equipment as well as food supply. Officers who had grown used to relying upon them for most things enquired about boots with which to meet the arduous conditions of 'The Veldt'—which was to the Boer War what 'The Trenches' were to the 1914-1918 War. And boots of a specially pliable kind of leather were evolved and became most popular. Though that war darkened the closing years of the Victorian Age, life went on in this country much the same as ever—the fighting was so far away and Fortnum and Mason supplied the needful delicacies here and at the front. Tinned foods came more and more into use. In this line Fortnum and Mason's were No. 1 in the world—Fortnum's tinned or potted foods were freely eaten even by hard boiled Victorians. And that is why in June 1886, a young gentleman from America who looked very smart, alert and businesslike, alighted from a four-wheeled cab at the front entrance of No. 181 Piccadilly. That was not the smartest nor fastest form of transport but this young gentleman needed it because he carried five cases of samples, all canned goods. He entered the emporium, a little on his guard, very polite but very firm, very pleasant but prepared to fight against what he was sure would be arrayed against him: the strong conservatism of British trade. His name was Mr Heinz. He displayed his goods and the firm of Fortnum and Mason took a look. They astounded him by saying 'We will take them all.' They knew a good thing when they saw it. And so those famous 57 varieties were sold in Piccadilly with such success that nine years later Mr Heinz opened his own London branch.

What were working conditions like in that stronghold of Piccadilly trade in the days of Queen Victoria? Much the same as they are today. There was the complete absence of fuss and bustle which marks true efficiency. The day began early then, however, at 7.45, when all preparations were completed by the porters and those who 'lived in'. By nine a.m. the heads of all departments and the partners themselves were busy. The senior assistants were at their posts in their swallow tailed coats. The juniors, who were called 'roundsmen', were already off on their daily job of calling on customers—at the Best Houses in Mayfair, Belgravia, Bayswater and Kensington, at Marlborough House, Clarence House (where the Duke and Duchess of Edinburgh lived) and at Buckingham Palace itself. Sometimes the orders from the Palace were very modest—'Two pots of marmalade, 1/8d' or 'Four bottles of oil at 2/6d.' The Prince of Wales however wanted apricot pulp, Parmesan and Gruyère cheese.

But fashionable people of all nationalities, resident nobility or those on a visit from abroad, preferred to call at the shop itself. To them it was the centre of Piccadilly, they met their friends, they saw novelties, and the folk from overseas regarded the place as being marvellous, a real piece of Piccadilly magic. Piccadilly has never been a woman's shopping centre—it is essentially a male street—but women could and did shop of course at Fortnum's. Men with great names, famous in every walk of life, who would never have entered an ordinary provision shop, went into Fortnum and Masons as readily as into their own club. They ordered all sorts of things—for the Victorians lived well and were hearty eaters—caviar, pâté de fois gras, Perigord Pies, guava jelly, Spanish hams, boars' heads, truffles, mangoes, Chinois and Carlsbad plums—everything was available in this Piccadilly emporium.

When Queen Victoria died and King Edward VII ascended the Throne, Britain entered that last decade of real greatness, glory, peace and plenty. There was still High Society, there were fabulous fortunes to spend on entertainment and to make London the gayest and most exciting city in the world in 'The Season'. Fortnum and Mason moved with the times. Nowadays you could just give them an order for a full banquet, or any meal you liked, and they would supply everything, down to the flowers, the toastmaster and the orchestra. In 1908 they opened another department to cope with the growing trade of those going on expeditions and cruises. Through Fortnum and Mason's Piccadilly went all over the world.

Their importance in the scheme of things was such that they became a target for the activities of the suffragettes. Mrs Pankhurst led her troupe of ardent vote-wanting ladies into Piccadilly and they hurled stones and bricks through shop windows but especially through those of Fortnum and Mason. In true Piccadilly manner that firm returned good for evil. When the ladies, who were arrested, came out of Holloway Prison, having served their term, Fortnum and Mason sent them a selection of delicious things to eat. Despite the fact that the 1914–1918 war changed the world, the banner still flew high over 181 Piccadilly. The food shortage and rationing hit them hard but they coped. And then, between the years 1923 and 1925 the firm underwent a change of its own design. The premises were entirely rebuilt—and there they still stand at 181 Piccadilly on the corner of Piccadilly and Duke Street. And the firm's activities have become all embracing —from those original candle ends much has sprung—and you can now buy anything you are likely to want in any line—if you are a lady you can have your hair done and you can lunch or have tea or dine in the delightful restaurant, where the service is quick and carried out by pretty and efficient young ladies—where a very nice orchestra plays melody in keeping with the surroundings and never too loud. When I was there the other day it played a selection of tunes from the old George Edwardes musical comedies at the Gaiety and Dalys—in perfect keeping with the place— and as it played 'Moonstruck' from 'Our Miss Gibbs I thought of my dear and much missed friend Gertie Millar who sang it and who was a customer of Fortnum and Mason's, before and during the time she was Countess of Dudley. Times have changed, prices have altered, values have changed too, but still the best is only good enough for this microcosm of Piccadilly. You cannot buy six dozen of excellent claret there for £5 nowadays—no Indian Rajah could send a lady, as a little token of his esteem, six bottles of champagne, a ham, a tongue, three tins of sardines, a box of fruit, a box of chocolate and a charming little basket of Turkish delight—at a total cost of £5.4.6d—as happened in pre-1914 days, when a golden sovereign went such a long way. But the quality and value are still there. What strikes you when you enter this centre of Piccadilly commerce is the quietness—for instance, the cash registers have no bells—and the good looks, cheerfulness and quick service of all the staff.

People like shopping here. It forges a link between Piccadilly and British people abroad. My old friend Charles S. Brown— with me now almost the last survivor of the old Gaiety Theatre company—although he now lives in New York still deals with Fortnum and Mason's. He sends me a hamper from there every Christmas, bless him. He could send one from New York—but he wants the best. That is the sort of man he is, this very English Old Carthusian. There is a customer in Los Angeles who has fresh Dover soles flown over to him from Fortnum and Mason's.

In that place, the past and the present mingle and the best of both is preserved. Fortnum and Mason's neither forget the past nor ignore the present. On the sixth floor they now make their bread and confectionery and that department is presided over not by a master baker or confectioner, but by the Groom of the Pastry—a title which existed when a Fortnum worked in St James's Palace and which they keep alive to show their unbroken link with Piccadilly. There is no longer any of the original family in the establishment. The High Command today is vested in that Canadian Prince of Industry, Mr Garfield Weston, under whose control since 1951 that same tradition and service has been carried on. And so although there is today no Mr Fortnum and no Mr Mason, Fortnum and Mason's still goes on in Piccadilly as it has done through twelve reigns and one hopes that one will never say Goodbye to it . . . until Piccadilly itself passes away.

3

Piccadilly Goes On

'This day, by the grace of God, the good will of my friends and £5 in my pocket, I have opened my bookshop in Piccadilly'. Thus wrote John Hatchard in his diary on 30th June 1797. And thus was founded the second enduring Giant of Piccadilly, for the shop flourishes in Piccadilly today. It came into being one hundred and nine years after Stewart's, and exactly ninety years after Fortnum and Mason. There had been many more traders in the interim, but none of them had lasted until Hatchard's came along. Fortnum and Mason's catered for the body, Hatchard's catered for the mind. Both carry on today still almost on the original spots and are in character and spirit unchanged despite the changing world about them.

When food had broken the ice, there was an invasion of the eastern end of Piccadilly by booksellers and bookshops, which were of course nice, respectable cultural sort of places such as could be tolerated by the nobility and gentry on their doorsteps or not too far away. Many of these booksellers were also publishers, for it was the time of the Pamphlets, which so inflamed political opinion. Politics was a very strong force and it flourished in Piccadilly. There was Wright's bookshop at 169 Piccadilly, where *The Anti-Jacobin* was published—quite forgotten today no doubt, yet George Canning inspired it and he lived in Albany, just across the road from Wright's shop. No doubt he was always popping in. There was a rather unseemly row in that shop which also spilled over into Piccadilly. William Gifford, son of a Devon glazier and once a shoemaker's apprentice, became a famous critic, editor of *The Anti-Jacobin* and was first editor of *The Quarterly Review*. He fell foul of another critic, one John Wolcot, who wrote under the pen-name of 'Peter Pindar'. Gifford wrote an 'Epistle to Peter Pindar' in which he said

'Thou canst not think, nor have I power to tell
How much I scorn and loathe thee—so farewell.'

Wolcot did not like it. He waited for Gifford outside of Wrights and when Gifford went into the shop he rushed after him, and hit him on the head with his stick. But Gifford, whose hands and arms had been strengthened by his work at bootmaking and also at sea, was far too strong for Wolcot, bustled him out of the shop and threw him into the gutter. Not a very dignified scene for a bookshop or for Piccadilly. *The Anti-Jacobin* finished publication the year before Hatchard's opened. Ridgways was already established. Almon had an establishment opposite Burlington House but he had gone and was succeeded by Debrett, who had been in partnership with him. They had their opponents too. 'A Letter to Edmund Burke', published in 1782, refers to 'that common sink of filth and fiction, the shop of Almon and Debrett in Piccadilly'. This arose because Almon's, which as a firm was devoted to the Whig cause—had published 'Letters in Favour of Wilkes' in 1764.

A very old Piccadilly firm was Hoby's the bootmaker. Mr Hoby was a bit of a character and a great favourite who had his place of business at 160 Piccadilly. Byron mentions him in some of his poems. But he opened a few years after Hatchard's. He had a sense of humour. A very junior ensign, equal to a 'one pipper' today, who was a customer, expressed great dissatisfaction with Mr Hoby's work—and Mr Hoby made boots for all the great people. So the king of the bootmakers, when the ensign said he should withdraw his custom told his assistant, in front of the young man, to put up the shutters, all was over—he was a ruined man. There are other old inhabitants of Piccadilly like the firm of Lincoln and Bennett, but it was the bookshops which mattered, for they added something to the general saga of Piccadilly and it was in them that so many of the famous and great gathered, down the years. And nowhere or in greater force than at Hatchards.

There was a time of course when the printing, publishing and sale of books was almost entirely confined to the City of London, even though Caxton had set up his printing press in Westminster. In the reign of Queen Elizabeth I, the centre of the book trade had been around St Paul's, although it was already seeping into Holborn and the Strand and also into Little Britain. St Paul's Churchyard was the great book centre and that received an almost fatal blow when the Great Fire of 1666 destroyed it—and also many of the books which the booksellers rushed into St Paul's for safety. But when the terror of the Fire and the Plague had died away, booksellers, like good conservative Londoners, returned to practically the same spot and settled in Paternoster Row—displacing the mercers and soft goods men who had been there. Paternoster Row, despite another disastrous fire, still hangs on to some of the book trade today. In the reign of Queen Anne it was supreme, but adventurers were breaking away. Rivington opened there in 1711, but the great Jacob Tonson moved to the Strand and Barnaby Percival Lintott opened in Fleet Street, between the Temple Gates. Edmund Curll, who became rather notorious was at Temple Bar and some had already put up their signs in Covent Garden. One man, more enterprising perhaps than all the rest, Dodsley—an ex-footman turned poet—actually opened in Pall Mall in 1735. His establishment was the farthest west.

Booksellers in the early days, and for many years afterwards, were much more than mere sellers of books and publishers. Their shops were used as clubs by authors, wits and men of fashion, who frequented them as readily as they did the coffee rooms. Each shop had its back parlour and any man of learning and wit was welcome. The day of the literary or social club was not yet come to strength. It was in the back parlour of Tom Davies' bookshop in Russell Street, Covent Garden, that Boswell first met Dr Samuel Johnson.

In January, 1782, a printer named Bensley, who had an establishment in a court off the Strand, took on a new apprentice whose name was John Hatchard. The lad was fourteen years old and was starting to earn his own living. He had been a pupil at the Greycoat School. But young Master Hatchard did not like printing—perhaps he did not like Bensley either—and in less than a month he was home again. His father had to find him another job. He went on trial to a Mr Ginger, who was a bookseller and publisher with a sound connection and a shop in Great College Street, Westminster. Master Hatchard joined Mr Ginger on 17th June 1782. Apparently he liked the business, for in the September he was bound apprentice. Mr Ginger did not control a famous establishment and did not count great people as his customers, but somehow young Hatchard got an insight into what bookselling and publishing could be, and he became acquainted with a young man who dealt at the shop whose name was George Canning. And a great deal came of that later. John Hatchard served Ginger faithfully for just over seven years. He formed the habit, which he never gave up, of keeping diaries in penny exercise books.

He wrote down a memorandum of a most important day: 'Apprenticeship expired October 18, 1789, which was served duly and truly, and on 19th my friends congratulated me (at my father's expense; a good supper and a flowing bowl of punch, with some good songs, toasts and sentiments). On the 26th day of the same month was situated as shopman with Mr Payne, Bookseller, Mews Gate, Castle Street, St Martins. On 2nd day of December 1789, I took up my freedom at the expense of my father, which cost about five pounds.'

Thomas Payne was a most notable bookseller, who was renowned for his honesty which was repeatedly put on record by eminent men. Great scholars and men of letters congregated in that shop in Castle Street (where the National Gallery now stands) which was shaped like an L and which became known as the Literary Coffee House. Young Hatchard was in contact with the lions of literature and learning of his day. The example of Mr Payne and the atmosphere of his surroundings planted in him a quality which was also inherent, for it never left him all his life. He made friends and connections which were useful to him in his future career and there is no doubt that he was happy. And he must have known he was doing well and establishing himself because after being employed by Payne for less than a year he married, on 11th July 1790. His wife's name was Elizabeth Lambert and he writes, 'having come to man's estate I have only to hope for the blessing of God, long life, health, prosperity and happiness.' He was not disappointed. He worked for Payne at Mews Gate for almost eight years and until he had reached the age of twenty-nine, when he felt he should put his own fortune to the test. He had of course chosen to carry on as a bookseller. But where should he open his own shop? He had plenty of choice. He could go to the Strand, into the City itself, to Paternoster Row, or he could follow the sun and the trend of building expansion and move westward. He might go to Pall Mall—he might go to Piccadilly.

As has already been explained, Piccadilly was a very different place from what it is now when Hatchard explored it with a view to staking his claim, for like generations of young men later, he had decided to 'Go West'. There was no Regent Street. There was the eastern side of Piccadilly with the Haymarket, St James's Street, Pall Mall and Jermyn Street, and that square of habitation was the very pith of London's west end, wealth and nobility. Mayfair was further along, Belgravia only in its birth pangs and Piccadilly stretched as far as Hyde Park Corner, full of great houses and great people. It was already a very busy thoroughfare, for it had inns from which stage coaches started. There were indeed more inns in Piccadilly then than there are now, for they have blossomed into hotels. But it had already become one of the termini for travellers to and from London and provincial cities. 'The White Bear' Inn properly belongs to Piccadilly Circus and will be dealt with later but it was then reckoned as part of Piccadilly because, when Hatchard's started, there was no Circus at all. There was a 'Black Bear' too near its white rival. There was, in Piccadilly itself, the Gloucester Coffee House and Hotel, spelt 'Gloster' in those days and for a time known also as the St James's Hotel. That stood upon the corner of Berkeley Street and is still there today as the Berkeley Hotel. Its linkmen and porters carry the signs of its antiquity in their picturesque old English livery. In 1805 it advertised 'good soups, dinners, wines and beds'.

There was the 'Three Kings', at No 67, now Hatchett's Restaurant. From there General Palmer started the mail coach service to Bath. Where the Ritz Hotel now stands was 'The Old White Horse Cellar' then No 155. This was one of the famous coaching inns of England. It was there in 1720, and a description in 1805 in a sort of superior guide called 'A Picture of London' says 'This house is well known to the public on account of the great number of stage coaches which regularly call there. In a pleasant coffee room passengers can wait for any of the stages and travellers in general are well accommodated with beds.' The old time travellers were, it would seem, a good deal more fussy about their beds than their descendants today and hotels do not now make a feature of the comfort of their beds in their advertisements. It might not be a bad idea if they did and lived up to it. Down at the Hyde Park Corner end of Piccadilly were a cluster of eight taverns, all of which have vanished. But they included the well known 'Pillars of Hercules'—where Fieldings 'Squire Western' called and chatted with the landlord, where the Marquis of Granby (who gave his name to so many public houses) was a constant visitor and to which Sheridan and Captain Mathews repaired when the duel over Miss Linley was interrupted. There were records of 'The Pillars of Hercules' as early as 1676.

When John Hatchard surveyed Piccadilly with a view to

starting in business it was of course a busy flourishing place which despite the stage coaches and their bustle of coming and going still held to its great quality and what might now be called its 'smartness'—although that was then supplied by lineage and breeding rather than riches and show. There were bookshops there already, but that did not deter him—it probably encouraged him—and so by the 'Grace of God, the goodwill of my friends and £5 in my pocket' Mr Hatchard ventured his all. On 1st July 1797 he took a shop which had lately been run by Mr White at 173 Piccadilly and paid £31.10.0d. for goodwill and £40 rent per annum. From the beginning he prospered. Friends helped him, as did his ex-employer Tom Payne who did not even object to some of his customers transferring to Hatchard.

It should be remembered that he was not only a bookseller but a publisher too. He saw his way quite clearly. In religion he was Evangelical and his politics were Tory. It was at those two bodies of thought and opinion that he aimed and it so happened that they were in the ascendant. The Tories were most active and they were determined that the horrors of the French Revolution should not be repeated here. Hatchard had hardly opened his shop when he published a Pamphlet entitled 'Reform or Ruin; Take Your Choice'. It was written by John Bowdler, who was the father of the better known Thomas Bowdler, who performed the expurgations on Shakespeare. This pamphlet was a tremendous success and Hatchard admitted it formed the basis of his fortune. Almost immediately he was made publisher of *The Christian Observer* and also of the 'Reports of the Society for the Bettering the Condition of the Poor'. This had been formed by Wilberforce in 1796, with Sir Thomas Bernard, F. J. Eliot, who with Charles Grant, James Stephens and Zachary Macaulay, formed the hard core of what was known as 'The Clapham Sect', dedicated to reforming the Church of England from within. The amazing Hannah More was a great supporter, not that she lived in Clapham at any time. John Bowdler of pamphlet fame was also a Clapham Secter. They were not a sect, but were very important. Indeed, the whole of the Low Church Party which had based itself on Rivington's bookshop in St Paul's Churchyard, left there and transferred to Hatchard's in Piccadilly. Hannah More had a good deal to do with this and she must always be held in respect by anyone who writes, likes or deals in books for her ambition to come to London and 'see the Bishops and the bookshops'. She had much to do with the career of Thomas Babington, Lord Macaulay—no stranger to Hatchard's either. Wilberforce had an office there. The very important people who formed this sect treated Hatchard's as a species of club—which suited its proprietor. He regarded them as people to be given the best service, and we find that Wilberforce himself borrowed half-a-guinea—charged of course to his account, and a Richard Heber, whose brother was a Bishop—had 2/- charged to him, as 'cash for gloves'.

Hatchards was already famous, and Sydney Smith, who ran *The Edinburgh Review* took a critical shot at its patrons in 1810. 'There is a set of well-dressed prosperous gentlemen who assemble daily at Mr Hatchard's shop' he says, 'clean, civil personages well in with the people in power, delighted with every existing institution and almost with every existing circumstance; and every now and then one of these personages writes a little book and the rest praise that little book, expecting to be praised in their turn for their own little books, and of these clean books thus written by these clean, civil personages so expecting to be praised, the pamphlet before us appears to be one'... But although his picture is true in the main if slightly malicious, he is not quite right. One of the things which concerned those people meeting at Hatchard's and for which they worked, was the Abolition of the Slave Trade.

What sort of a person was John Hatchard? He was handsome, with a fine face and noble head, and his sterling character looked forth from his eyes. He had, in his business associations and with his firm religious beliefs, much to do with the Church and his clothes reflected that. 'He was invariably dressed in black. His coat was of the style of a bishop's frock coat, waistcoat buttoning to

Clarendon House

Clarges House

Piccadilly, near the Circus, in 1894

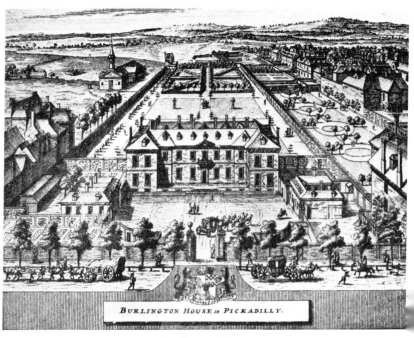

BURLINGTON HOUSE in PICKADILLY.

Burlington House

the throat with an entirely plain front and knee breeches and gaiters'. He looked what he was—completely trustworthy and reliable. Dickens tells us that the public always trusted 'buttoned up' men—and such was John Hatchard.

Not only literary people forgathered at this kind of club with no subscription or entrance fee, which was Hatchard's book shop. An organisation which had nothing whatever to do with litera- ture met there and indeed became established for what it still is today—the Royal Horticultural Society—which really got going 'at a meeting held at the house of Mr Hatchard, the Publisher, in Piccadilly' on 7th March 1804. There seems little in common between Piccadilly and horticulture, but that was where the famous society blossomed, although the field which once formed Piccadilly had long since been lost to sight and even the bugloss bloomed no more. But London and Londoners must have their horticultural pleasures: in no other city in the world will you find so many window boxes or such ardent cultivation of plants and flowers of all kinds in areas and basements. It always astonishes the foreigner.

Such was Mr Hatchard's success that he moved to larger premises in 1801, when he had been established for only four years. He moved from No. 173 to No. 190 buying a 24 years lease for one thousand guineas, half paid on the spot and the other half within two years. So rapidly had that original capital of £5 increased that John Hatchard felt no qualms.

These early years of the 19th century were a boom time for books. It was estimated that in 1816 no less than 800 new books and pamphlets were issued every year at a turnover of £2,000,000 and that in London no less than 2,000 people were employed in the trade.

Hatchard was now in the very front rank, if indeed he was not the premier bookseller and publisher. It was reported in 1816 that 'Nicoll in Pall Mall is bookseller to the King, Hatchard to the Queen, Murray to the Admiralty, Black and Co. to the East India Company and Egerton to the War Office'. But a note adds 'The shops which are frequented as lounging shops, and which are provided with all new publications, newspapers, etc. are Ridgeway's, Stockdale, and Hatchard's, all in Piccadilly'. So Piccadilly was the centre of literature. Hatchard kept up that club and lounge meeting place atmosphere always. And everybody who was anybody—of his way of thinking—came along Piccadilly and called in. Disraeli said 'Debrett's was the chief haunt of the Whigs, Hatchard's, I believe, of the Tories. It was at the latter house that my father Isaac D'Israeli made the acquaintance of Mr Pye.' He had been Poet Laureate since 1790 and he wrote deplorable verse. Hatchard would have liked to publish Byron, but that was done by Murray's, so he had to be content with the Poet Laureate, bad as he was. But he did publish the works of the great poet George Crabbe. In 1807 there appeared a volume of his poems and two days after a review of them appeared in *The Edinburgh Review*. Hatchard sold out the entire first edition. Crabbe's piety and high moral tone no doubt appealed to Hatchard. Beloe, an early customer of his who had also been a customer of Tom Payne, issued a list of booksellers, anonymous but adjectivally described in a book of his, and in this Hatchard appears as the 'Godly Bookseller, a worthy and conscientious man'.

Hatchard's stock and undertakings were far reaching. His catalogues were voluminous and all embracing, ranging through every conceivable field of literature, even to plays and treatises on how to prolong one's life. There were many sermons too. Hatchard was one of the mostly highly respected sons of Piccadilly.

Yet he did not escape calumny. In 1817 he was involved in a libel action which must have shocked him profoundly. It was all because of an uncorrected error in the 'Tenth Report of the Directors of the African Institution', which was said to contain a libel on the 'Aides-de-Camp of Sir James Leigh, Governor and Commander-in-Chief of the Leeward Islands and the Grand Jury of the Island of Antigua'. On a technical point Hatchard lost, although his counsel's eulogy of his character was accepted by all and he left the Court without a stain on his character. Wilberforce said that his friends would not see him suffer and kept his word. Hatchard did not suffer. He moved to another shop at No 187 Piccadilly and there this true Piccadilly firm still is today.

The Royal Horticultural Society was not the only society unconnected with literature to be nurtured at Hatchard's. There was another which started with tea and buns but did not become royal; indeed there is no record of what became of it. It is quite intriguing however, for it was called the Outinian Society. It existed, the rules said, for the promotion of marriages and its object was to ascertain, by enquiries, the suitability of would-be contracting parties—and to advise and supply helpful information to those who wished to marry. One wonders if Mr Punch's famous advice was ever used? Mr Hatchard lent his premises and is said to have 'lent his initials', whatever that might mean, to this project. Many wondered why such a good man of business and such a very respectable and upright man should have been connected with it any way, not that there seems to have been any harm. But doubtless Mr Hatchard made a small charge for the use of the premises and his time. Hatchard's in 1817 looked much the same as Hatchard's of today. But there was a porch outside the shop under which the servants of the customers could shelter, and a fireplace inside, which has been restored, a large table which bore all the newspapers, and chairs for the weary to rest in.

The firm has numerous relics of its customers, kept in an old leather-bound book. There is the following letter:—

'Walmer Castle. Sept 19, 1833

'Mr Hatchard,

I beg you to send to my house in London to be forwarded to me here

Hamiltons Men and Manners in the United States
De Haussey Sur L'angleterre
The pamphlet recently published on the last Session of PARLT.

Your most obediant Servant
Wellington.'

Wellington had been an early customer of Hatchard's, arriving on horseback to make his purchases. Fortnum and Mason's and Hatchard's between them have seen every form of transport pass along Piccadilly—wagons, wains, carts, pack horses, great travelling coaches, saddle horses, sedan chairs, and then, when Hatchard arrived, lighter carriages, curricles, phaetons, all the various forms of carriages used before the motor took control. Both those firms saw the stage coaches bow to the railways and then in turn the arrival of air travel open up the world.

But there are all sorts of handwriting in that prized book—and in contrast to the short and explicit style of Wellington comes one from the Earl of Grosvenor, dated Eaton, Jan 1st 1833.

'Dear Sir,

I have desired my servant to deliver to you two more copies of the Chronological Chart on Rollers to be sold at 15/- each—you are quite at liberty to mention my name as the Compiler which might facilitate the sale with some of my acquaintances—Believe me to remain very faithfully yours,

Grosvenor.'

Wonderful names jostle each other, the Duke of Richmond, the Duke of Leeds, Winchelsea, Anglesey, Londonderry, Liverpool, Lord Spencer and Lord Willoughby de Broke; Lord Clancarty, Earl Bathurst, Lord Saye and Sele. Many, many more, some scarcely decipherable, but finally made out as Bolton, Decies, Hotham and Lauderdale. There are many Bishops, as one might expect and there is W. E. Gladstone, in 1834, who was then a Tory. And there are Peel, Palmerston, Derby and a very different kind of nobleman, Lord Henry Seymour, who was a real exotic character. There is no signature of Macaulay, who was a customer. He probably called in himself and took the books away with him. Since he was a little boy Hannah More had been buying books for him at Hatchard's. She was most concerned about him. When he was six she wrote to him 'Though you are a little boy now, you will one day, if it please God, be a man, but long before you are a man I pray you will be a scholar. I therefore wish you to purchase such books as will be useful and agreeable to you *then* and that you will employ this little sum in laying a corner stone to your library.' And a couple of years later she wrote to him again complimenting him on two letters free from blots which had entitled him to another book. She told him to go to Hatchard's and choose and gave him good advice to help the selection. Master Macaulay—reading epics and forming them in his own head—was apparently neglecting prose, for Hannah wrote to Zachary Macaulay, 'I do not find he has been to Hatchard's for a book yet. He could not determine his choice when here. He is not to be circumscribed in anything within two guineas; but I wish he would condescend to read a little prose.' Thus was Macaulay's love of books firmly cemented. His friendship with Hatchard's grew closer and closer and he actually did some work in the shop, acting as index maker to his father and John Hatchard. It is probable that it was to Hatchard that he first confided his intention of writing his *History of England*. The Hatchard family had in the 18th and early 19th century lived over their shop in Piccadilly. Then they moved to Clapham—a suitable move seeing the close connection with the Clapham Sect. The Macaulays moved there in 1802 and often young Macaulay would travel down with his friend Hatchard. Later Macaulay moved into Albany in Piccadilly. He wrote his history and Hatchard's published it. The first two volumes of this monumental work were published in 1848 and were very successful.

At this time John Hatchard was nearly eighty. His children were middle aged. His eldest son, also John, did not succeed his father in the business but went into the Church, being educated first at Oxford, then at Cambridge, where he took his B.A. and M.A. degrees. He became Vicar of St Andrew's Church, Plymouth where he remained until he died. It was the second son, Thomas, who carried on the firm. He was born in 1794 and went into the business as soon as he was old enough to do so. He married in 1815 and had four children, a son and three daughters. The son became the Bishop of Mauritius. It is a pity his grandfather did not live to see this, for it would have filled him with pride. Thomas was not quite so severe in his dress as his father. He wore a blue dress coat with a velvet collar, gilt buttons, white cravat, yellow waistcoat and brown nankeen trousers. But he carried on the same views, tradition and benevolence.

Martin Tupper, some of whose works Hatchard's published, described John Hatchard. 'When that good old man, Grandfather Hatchard, more than an octogenarian, first saw me he placed his hand on my dark hair and said, tears in his eyes, 'You will thank God for this book when your hair comes to be as white as mine'. Let me gratefully acknowledge that he was a true prophet. When I was writing the concluding essay of the first series my father (not quite such a true prophet as old Hatchard) exhorted me to burn it, as his ambition was to make a lawyer of me.'

Although Hatchard was not quite so old as Tupper made out, it is a charming picture and tailpiece. For the great bookseller died on 21st June 1849 having run his business for more than fifty years. He had seen many changes, for the world at that time was a melting pot and Piccadilly one of the channels through which the material poured. He had seen the balance of social power shift and change and the rise of the Middle Class. He had risen from errand boy to be the most respected bookseller and publisher in London. That £5 with which he had started had now increased to £100,000. And all that had happened in Piccadilly. His son Thomas had not his father's stature in any degree beyond honesty and integrity. He ran the business well and efficiently and he died in Brighton on 13th November 1858. And the male line of the Hatchard's was now extinct as far as the business was concerned. But Henry Hudson, a great grandson of John Hatchard, was there and he carried on efficiently too. Hatchard's ceased to be publishers but they never ceased to sell books.

As in the history of nations, when a man is required to take charge and carry on, one arises, so it has happened in the history of Hatchard's. Down in Bristol was a bookseller named William

Mack, who had invented those pleasant social things called Birthday Books. He had taken on an errand boy—whose age at the time was fourteen and whose name was A. L. Humphreys. Mr Mack decided to sell up his Bristol business and come to London, where he had an agency—carried on by his sons—in Paternoster Row. He took the errand boy to London with him. That boy's imagination was fired by the thought of London and the idea of Paternoster Row in particular. He suffered considerable disillusionment, but he worked on, and he developed a great love for London. When free on Saturday afternoons he would walk about the city and then he penetrated the West End. He went along Piccadilly which gave him a thrill and he got an even greater one when he saw a shop about which he knew something—a grand, dignified shop with black and gold pillars—and the name was Hatchard. He stood in awe. This was where they had published *The Peep of Day*—a book he had seen at home, and which had impressed him. He gazed at Hatchard's a long time. Young Humphreys earned 15/- a week with Mack. He wanted a rise, asked for it, was told the business could not stand it and was very disappointed. A few days later a friend of his showed him an advertisement in *The Publishers Circular*. The date was 15th October 1881. It said 'Wanted, a Junior Assistant, aged 20 to 25. A good writer, quick, active, industrious, and thoroughly steady and respectable, with some knowledge of the retail trade. Apply by letter only to Messrs Hatchard's, 187 Piccadilly.' He wrote at once, he could not wait—he got an answer—he got the job. Neither he nor the manager who offered him the princely wage of £1 a week realised what was to come of this engagement. Truly there is a tide in the affairs of men. . . .

He himself has left us a picture of what Hatchard's was like when he entered it. 'The building at 187 Piccadilly where the business was conducted was then one of the old residential houses and in former days the Hatchard family lived in a large part of the front upper floors. At the back and on the lower floors there were heaps of narrow staircases, dark corners, and low ceilinged attics all fitted with books. An atmosphere rather sombre and religious hung over the whole place. The assistants seemed to me to be all very old men either with beards or side-whiskers. Some of them treated me at first as being entirely beneath their notice. However, I soon made friends and disarmed criticism. A new and vast world of books was now opened before me. Whereas up to the day when I went to Hatchard's the books I had handled were trifling things such as are used for village Sunday School prizes, here in Piccadilly I saw the best of everything. It was of course bewildering at first for a boy who was only sixteen.'

How right was Mr Humphreys about the best of everything—that is, or has been up to now, the destiny of Piccadilly. He gives his own secret away—he had that heaven sent gift of being able to make friends. And make them he did, for himself and for Hatchard's. He was also amazed at first at the people who came to buy books. He saw the great ones of the land alighting from their carriages and coming into the shop. He says 'The great and good Lord Shaftesbury looked sometimes, so I thought, so downcast because the wretchedness of the world was almost too much for him to bear.' Neither he nor the noble Lord had any idea of Eros arising in those days—to make Piccadilly Circus the centre of the world in which the Earl saw such wretchedness. 'Lady Mount Temple,' says Master Humphreys, 'one of Ruskin's great friends then an old lady but who carried herself with most wonderful dignity, was one of the most striking people I can recall.' He gives another glimpse of the times, 'Then there were certain folk who would now and then drive up in state with two powdered footmen in breeches and white stockings standing up behind.' He recalls a crowd gathering to watch this—so it would appear that some of the pomp and circumstance, once part and parcel of its everyday existence, had gone from Piccadilly in the 80's. Not so long before footmen so dressed were the rule rather than the exception. Had not Hatchard's provided a bench for them to rest upon whilst their employers were in the shop?

Humphreys had that supreme quality for anyone dealing in

books, not often found today, it is feared: he had a great love for books himself, and for everything connected with literature. He still explored London and spent a lot of time in now vanished Holywell Street, which was the heart and centre of the second-hand book trade. Aldwych now covers its site. He read the classics in cheap or secondhand editions. He could not afford more than 6d. There was hardly a secondhand bookshop in London whose contents, as displayed in the window or on shelves outside or in the doorway, he did not know by heart. He looked so friendly and so anxious to please that even exalted customers took notice of him and that ability to make friends worked always. The Duchess of Rutland of the period who did much good work asked him for advice as to what books she should put into some of the institutions—reading rooms for working girls—in which she was interested. His answers were so good and so much to the point that she thanked him publicly by name and in print. All this sort of thing was noticed by Hatchard's. He gained advancement.

Many of the customers now began to ask for him by name. Amongst those who did so were the Ladies Cynthia, Helen and Hermione Duncombe, three of the most lovely women of their time. Lady Hermione became the Duchess of Leinster. He gained kudos too through Lady Brook, who became Lady Warwick. She came to the shop and asked for a very obscure book to be got for her the following day without fail. Young Humphreys' habit of staring in bookshop windows and his impeccable memory stood him in good stead. He believed he knew where it was, rushed off, got it and Her Ladyship had her book the next day. She was so impressed that she asked him to help her build and found a library. That was one of the first of many such tasks he undertook for Hatchard's. He built up a branch of the business along these lines and loved doing it. Lord Stanhope's library at Chevening, Lord Derby's, at Knowsley, were two in which he had a hand. And when the Edwardian days were coming near and books became important, Humphreys began to supply and

c*

to stock libraries at many great houses and for many great people.
What was his status with the firm now? A gentleman named
E. A. M. Shepherd, who had been apprenticed to Thomas
Hatchard, was running Hatchard's. The firm prospered in the
main but had its ups and downs.One day in March 1891, into the
shop strode Alfred Taylor, a former manager of Hatchard's who
had ridden up on horseback. He asked to see Shepherd and told
him that Hatchard's was for sale—it had been advertised in *The
Times* that morning. The family was selling out. Taylor said to
Shepherd, 'You must buy it, and I will help you'. They made the
purchase and did more; they made young Humphreys a partner.
He was now the moving spirit of the place and great people came
to see him. On a spring afternoon in 1893 he was in his office and
two visitors were shown in. One was a Member of Parliament,
James Rochefort Maguire. The other was a man who despite his
rather high voice and not robust body—nevertheless exuded
power, for he was Cecil Rhodes. He wanted a library in his house
overlooking Table Mountain which should contain every book
which Gibbon had consulted when writing his *Decline and Fall*—
which had almost paralysed Rhodes's imagination. This was
indeed a task. But Rhodes came to Hatchard's to do it and
Humphreys, for Hatchard's, undertook it. He also formed an
influential working committee, and the job was done. Humphreys
ran Hatchard's during the glittering nineties, so often called
'naughty' with little reason but truly glittering in so many ways.
The names of Hatchard's customers are a roll of honour: Andrew
Lang, Frank Danby, Captain Harry Graham (who wanted a list
of the Hundred Worst Books), Rudyard Kipling, W. L. George,
George Moore and Rhoda Broughton. There were also 'Victoria
Cross', Hall Caine, Mrs Humphrey Ward—so many, many more
—in fact everyone who mattered. Oscar Wilde's last visit to the
shop was the night before *The Importance of Being Earnest* was
produced at nearby St James's Theatre. And if ghosts come to
Hatchard's, as well they might, they would include Sir Gilbert
Parker, Robert Hichens, Maurice Hewlett, Anthony Hope,

Ronald Firbank, Fergus Hume, Phillips Oppenheim, G. K. Chesterton and E. V. Lucas.

Mr Humphreys was indeed the vital spark of Hatchard's until he retired in 1924, one of the best known men in Piccadilly. The two sons of Edwin Shepherd carried on and Mr E. W. Shepherd, who joined the firm in 1891, completed over 50 years' service with it, holding the Royal Warrants for Kings George V and VI.

Hatchard's today is a place of quality. Although the celebrities do not lounge in and out and sit and read the paper, there is still a charming room, full of atmosphere, where friendly gatherings are held, where people who love books meet the men and women who write them, and where that spirit which fostered the Royal Horticultural Society still lingers. There is still about Hatchard's the original atmosphere of the bookshop of the period when it first came to Piccadilly and such places were unofficial clubs. Customers in that shop do not seem so much customers as members using the club premises. There is no hurry, no rushing about, but the service is quick and unobtrusive. Indeed, the books themselves seem to take on life and to communicate with you. They are not just pieces of merchandise, but something endowed with humanity.

And in 187 Piccadilly the spirit which has been with Piccadilly since its creation is still strong. The ghosts are there and so is the living present. Yesterday mingles with today and Modernity rubs shoulders with Olden Times. That, indeed, is the essence and part of the magic of London, and it can be sensed so strongly in that very English bulwark of this English thoroughfare with the curiously foreign name.

4

Victorian Piccadilly

Piccadilly, in Victorian times, must have been the richest street on earth. A claim might have been put in for Park Lane where millionaires resided who had made millions quickly—some of them—and whose money was in opposite ratio to their birth. But in England then, birth still mattered and in Piccadilly still many of the great families held on and their wealth was prodigious if it was not lavishly displayed. Of course the thoroughfare was changing, it was always changing, it is doing so still—and commerce was steadily infiltrating. For Victorian times were the greatest of the commercial period of our history. And entertainment crept in as well. This began in a very small and odd way at the far end, at Hyde Park Corner. There was, in the early 18th century a place there called 'Winstanley's Water Theatre'—which was full of mechanical devices which amazed generations who had not been used to machinery. In 1713 it advertised a marvel: 'Six sorts of wine and brandy, to drink the Queen's health, all coming out of the barrel, with bisket and spaw water; and as peace is inlarged; there will be added Claret, Pale Ale, Stout and Water, playing out of the head of the barrel when it is in the pulley.' Some may remember, in far more recent times, the same trick being done with a kettle—and probably done by the same means. Winstanley and his magic are quite forgotten now but he planted a seed of magic in the magical mile which came to bloom a little lower down the road. For one of the giants of entertainment which flourished in Piccadilly was the Egyptian Hall. Piccadilly stood for nobility and in natural sequence for culture. It has been shown how, with the exception of food and catering, the early outcrop of commercialism in Piccadilly was literature: bookshops and publishers. It is worthy of note, too, that Chapman and Hall, great publishers indeed, had their establishment in Piccadilly—almost where Hatchard's stands today and that from there issued *Pickwick Papers* and *Nicholas Nickleby* in their serial forms, so that Dickens can be claimed as of Piccadilly.

Culture stood high in the early 19th century, and the Egyptian Hall, one of the strangest places Piccadilly ever knew, had its roots in culture. It was built in the year 1812, from the designs of a Mr G. F. Robinson, and it cost £16,000. Its object was to be a museum of natural history and to house the collection of William Bullock, F.L.S., mostly gained from the South Seas, Africa and North and South America. For some reason which cannot be discovered this building was built to resemble something in the nature of an Egyptian Temple—or Pharaoh's Palace—whichever you fancied. It had no place or companionship in very English Piccadilly at all. On both sides of it, when first built, were gracious Georgian houses of red brick, with their little balconies, and then came this exotic affair. It was yellowish of façade, with a pillared entrance above which stood two gigantic figures, who might have been Pharaohs—who in turn supported on their heads a large canopy. There were big recessed windows with Egyptian style surrounds to them and there were hieroglyphics all over the place. Across the foot, beneath the feet of the mighty figures, the word 'Exhibition' was cut in stone. It may not have been genuine Egyptian but it was near enough to be Piccadilly Egyptian and looked upon with some awe by passers-by. The natural history

77

exhibits did not attract and were in due course dispersed and replaced by a strange gentleman known as 'The Living Skeleton'. He was a Frenchman, born at Champagne in 1798 and it was in 1825 that he arrived at the Egyptian Hall and became an attraction of Piccadilly. He was 5 feet 7½ inches tall—and he weighed only 77¾ lbs. It must hardly have been worth while. He was followed by numerous strange things in this strange Egyptian stronghold, of whom a notable example were the original Siamese Twins, in 1829, described at the time as 'two youths of eighteen, natives of Siam, united by a short band at the pit of the stomach—two perfect bodies bound together by an inseparable link'. They died in America in 1874.

But the most famous of all the earlier visitors to the Egyptian Hall was General Tom Thumb. His real name was Charles S. Stratton, and he came from Bridgeport, Connecticut. The great showman Barnum took him up and toured the world with this midget as an attraction, and the General, as he had become, was a phenomenal success. Barnum first brought him to this country in 1844. He did not come straight to London because he had made up his mind that Tom Thumb should appear before Queen Victoria, before giving public performances, but the Court was in mourning. He got a shock too in Manchester where he was told that the price English people were in the habit of paying to see giants and dwarfs was one penny per head. Barnum had made up his mind that the lowest price of admission would be 1/- and he was determined he would get it—and more. He came to London with the General and gave three performances at the old Princess's Theatre, in Oxford Street, which he regarded as publicity. The manager of the theatre was Maddox, who had gone down to see the General at Liverpool, where he had appeared a few times in a hall. Barnum boosted the dwarf—and great crowds came to the Princess's. But the astute showman would give only the three performances. He hired, instead, a great mansion, belonging to Lord Talbot, in Grafton Street, and there he invited the nobility—gentry—and the Press—to meet the little man. And they came.

They all talked about the amazing midget. Crowds flocked to the mansion, all to be turned away by polite but implacable butlers and footmen. If they had no invitation cards they could not come in. In a few days General Tom Thumb was the talk of the town, the talk of England. But Barnum knew that to get the fullest value he must have the approval of Queen Victoria. He refused to be daunted by the fact that the Court was in mourning, in point of fact, this was very often the case, so deep and widespread were the family ramifications of the Queen. The showman enlisted the aid of everybody possible. He got hold of the American Minister to the Court of St James's, one Edward Everett, a tough customer but one who succumbed to the combined wiles of Barnum and Tom Thumb. The General delighted him and he promised to do his best. Barnum had a real glimpse of British wealth and power when the Baroness Rothschild summoned him and the General to her presence. The American was dumbfounded at the splendour, the riches—it was like entering Aladdin's Cave—and at the end he was given a purse full of gold.

Barnum decided that General Tom Thumb could now be exhibited. So he decided also that the right place for this debut was Piccadilly. Consequently he took the Egyptian Hall. He took, of course, one of the large rooms—there were other smaller ones. In one of those a painter named Haydon was exhibiting a picture of his, an immense and massive work of art. Large pictures were fashionable then and this was something similar to those huge canvasses painted by Doré. Haydon considered it a masterpiece and hoped to make money, of which he stood in sore need, by exhibiting it at the Egyptian Hall. But nobody wanted to see the picture—they all wanted to see the dwarf. Haydon had the extreme mortification of seeing crowds pass by his hall without a glance, all intent on seeing General Tom Thumb. Filled with frustration and despair he committed suicide.

Whilst General Tom Thumb was drawing crowds, and shillings, into the Egyptian Hall, what Barnum had hoped for came about. He met Mr Charles Murray, Master of the Royal Household, at the American Ambassador's. He told Mr Murray he was going to take the General over to Paris as Louis Philippe wanted to see him. Murray swallowed the bait and was sure that Her Majesty would want to see the celebrated dwarf before the French king did so. Soon afterwards, a note was received, bidding Mr Barnum to bring his tiny protégé to Buckingham Palace to appear before the Queen. Her Majesty intimated that she wished him to give his usual performance and not one primed and altered by Royal Limitations of Ceremony. The visit was a great success, the Queen unbent and both Barnum and Tom Thumb gave lively satisfaction.

Barnum had made full use of this situation. On the night when the visit was paid to Buckingham Palace, a large bill was displayed on the door of the Egyptian Hall which told Piccadilly and all who passed by, 'Closed this Evening, General Tom Thumb being at Buckingham Palace by Command of Her Majesty'. Queen Victoria was delighted with the little man, who visited the Palace three times, and Barnum had to take the largest of the halls in the Egyptian Hall to try and accommodate those who flocked to see the General. Phineas T. Barnum and General Tom Thumb were both figures of Piccadilly.

But what many people, now in their declining years, will remember about the Egyptian Hall is that it was London's home of magic, so suitably situated in Piccadilly. Two master magicians, whose names were Maskelyne and Cooke took it over, made it a place of wonder and remained there for years as one of the institutions of London. They could not have chosen a better place. It was billed as 'England's Home of Mystery' and it was so indeed. The place was dark and dingy—those clever men Maskelyne and Cooke did not waste money on making it bright with paint and shining with light. They knew that its dark, rather cavelike atmosphere would induce the right feeling in the audience, and, when you entered, you felt that you were in a place where magic was to be expected. There was suspense in the air, with no hurry and bustle but a sense of timelessness and of brooding, as though great jinnees were still imprisoned in bottles and jars, waiting for the mediums of magic, Maskelyne and Cooke, to unleash them. This was a place, you felt, where anything could happen—and believe me, it did. You stepped out of the whirl of Piccadilly into another world.

The entertainment was most refined. It was of the drawing room variety which Victorian days demanded and which in Edwardian days was required, for children and everyone went to the Egyptian Hall. The most amazing things happened. A man named David Devant, afterwards to become a partner, did wonderful conjuring and kept so many plates on the spin altogether at the same time that the senses reeled with them. He never let one fall down. There was a remarkable organ; there was a kind of trick orchestra which really was the forerunner of that marvel of the films, stereophonic sound, for it played 'The Death of Nelson' from all sorts of unlikely places in the building and filled its listeners with wonder. That organ, too, pealed out 'The Bay of Biscay' with terrific effects in the way of thunder and lightning, more than a little frightening to nervous children who got some strange thrill out of it all the same.

There was also an entertainer at the piano there for a long time whose name was Mel B. Spurr, the Mel being a corruption or abbreviation of Melancthon, a most extraordinary name for a boy to be saddled with. At the time of his birth his parents, good honest and God-fearing Yorkshire folk, were deeply interested in D'Aubigne's *History of the Reformation* and especially in the life and character of Philip Melancthon. Mel B. Spurr became an entertainer of the same kind as George Grossmith of Gilbert and Sullivan fame, and Corney Grain, who crosses the Piccadilly story later. Such 'acts' were immensely popular and Mel B. Spurr was one of the very best. His face was most expressive; it was like indiarubber and he did as he liked with it. He could sing, he could act, he had complete mastery of the piano and he wrote much of his own material. He was a fixture at the Egyptian Hall for eleven years. It may well be that there remain ladies and gentlemen of

mature age who recall this man at the piano, reciting one of his
most famous pieces to musical accompaniment:—

  'Listen to the water-mill
  Through the live-long day.
  How the clicking of its wheel
  Wears the hours away
  Languidly the autumn wind
  Stirs the forest leaves
  From the fields the reapers sing
  Binding up their sheaves;
  And a proverb haunts my mind
  As a spell is cast
  "The mill cannot grind
  With the water that is past". . . .'

That was amazingly popular: amateurs used it at musical
evenings, concerts and the like all over the kingdom, but it
originated from Mel B. Spurr in the Egyptian Hall in
Piccadilly.

When the cinema came into being—a thing regarded as a
miracle at the time, the Egyptian Hall, under Maskelyne and
Cooke, was one of the first places to show it. It was called the
Bioscope. The pictures were blurred and flickery and all the
figures moved jerkily, spasmodically as if in a desperate hurry
through sheets of torrential rain. There were pictures of news
value and there were little comedy items and dramas which
always developed into a 'chase'. But the high spot was when a
railway station was shown and a train came full tilt apparently
straight at that wondering audience. Even strong men turned
pale, children screamed and were taken into anxious, motherly
arms and some even sought the exits in flight. But the hard core
and set piece of the show was a sketch staged by Maskelyne called
'Will, the Witch and the Watchman'. One does not recall the
plot, but that does not matter—it was merely a vehicle for magic
—and absolutely unbelievable things happened before your very
eyes. The leading roles were a sailor and his lass, a butcher—

played by Maskelyne himself, in striped apron complete—a Witch, also played by Mr Maskelyne, who also played a full human sized monkey, and probably other parts as well, and an old fashioned watchman (of the 'Charlie' variety) who was a stooge, whose job it was to be mystified, made a fool of, bamboozled, scared and horrified, and who registered terror, amazement, fear and amusement as occasion demanded. The scene was a village green and in the midst stood, very oddly, a large cabinet. For this sketch was the demonstration of that world famous Cabinet Trick which had brought magical eminence to Maskelyne and Cooke. It served amongst other things as the lock-up. And although you could see all around it and underneath as well, and right through it when it was opened to reveal its partly steel barred cage interior, yet the power of magic was such that the performers were no sooner in than they were out again—or they vanished into space before your very eyes. The Witch was locked in—you saw her—yet a second later, when the doors were thrown open, she was not there but a huge monkey was there instead, and you saw the Witch fly through the air on a broomstick. And that monkey changed into all sorts of people whom you never suspected were there at all. It lost its tail, and the tail, without any visible means of support, leapt all over the stage, rose in the air, performed all sorts of weird things which no respectable tail not attached to a body would have dreamt of doing, whilst Will, the Witch and the Watchman and All Concerned, even the monkey himself from time to time, tried to catch it but could not. Children were pleasantly frightened or filled with amazed delight and grown-ups, who would not have shown their feelings for the world, felt exactly the same as their small charges but strove to maintain an air of adult patronage and all-knowing expression, out of which they were often bounced. That smallish, dark, dingy hall, with its not too comfortable seats—there was a row or two of special stalls in light oak, across the front where the elite sat—held all the mystery of a simpler world, not yet accustomed to flying, radio, internal combustion engines and H-Bombs or Sputniks, and was none the worse for adoring the Maskelyne and Cooke type of magic instead.

Those stalls and many of the posters are treasured possessions today in the keeping of the Magic Circle, the super club of Magic and Mystery. I had the thrill of sitting in one recently myself, although I don't think I ever reached that eminence in the Egyptian Hall. When the curtain fell on 'Will, the Witch and the Watchman' the National Anthem blared out on the vast organ and it was all over. Many children kicked and screamed and did not want to go—they wanted to stay and see it all over again— and they were borne forth into Piccadilly thus protesting, but calmed their cries at the sight of the windows of the great taxider-mist Rowland Ward, next door. There, where wild animals were seen in the most lifelike form—where a great bear reared itself aloft and where a ferocious lion, with every semblance of life, had leapt on the back of a terrified horse, with eyes wide and nostrils agape, who galloped for dear life in suspended action, whilst great wounds seemed to flow with blood where the lion's talons had clawed it- -they stifled their cries. Then, into broughams, private or hired, into buses or on foot to a teashop, with eyes which did not see Piccadilly itself but were crammed with the magic it had held in the Egyptian Hall. Later, the firm became Maskelyne and Devant. But the Egyptian Hall departed in Edwardian days, when so much of Piccadilly was rebuilt, in 1905. Shops and offices called Egyptian House fill the site today. Maskelyne and Devant moved to the St George's Hall in Langham Place or upper Regent Street—where they remained for years, altering in personnel but never in quality of magic. But the St George's Hall never had the same authentic magical surround that the Egyptian Hall provided —for one thing, it was not in Piccadilly. The other giant of entertainment which Piccadilly provided was held in the St James's Hall. The Egyptian Hall was on the south side and the St James's Hall almost opposite on the north.

Just as there had been several departments or halls in the Egyptian Hall, there were two halls in the St James's Hall, and it was in the lesser that the entertainment flourished, for the St James's Hall was the London home of nigger minstrelsy. It began its black-faced career in April 1859 right in Victorian days and it only ended them on 9th April 1904 when demolition began to make room for the monster Piccadilly Hotel. For forty-five years it was the centre of the kingdom of burnt cork, indeed, the holy of holies. It was small, plain and undistinguished and it had only a tiny stage. The minstrels did not go in for scenic effects, build-up and bally-hoo; they just relied on personal talent, which shone there for nearly half a century. The first Minstrels ever to appear there, on 11th April 1859, were Raynor and Pierce's Christy Minstrels, eleven in number. That name 'Christy Minstrels' is a bit misleading. There was a troupe so-called but they never appeared in this country, only in America, the original home of nigger minstrelsy. But the name became generic and descriptive and was adopted by many troupes. Both Raynor and Pierce had been members of Edwin P. Christy's troupe so they had some right to the title. To most people Christy Minstrels just meant men with blacked-up faces. Raynor and Pierce took the smaller St James's Hall for four months only and were an outstanding success. But bad luck smote them half-way through their season, for Pierce died suddenly. He was a very devout man and had been ailing for some time. He had not been able to appear on the stage during the week which led to his death, but on the Sunday he felt impelled to go to Church. He rose from his bed, went to church and worshipped with a strange fervour. On leaving at the end of the service, he clasped his hands suddenly, turned his eyes to the sky and dropped on the pavement, dead.

Raynor was determined that the show should go on. He cabled to other leading individual minstrels in America to come over and join him. Only one could—or would—come and Raynor had not cabled him at all but he had heard what was going on. His name was George Washington Moore. He got on a boat, came over on speculation, presented himself to Raynor and assured him that he was just what the show wanted. Raynor gave him the job. Moore had started in a circus where he drove forty ponies all at once, which gave him the nickname by which he was always known—'Pony' Moore. He was an expert banjoist and could sing well but he fancied himself chiefly as a comedian. His starting salary at the St James's Hall was fifteen dollars a week which worked out then, in English money, at less than £4. But he made a big personal hit. That original season of four months extended itself to fourteen. Then Raynor went home to America and the company disbanded. Other troupes followed, always with success. The Nigger Minstrels with their good, clean and artistic show were just the thing for most Victorians. But Piccadilly had impressed itself on Pony Moore's mind. He came back, five years later, in 1864, with another combination. He had three partners, Crocker, Hamilton and Ritter. They announced that they were at the St James's Hall for a short season, and had an immense success. The hall at that time held 550 people only and Moore said that the stage was about as large as a full sized billiard table. Moore took a lease of the hall and worked wonders. They built a bigger and better stage and somehow they increased the seating capacity to nearly 900 people. The prices were 3/-, 2/-, and 1/-. They added a few of what they called 'arm chair' stalls and this brought the money capacity up to £90 a performance. In light of capacity figures of today it seems incredible that such an institution could have carried on with success, and made fortunes. But the spending power of money was amazing then as compared with today.

The little St James's Hall was underneath the big one, in which great artists like Sims Reeves, Santley, Madame Patey, and Signor Foli gave ballad concerts and where big meetings were held. At one such, which was addressed by the Rt Hon. W. E. Gladstone the cheers, hullabaloo and stamping of feet were such that the minstrels underneath sent up a strong protest.

The business manager of this outfit was Frederick Burgess. The minstrels provided entertainment which was completely Victorian and completely of Piccadilly. People who never visited a theatre or music hall flocked to see them. They sat around the stage in a half circle with the Interlocutor (or compere as he would be called today) in the centre. The funny men—called 'Corner Men'—sat at each end, as the name implies. More fantastically dressed than the others, they cracked gags, they asked riddles, they scored off the Interlocutor, they banged tambourines, clattered their 'bones' and were most animated. There was nothing 'relaxed' about them. Had there been, the audience would not have stood for it. The rest of the company sang and played instruments. Their harmony was perfection—they blended their voices like a great organ. There was a large dose of sentimental songs amongst the 'plantation' melodies—and 'black-faced' boys with soprano voices, in Eton suits and collars and white gloves, sang tender ditties about their mothers. All the troupe were expert solo performers. After the interval they showed what they could do individually—and they could do practically everything—and the show wound up with a screaming farce of complete absurdity. Pony Moore as a comedian attained great fame, and from start to finish of the show there was not a vestige of vulgarity or suggestiveness of any kind. Their success enabled them to get the best artists. Burgess became a partner and then Moore threw over the name Christy Minstrels and they became the Moore and Burgess Minstrels. These two men were the direct opposites which form the ideal combination. Moore was a man of immense hospitality and his Sunday parties at his house, Moor Lodge, in the Finchley Road were terrific affairs. Burgess was a man of solitary tastes. He knew everybody but always kept himself to himself. He dined alone at Simpsons in the Strand, always at the same table. He was a man of culture and education and had a remarkable collection of rare books and prints. Moore was the complete Bohemian—and the performer. Burgess never performed. They assumed the title of Moore and Burgess Minstrels in 1871 and became one of London's most popular, enduring and celebrated entertainment features. Both Moore and Burgess must be counted as men of Piccadilly. Stars emerged from their company and the greatest of them all was the incomparable Eugene Stratton who joined them in 1881. He married Pony Moore's daughter and became one of the greatest artists who ever graced British music hall. When he left the Minstrels he tried to play with a white face. It was no good. As soon as he blacked up he was at the top, with the wonderful songs of Leslie Stuart as his material. That minstrel troupe from its small beginnings became a limited company with distinguished people on the board. Pony Moore retired in 1894 when seventy-four years old.

Something had gone of course from the Moore and Burgess Minstrels. Its moving spirits had gone. Also it was over capitalised. The actual Moore and Burgess Minstrels ended in 1900. But the Mohawk Minstrels had come in. They had begun at a part of the Agricultural Hall in Islington called the Berners Hall which was to North London what the little St James's Hall was to Piccadilly—only it was not underground. The Mohawks had been founded by James and William Francis, who in turn were joined by Harry Hunter, who not only wrote magnificent songs but sang them superbly. They were rivals to the Moore and Burgess, although not so well situated, but they moved into a larger hall, also part of the Agricultural Hall and filled it with audiences numbering over 3000 people. Then David Day, who like the brothers Francis, had much experience in music publishing, joined the Mohawks as well. From this minstrel troupe came the great music publishing firm of Francis, Day and Hunter which flourishes today. So when the Moore and Burgess Minstrels came to an end, the Mohawks moved in and absorbed the name—and remained at the St James's Hall until its end. Pony Moore died in 1909 at the age of ninety—Burgess had died in 1893, aged 68.

When the Moore and Burgess closed down, the troupe numbered thirty as against the bare dozen with which they had started. Both they and the Mohawks used the same boast—that 'they never sang out of tune or out of London'. The first half was true but as regards the second, they would sometimes take a little tour. But they took the atmosphere of Piccadilly with them when they did so. They wrote a page which shines in the history of British Entertainmant. Today minstrelsy has gone—the B.B.C. had the Kentucky Minstrels and B.B.C. Television has an excellent show called 'The Black and White Minstrels' a modern variant of the old idea—but apart from the excellence of the singing, not quite the same. Minstrelsy has gone—it belonged to another age —and you would not be allowed to call them nigger minstrels nowadays—it might offend the ladies and gentlemen of colour— so it is really impossible to revive them. Nigger Minstrels they were—no other name was possible and although there were many all over the kingdom—their capital and their real origin here was in Piccadilly.

That remodelling of Piccadilly which took away the St James's Hall also removed the St James's Restaurant which was part of the composite building. 'Jimmy's', as it was popularly called, was opened in April 1858 and cost £60,000. It had entrances both in Piccadilly and Regent Street. It became synonymous with gaiety and seeing 'life'—that life which was frowned at in the Victorian homes. It did well and in 1875 large new dining rooms were built, to make it rival the Criterion Restaurant. Jimmy's led a double life. In the daytime you could take your wife there— your maiden aunt if it came to that—and a bishop would not have felt out of place. There was a large sprinkling of men-about-town and maybe sportsmen but it was all decorous. Perhaps a pretty large proportion of champagne was consumed, but its food and wines and cooking were all impeccable. At a luncheon party there, the great John Hollingshead founded the Gaiety Theatre, and nowhere could have been more suitable. There was always a sparkle about Jimmy's and it was not cheap, even in those days. But, when night fell, it underwant a striking change. It became intensely Bohemian. It was a good place for a man to dine alone; if he did not want to remain alone, he would soon find a companion of the opposite sex. No gentleman would take his wife to Jimmy's in the evening but he might take somebody else's wife—

that had been known. The ladies one met there were very free from inhibitions—there was little of the so-called Victorian severity and starchiness about them. They were dressed in the full flight of fashion and perhaps a little overdressed too, and where they could they made full display of their anatomical charms. Most of the ladies who were said to be 'On the Dilly' liked to go to Jimmy's; to be escorted there, or even casually met there by a gentleman marked them as successes in their own line of business. There was noise, chatter, laughter, and popping of corks and, one presumes, a good time was had by all.

There was no sign of riotousness as yet—that came later, when it came at all. Jimmy's was a strange magnet for young men who had been 'Up West' and celebrating. It drew them relentlessly, as Eros does today. A gang of them might, around eleven oclock, try to force their way in the back door, in Regent Street, to be resisted by the chuckers out stationed there for that purpose. But from midnight there seemed to be a strange flood tide which set towards Jimmy's formed of all sorts of people but mostly young men out for a good time and ladies who were very intimate with the neighbourhood and who desired the better acquaintance with those young men in evening dress—and with golden sovereigns jingling. And you would observe, as if from nowhere, policemen from neighbouring Vine Street but seeming suddenly to embody themselves out of the thin air—the old fashioned policeman had the trick of doing this but his modern successor does not seem to have mastered it. There would be a sergeant or an inspector, too, and they would be an unobtrusive bodyguard to Jimmy's. And if the fun inside grew too fast and furious, well, they would remove the core of the trouble, but only if asked. If anyone tried it on in Piccadilly itself, he or she got short shrift. And then—at 12.30—Jimmy's would disgorge its patrons; the long line of hansoms and four-wheelers right down the middle of the street would spring to life as the doorman whistled his distinctive blasts—one for a hansom—two for a four-wheeler—no taxis then—and into those cabs got the ladies of the Dilly, rather proudly, and very dignified, helped in by the linkmen as if they were duchesses, and their escorts telling the man where to drive and dispensing handsome tips all round. By 12.45 it was all over and only the parade of the ladies who had not been in Jimmy's went on. There is no equivalent to the St James's Restaurant today.

But what of the men who normally used Piccadilly during the day, in Victorian times. The ladies, save those who used it for business purposes, can be ignored as they will be met with in a more suitable street—Regent Street. Piccadilly was and still is a male street. Its shops do not cater overmuch for ladies. But for men there is much, and the Burlington Arcade, despite its fancy shops and jewellers, is governed really by men's haberdashery—the finest in the world.

The men of this country had walked along Piccadilly since the Empire had begun and when Victorian times came, although there were changes, the men were much the same. They rode in their carriages, their broughams and some of them still rode on horseback. They were in the very centre of their capital and this street was still the abode of nobility—ducal palaces still flourished there. These men were the sons and grandsons of those who had seen Great Britain through what had then been her darkest hour— when Britain stood alone against a world in arms, deserted by her allies and those who should have fought for her—her Navy arrayed against the French, Spanish and Dutch Fleets—her army facing the greatest military genius the world had then seen— Napoleon Bonaparte leading a mass of victory-swollen and revolutionary people, believing themselves to be invincible. But this country had destroyed the menace and grown greater. And the Victorian men who frequented Piccadilly were different from those men of the Georgian and Regency days who had fought 'Boney'. They were much more quiet, much more sober and in many ways much more respectable. They were essentially English —the word British was seldom used. Waterloo was still a living memory—England was on top of the world and those Victorians thanked God for it.

They dressed formally—and their fashions changed little. The chief change was in the matter of whiskers. The Victorians were not a clean shaven people. They liked hair on the face and that hair varied. The wonderful creation of 'Lord Dundreary' by Sothern in a play called *Our American Cousin* at the Haymarket Theatre popularised a kind of whisker called 'Dundreary' and they were all the rage. They were curious things, being divided in the middle and tapering to a point. 'Lord Dundreary' was himself what was known as a 'heavy swell' and there were plenty like him in Piccadilly. Those whiskers were also known as Piccadilly weepers. The Crimean War popularised beards, when many men had discarded them but still kept the moustache. The necessity for keeping warm made beards almost essential in the bitter Russian winter and the fashion grew and was largely followed. Many elderly men kept to 'mutton chop' whiskers too. The senior gentlemen of Piccadilly in Victoria's time were very largely bearded or whiskered. They were divided into two political classes, Conservatives and Liberals. The day of Labour was not yet—especially in Piccadilly. No man with any pretence to gentility or to true Piccadilly style would have walked down that august street unsuitably attired. Suitably attired meant tall hat, frock coat, waistcoat, dark or striped trousers, not turned up but falling over the boot, shining white linen collar of all sorts of designs, white linen shirt with stiff front and cuffs, resplendent cuff links and shirt studs and a quiet tie set off with a tie pin. That tie could be of many varieties but it must not be coloured. To wear a coloured tie with a frock coat was just not done. It could be black, black and white, grey, grey-black and white—it could be slim or full, it could be an Ascot or a cravat. It could be silk or satin. The pin could follow the wearer's taste. It could be a large diamond— a horse's head in gold, a fox, a horse at gallop, a post horn, a hunting horn, a horse shoe—sometimes of diamonds, or it could be a pearl pin and sometimes just a plain gold pin with a knob. You suited yourself about that. Across the waistcoat went a watch chain of gold described as an Albert, because it was popularised by the Prince Consort. He knew Piccadilly and he had established some culture there in the form of a Geological Museum, which had a frontage in Piccadilly and an entrance in Jermyn Street. But that was never very successful. The Albert was a very nice watch chain, not too heavy and with a special bar attached to a chain—a sort of anchor to prevent thieves getting away with it easily. Often it was passed through a special buttonhole. Those men all wore gloves—to go down Piccadilly ungloved was a solecism not to be endured. They all carried sticks or umbrellas and the designs thereof were a matter of individual taste. Their boots were always black and they often wore spats. Sometimes the boots were of leather: box calf or patent leather. Sometimes they had fancy tops, if the wearer was inclined to dandyism. In winter their overcoats varied. They could be Chesterfields, with a velvet collar and sometimes velvet cuffs; they could be Raglan, looser in cut and with pockets on the slant instead of across; and sometimes in the winter they wore heavy ulsters and fur collared and lined coats, which had large collars and looked very rich, and were very warm and comfortable. A man of mature years seldom wore a bowler in Piccadilly but a younger man might do so and also a lounge suit, if not of too countrified an air. But mostly the tall hat and the frock coat was the wear. And in the pockets were five pound notes and golden sovereigns and half sovereigns carried in special metal purses called sovereign cases.

For men, dignity was the thing. You did not smoke a pipe in Piccadilly. But even those staid elders of Piccadilly relaxed for Queen Victoria's Diamond Jubilee. They even wore red, white and blue rosettes in their buttonholes and cheered Her Majesty to the echo. Her Majesty was not a habituée of Piccadilly but she knew it pretty well. She passed along there twice in glory—on her First Jubilee in 1887 and her Diamond Jubilee in 1897. The decorations were marvellous.

For many years peace reigned in Piccadilly. The little distant native wars hardly caused a ripple. But then came the Boer War. This was more serious but Piccadilly met it as it had met other troubles. A lot of the young men who were regular passers-by on their way to the clubs were missing—and many found graves in the distant veldt. But their elders kept their heads up during the dark days, and some were very dark. They believed in Buller, and they believed in 'Bobs'—Field Marshal Lord Roberts the invincible. They believed in this chap Kitchener too, who had shown the Dervishes where they got off and avenged Gordon, and a chap named French, and 'B.P.' They also believed in the British Army, which was, according to Kipling and Sullivan, composed of absent-minded beggars wiping something off a slate, and they contributed handsomely to funds. Some of them wore black bands round their arms—which meant that a son would never be seen in Piccadilly again—but they kept their chins up and they endorsed their Queen's dictum—that there was no depression in her house. And although taxes rose there was no depression in Piccadilly . . . bound to win in the end. . . .

When night fell, the ladies of the Dilly came out as usual, war or no war, as they had been doing ever since Piccadilly began, and started their slow, stealthy prowl, like wild beasts of prey along that northern side of the magic mile, and the hansom cabs came along, in endless chains, like so many fireflies up that little hill in the middle of the thoroughfare.

5

Victorian into Edwardian

To get a true picture of those Victorian days in Piccadilly, it is necessary to remember that although Piccadilly was still the residence of nobility there had been infiltration not only of commerce and amusement, as has been shown, but of some of the rich City folk, the men who had played the leading part in making the might of the British Empire. And to them Piccadilly was the centre of that Empire. They were men of the utmost integrity. Their word was their bond. They regarded themselves as the salt of the earth, a state which applied to all Englishmen and inhabitants of Great Britain; though maybe the Irish in the main did not subscribe to it. And although those Victorians' grandfathers and great grandfathers had stood against the world in the Napoleonic Wars, it is often forgotten today that—outside these islands and the Empire—the Boer War was regarded as something likely to see the downfall of proud Britain. Foreign powers, jealous of the British might, rejoiced at the early military setbacks —or what were called, in a new parlance—'reverses'. The British could not of course be defeated, according to their own lights, but they could meet with reverses. The men in the clubs in and around Piccadilly, in their great houses and in their offices in the City were aware of the truth but no thought of defeat crossed their mind. They stuck flags in maps and waited for better news. There were, during that conflict, a large and growing body of people known as 'Pro-Boers' and 'Little Englanders'. They firmly believed England was wrong in attacking the Boers—although of course the start was the other way round—and wanted peace made and the Boers to have absolute Freedom. They found little support in and around Piccadilly.

But the foreign Press gloated. The military experts foretold British doom. Count Bulow, the German Foreign Minister, said, 'The vast majority of German military experts believe that the South African War will end with the complete defeat of the English.' Most Continental Powers confidently expected this to be the break-up of the British Empire. Germany and France kept up a continual and bitter attack on this country in their Press, and a large party in Russia urged the Tsar to step in at this critical juncture and seize India. The French vilified Joseph Chamberlain, the Colonial Secretary who was universally held to be the man who made the war. They always called him 'Sir Chamberlain'. Only Austria remained friendly to us in Europe, and Japan in Asia. Chamberlain had proposed, shortly before, an alliance between this country and Germany. The Boer War caused the Germans to turn down the idea with ridicule. Had they not done so, the whole history of the world from that date might have been altered. In America, although there was sympathy with the Boers because of American dislike for 'colonialism', there was no active animosity. Indeed the Americans remembered that this country had not intervened in their war with Spain over Cuba for which they had some gratitude. And Kipling was very largely read in America and his views had great power. That celebrated war historian Admiral A. T. Mahan wrote to Lord Roberts, 'It is a time of deep disappointment and sorrow, not unmingled, I fear, with something of humiliation, of chastening; but I am persuaded that your noble people will come out of it purified and nobler to resume its beneficent work in the world. With my prayers for the success of yourself and your cause, which I believe the most and

Georgiana, Duchess of Devonshire

Samuel Foote

Hyde Park Corner, about 1750

Devonshire House

best of my countrymen recognize to be that of equal rights and human welfare.'

Piccadilly and its people set its teeth and faced up to the war—they played no active part because that war was far away—but it 'carried on' which was recognised as the true British way. All the social life went on as usual—save where mourning had stricken a family by a son lost in the mists of war. All the big sporting events took place as if nothing was happening, and the coaches lined up at Fortnum and Mason's for the Derby and for Eton and Harrow at Lords. The carriages passed up and down and rolled around Hyde Park at the fashionable hour—the broughams, victorias, landaus and the occasional phaetons. The traffic was horse drawn but towards the end of the era a few motors were breaking in. But you could cross Piccadilly wherever you liked and not be in any danger although it was regarded as a very busy thoroughfare —and it was. The buses were horse drawn—no trams ever invaded that select district. And the omnibuses were either those of the London General Omnibus Company or the London Road Car Company. The latter had little Union Jacks flying from small poles on their tops, just by the driver—and many of these were seized by an excited public when Mafeking was relieved—and carried in procession. There were pirate buses too, who vied with the established lines and tried to race the regular buses to the recognised stops and collect the bulk of the passengers. Those horse buses were of course much smaller than the vast motor buses of today—and they were pulled by two horses. The driver was usually a very cheery chap, with a rubicund face—for he was exposed to all weathers—and pretty smartly dressed. Some of them wore toppers made of felt—some actual silk toppers— rather the worse for wear—and a large proportion wore bowlers. They sat well tucked up on their driving seat high above their horses with many rugs around their knees and up to their waists. Passengers on the front seats on top liked to talk to them and indeed they were most amusing. They retained a strong dash of the old stage coaching days—as typified by Tony Weller. The conductors were rather more morose but did their work admirably and were most polite—unless provoked by being poked in the back by umbrellas or a string of absurd questions. And in those distant and primitive days buses actually stopped wherever you wanted them to, to allow you either to enter the vehicle or leave it. Piccadilly was not such a crowded route in those days as it is now, but there were still plenty of buses and one knew them not by numbers but by colours—red, chocolate, blue, yellow, green, black, etc. But by way of comparison with today there was in 1888 a service which ran from Hammersmith to Liverpool Street —the forerunner of the No. 9 service today. The distance is 7 miles which the horse bus covered in 70 minutes; they ran every 4 minutes and the fare for the entire distance was fourpence. This particular service is perhaps the senior of the lot. It passed down Piccadilly and in 1888 the average rate of progression for a horse bus, in town, was just over 5 miles an hour. This speed, however, was often exceeded when they raced with the pirates. And the average cost in fares per mile was rather less than a penny.

There was seldom any traffic congestion in Piccadilly unless some big event was toward—although there were small jams at times at the junction with Park Lane—but nothing compared with today. The buses were not nearly so big, and the horse traffic not so vast. Those buses carried advertising then as now. A picture of one at the turn of the century shows advertisements for Sanitas, Pear's Soap, Zebra Grate Polish, Horlicks Malted Milk, Heinz 57 varieties, specially mentioning tomato soup and baked beans (it may surprise many to know that baked beans have been on the market for so long but they made their entrance it will be remembered by Piccadilly and Fortnum and Mason's.) There were also advertised the Remington Typewriter and Colman's Wincarnis. These were on a bus which ran from Camden Town to the Kent Road, via Piccadilly Circus. Other advertised goods included Quaker Oats, Hudson's Soap, Nestlés Milk, Champion's Vinegar, Fry's Pure Cocoa, Mellin's Food, Reckitt's Blue, and Oakey's Knife Polish, also Colman's Mustard. All goods were delivered by horse and cart—unless the delivery was done by hand. I remember seeing women delivering milk in the Piccadilly district, which they carried in covered pails slung from each end of a yoke worn across their shoulders. Traffic was not very difficult to control and the police were most efficient. They seemed larger men than they are nowadays and many of them were bearded. One of the sights of London was a mounted policeman—who still commands attention today but chiefly because he rides a horse in a machine age. In those days he still was a notable figure. He wore a helmet, not a cap, his horse was a beautiful animal— they still are—but the thing about this policeman that was different was that he wore a sword. It had neither a sharp cutting blade nor a very acute point, but it was a sword—indeed, a cavalry sabre. So those who imagine that our police were never armed are not quite right. Today the mounted man carries a long, sword-like wooden baton—a pretty deadly affair. Sometimes a rakish looking dogcart would flash by at a good eight or ten miles an hour, en route either for the country or the park, with a Dalmatian dog running between the wheels just behind the horses hooves and apparently liking it. And although the white-stockinged, knee-breeched powdered hair footmen and coachmen had gone from the carriages—the coachman still wore his smart livery, his blue coat and plated buttons, his tall hat with cockade and his high boots with the buff turnover tops. This too was repeated in the footman who sat beside him, who opened the doors, kept the lady's dress and the gentleman's coat from muddy wheels, carried parcels and stowed them in the vehicle with care and in the winter wore, as did the coachman, long overcoats reaching right down to the heels, which looked very smart indeed. Often they wore fur capes too. The stately progress of a good carriage of any design, with its pair of perfectly matched horses, and its coachman and footmen had something about it which no limousine, however smart and expensive, has ever captured. You see, it was alive and vital.

The roads were apt to get muddy but there were plenty of men to clean them and what were known as 'street orderlies'—men and boys in red jerkins, rather like a Russian blouse, dived in and out of the traffic, under the very heads and hooves of the horses themselves and scooped the manure by means of brushes into a metal receptacle very like a large dustpan. There was a crossing sweeper in my very young days who swept his crossing at the junction of St James's Street and Piccadilly and did very well. And one other note about the buses: just before Christmas every bus in London burst out into decorations of blue and yellow ribbons—they were tied in a bow on the whip—the driver and conductor wore a knot in their buttonholes. The reason for this was because each of them—every driver and every conductor— had been given a brace of pheasants by Mr 'Jimmy' de Rothschild —who lived in Park Lane and had a soft corner for London busmen. Blue and yellow were his racing colours. You won't find anything like that in London today.

A man who often passed along Piccadilly was to become a national hero in the Boer War. His name was Robert Stephenson Smyth Baden-Powell and he lived in Knightsbridge. He was a soldier; at the time when he took over the defence of Mafeking he was forty-two years old and a Lt.-Colonel in the Dragoons. An Old Carthusian, he had seen much service and had already had a most distinguished career. His defence of that small town did much to keep up the prestige of British arms throughout the darkest days of the war. When Mafeking was relieved London went mad, and that story belongs properly to Piccadilly Circus, and will be told in due course. Maybe the defence of Mafeking is half-forgotten—recently I heard a BBC personality describing battles of the first world war as being 'as distant as Agincourt'— but the Boy Scouts are still with us and 'B.P.', as he was affection-ately called, founded that world movement. Robert Stephenson the great railway engineer was his godfather.

Piccadilly in late Victorian and early Edwardian days was so full of personalities that there is not room even to list them. But two are perhaps typical and both belong to the theatre. One is George

Alexander—to become Sir George Alexander—whose theatre, which he made so distinguished, was the St James's in King Street, adjacent to Piccadilly and absolutely of the right type and atmosphere. Sir George Alexander himself might well stand for the very embodiment of Piccadilly, for he was handsome and distinguished, with perfect manners and perfect attire, never hurried, never losing his sang froid and with a belief in tradition and good behaviour which shone like a diamond. He was indeed 'West End'. His likeness to Piccadilly did not escape his great chief, Sir Henry Irving, under whom he won his spurs. Irving cast Alexander for the part of Macduff in *Macbeth*. He watched the young man rehearse and having formed an opinion, he called him over. 'Yes, yes, yes Alexander', he said, 'very good, very good indeed. I see what you are driving at. But—Macduff, you know—a man of a violent age, a man of blood and steel, used to keeping his own head with his own sword—a man of battle and slaughter—hardly anything of Piccadilly. . .' which puts another angle on the criticism once made of him to the effect that 'George Alexander does not act—he behaves.' One could do with more behaviour of that kind on our stage today. Alexander was the idol of the ladies and the envy of the men; he was the best dressed man in town and he set male fashions. And the other man who was so redolent of Piccadilly died only recently at the ripe age of ninety-five. He was an actor of the actor-managerial regime and he often played at the St James's Theatre with Alexander and was often in Piccadilly. His stage name was Allan Aynesworth and he was, on and off the stage, a man and actor of distinction, quality and charm. Like Alexander he was a living example of the Age of Dignity—which Piccadilly could typify.

His real name was E. Abbot-Anderson and he was born at the Royal Military College, Sandhurst, third son of General E. Abbot-Anderson, who was in command there. His family mixed military and medical tradition and real old time Conservatism. He was educated at Chatham House and in Germany and France. He became interested in the theatre through the Comédie

Française. He revered its tradition and something of the classical manner remained with him to the end. He embarked on a stage career, and that took courage in those Victorian days, when it was not considered respectable to be connected with the Theatre and his whole background and training was against him. But he succeeded. He became a splendid actor. This is not the place to trace that long successful career, both as actor and actor-manager, but he always seemed at his best when playing either at the St James's or the Haymarket Theatres—two playhouses in the vicinity of Piccadilly. He was the original Algernon Moncrieff in *The Importance of Being Earnest* at the St James's—and those who saw him in *The Second in Command* at the Haymarket or in *The Dover Road* will never forget it. He was a very handsome man and had there not been something of the aura of an actor about him, he might have been taken for a general or an admiral. There was never anything meretricious about him or his work. He did at times allow himself a little eccentricity in the matter of hats, which seems to be the prerogative of genius. He wore a kind of 'trilby' hat which was closely folded and came to a sharp point fore and aft. It is impossible to describe it exactly—nobody else ever wore one—it is doubtful if anyone else could ever have done so. He was one of the very first to follow the lead of King Edward VII and wear a green velour Tyrolean hat—and how it suited him! He was essentially English and yet he only referred to his country as 'These Islands'. He had a detestation of the English climate. Once he greeted his dear friend Norman Forbes at the Garrick Club— 'Norman, my dear boy, how are you?' 'I have a slight cold, Tony,' replied Forbes—Aynesworth was always Tony to his friends. 'Ah,' he exclaimed with anguish, 'the sickness in these islands . . .'

He had a distinguished career on the films as well as on the stage. His entry into that sphere is an amusing story. At that time he regarded films as being slightly vulgar and refused to regard them as a form of entertainment, 'theatre' or art in any form. But one of the early pioneers of British pictures wanted him and his name because both would add distinction to the early silent films. The management of the firm asked to see him and were accorded an audience. Knowing nothing of films at that time, he was courteous but aloof and listened to all they had to say with a quiet, attentive dignity. When they had finished he enquired: 'And what would be the remuneration?' They named a figure which to them seemed very high. 'Oh, no, no, no' said Tony Aynesworth, shaking his head, 'I should require five times that sum before I jiggered about in front of your magical lantern.' And he got it. He was a great comedy actor in a great period of our theatre, and Piccadilly was the ideal background for him.

You would meet the elders of Piccadilly as you walked along, men of position and standing whose features, whether whiskered or not, seemed far more in the patrician cast than one sees today. And you would see the young men, strolling to and from their clubs or going about some business. They were all quiet, all well dressed and all seeming much of a muchness on the outside, for they were the products of public schools, universities and the services, which seem to have the knack of putting a patina on their products. Yet those young men were of individual character underneath. A great number of them had private means or allowances. They rode to hounds, they shot, they sailed, they golfed; they played cricket and football and squash. They went through the London 'Season', from ball to ball and from banquet to banquet, reception to reception. They saw the same people and did much the same things at all of them. Many of them had professions—a large number were in the Army—but except for their bearing, this was never noticeable for the last thing in which they wanted to appear was their uniform. They got into mufti with all possible speed. Uniforms made them rather self-conscious. Some went abroad into the Indian Civil Service—into the Colonial Administration—and ruled alone, save for a handful of native soldiers over tracts of land larger than this country and brought law and order where savagery, slaughter and cannibalism had been before. They knew their West End intimately, but the extent of their peregrinations was the Gaiety Theatre at the east end of the Strand. Farther than that they seldom penetrated, unless a hansom took them to some City office on business. It was the ambition of ninety per cent of them to take a Gaiety Girl out to sup—at the Savoy, Romanos, or Rules—and many of them realised it. They knew the Empire Promenade, they knew the night haunts and they knew Jimmy's.

They were essentially English and would have hated to be unconventional or to be taken for foreigners. They wore good clothes, beautifully cut and it was permissible for them to wear lounge suits in Piccadilly—if not going to some social function. If so, then it must be a frock coat and topper. Their manners were as perfect as their clothes but their conversational powers were limited. But they were always self-possessed and at their ease. They would climb those wonderful staircases in the mansions of Piccadilly and Mayfair, make their bow and shake hands with their host and hostess, glance around, and then mingle with the crowd—they just had to be seen there in 'The Season' for everybody who was anyone was there. To many people not of the same social scale they seemed drones, but they were far from that. They all knew what to do when the time came, and they were intensely patriotic, although they never made a parade about it. But when, as in the Boer War, England wanted men, they were there—and many gave their lives.

You would also see in Piccadilly and the adjoining tributaries, quite a lot of reserved, detached and rather important looking men, different from the leisured classes but also different from the ordinary middle class pedestrian. They wore mostly quiet and unobtrusive clothes: black coats and waistcoats and 'pepper and salt' trousers. Sometimes they had a dog on a lead, sometimes they carried a parcel, sometimes they were just out for an airing or a shopping errand. They mostly vanished down side streets and slipped into quiet unobtrusive pubs where they were apparently well known and of some importance. They were 'Gentlemen's gentlemen'—and in Victorian days there were many of them.

They were remarkable characters—and P. G. Wodehouse has immortalised one of a later generation in the person of 'Jeeves'. He is idealised, but those men did their jobs superbly. They valeted their 'gentleman' and they looked after him like a mother. They knew all his secrets but disclosed none; they were ready to advise and their advice, based on long experience, was good. Sometimes it was tendered with great tact and in roundabout fashion, if it had not been sought. They did not get big salaries, but they got 'perks' and commissions and they did pretty well. Their manners were exemplary and they were sober and industrious. If they had a failing, and of course they had, it was an addiction to horse racing. There were no 'dogs' in those days nor football pools either. It may be that their 'gentleman' was no hero to them, but they served him like a devoted subject—and they were able to make his life very smooth. Mostly they were clean shaven. They shared one peculiarity with another set of men who could be met with in Piccadilly. This second variety were larger, more imposing men in every form and sometimes they had whiskers but you seldom met them with only a moustache. The peculiarity which they shared with the 'gentleman's gentleman' was that they wore bowler hats with morning coats and got away with what in other walks would have been a howling unforgivable social solecism. These men had large faces and moved with great dignity. They never seemed to hurry yet they moved from one place to another with remarkable speed. They were obviously men of substance and importance and tradesmen and the like touched their hats to them, to which they responded with kindly condescension.

Actually, they were butlers. Now in Victorian days butlers were butlers and English butlers were the finest in the world. They formed almost a definite stratum of society in themselves—they were entirely indispensable and were part and parcel of the great families and the great houses. They were never 'one of the family', however long their service but the best of them had the admiration and respect, not to say affection of their employers. In the household they ruled supreme. The housekeeper herself was just a grade below them. They were the top step of below stairs. They ruled the servants despotically but they were quite wonderful men. They, too, knew all the secrets, and never divulged them. No persistent newspaper reporter ever got a real butler to give the game away. They were, in their own sphere, strict disciplinarians. They presided over the meals below stairs but often when the lesser servants were served they themselves retired to eat their meal in the privacy of the housekeeper's room. They kept the household books and accounts, they had their own pantry, and there they themselves cleaned the silver—to see that it was properly done —and there was much silver on dinner tables in those days. They had the household keys, except those required by the housekeeper, locked the house up at night and saw that all was safe. Unless told they could go to bed, they would have stayed up all night.

They knew the etiquette of the times, they understood precedence, and no list of titles could appal them when it came to announcements. The character which Barrie drew in his play *The Admirable Crichton* was not overdone. But, of course, they were not all as cultured as that, by a long shot. They did not get large salaries, but they had 'perks' and tips. They controlled the household and they controlled the tradesmen, who had to please the butler if the custom of the family was to be theirs. It was all fish which came into the butler's net—and everybody serving the house had to 'take care' of him. That even went for the wine merchants, because the butler had control of the wine cellar. Tips were pretty good. There was far more entertaining at home in those days and not nearly so much entertaining at hotels. On special days like birthdays and family celebrations thirty and more might sit down to lunch or dinner and the average tip to the butler would be 10/- per head. When the family went to the country house and guests were invited to stay butlers did very well indeed. They could make or mar your pleasure, if it came to that. They were quite amazing people and the good English butler had no rival in the world.

There was however one curious gift which most of them shared, and that was a tremendous capacity for the consumption of alcoholic liquor. It has been stated that they had control of the wine cellar and they helped themselves lavishly to the contents. It is not too much to say that some of them were in a constant state of alcoholism. Yet somehow they never showed it but would carry on with immense dignity, receive and announce callers, control the staff, serve at the meals and never make a mistake. I have evidence of one at least who was drunk most of the time and yet never slipped up, whom we shall meet later. Butlers made money, despite their small wages of a nominal pound or two a week, and they saved it. They had to spend nothing unless they liked. And many of them married cooks and then took a lease of a house in the West End, in streets like Jermyn Street, and let the rooms off to single gentlemen of birth and position as 'chambers'. They served their clients well, the cooking was first class, the cleanliness unquestionable—and the discretion perfection itself. Some of them became greengrocers, which seems a strange calling for such men but many of them followed it. It appears to be a profitable trade. I knew one myself, in looks the ideal family retainer, who was a most successful greengrocer and also went into the tinned fruit trade and prospered amazingly. He served in his own shop and did it with such an air that suburban housewives felt they were people of consequence. Just a few butlers took pubs. And you would see a lot of them in Piccadilly.

In Victorian days there was another infiltration of commerce into Piccadilly and this was something of considerable importance because it spread through the length and breadth of the land. A shop was opened on the south side, only a few yards from Piccadilly Circus. It arrested attention of passers-by at once, for it was distinctively decorated all in white and gold. It was the beginning of a tremendous change in the eating out habits of this race, affecting men and women in business and trade and on pleasure bent. For that shop, opened in 1894, was the very first teashop of Messrs J. Lyons and Co Ltd. It is still there and bears a blue plaque to tell its story. That nationwide string of teashops controlled by Lyons started in Piccadilly. The firm knew what a wonderful jumping off board this was, and what importance it gave to such an undertaking.

Victorian Piccadilly was dignified and sedate; although there were shops and entertainments there were still magnificent residences and one saw wonderful sights. I have a recollection of having seen a goat there outside the Green Park. It was tethered and nobody seemed to think it strange. I never found out to whom it belonged or if it was kept there regularly. There was, of course, a cow not far away at the Horse Guards entrance to St James's Park and you could have a penny glass of milk drawn straight from it with no nonsense about hygiene, homogenising and the rest of it. Just plain milk straight from the animal. I had many a glass and came to no harm. But I don't know what the goat was for. And I remember so vividly walking along Piccadilly just before the Diamond Jubilee of Queen Victoria. I had been taken to see the soldiers encamped in Hyde Park and for a small boy this was a wonderful sight. As we walked down Piccadilly towards the circus, we saw the decorations which were being put in place and small bodies of troops were constantly going and coming—cavalrymen riding on some sort of business and single soldiers in uniform everywhere. It was an entrancing walk for a boy who adored soldiers and little thought then that he would be mixed up in two world wars. My mother and two of my aunts were with me and I know we had dinner in a restaurant called 'The Nelson' which seems to me to have been in a turning off Piccadilly just near the Church and that there were many courses at very cheap rate, to which I did full justice. I also recall the staff keeping us under constant observation and I did not know why. The reason was that here were three ladies dining in the West End without male escort—for by no manner of means could a boy of nine years be stretched into that. It was most unusual and I am really surprised they served us. But I recall asking why the waiters stared so and I was told that they were amazed to see a boy eating so much. I did not believe that, however, and I did not let it spoil my appetite.

I recall another day there at the absolute end of the Victorian era. The great Queen had progressed through her capital for the last time, on a gun carriage beneath the flag of her Empire. I had been taken to see it and shall never forget that day; a cold grey morning with low sullen clouds and not a sign of cheer anywhere. My family and myself were in deep mourning, as indeed was everybody else. The nation seemed still to be numbed. Victoria had reigned so long that it did not seem possible that she was mortal and would die. But no sovereign, however great and mighty, is immune. Even those golden sovereigns which were the standard of our prosperity met their doom. We stood in the front of the crowd that day and there was silence. Then from afar came the sound of a band playing Chopin's Funeral March. To say that there was a hush is to give no picture at all of the silence which obtained, broken only by the solemn music which came nearer and nearer and then the slow tramp of marching feet and the subdued clatter of horses hooves—even they seemed muted. The very air of London seemed to mourn, as that sad music lamented, and then—She came—invisible to us—wrapped in her flag, borne by the army she loved—for Victoria held the Army in higher esteem than the Navy. The last time I had seen her had been on her day of Diamond Jubilee—in St Paul's Churchyard— with the might and panoply of one-fifth of the world around her and kings and princes of many nations as her escorts. They were still there: the new King, her other sons, her grandsons and also the Kaiser Wilhelm of Germany, who gazed at that mass of Londoners with a hard-eyed stare and had that stare stolidly returned. It was as if this man was summing us up and we were also taking his measure. And—within such short time—the clash came. But we only stared at him that day. Then there was a burst of cheering from the crowd for a small man on a large horse, in field marshal's uniform. He raised his hand and hushed it—it had shocked him— but it was the spontaneous expression of approval of the London public for a man who had served them well and whom they loved—Lord Roberts, the beloved 'Bobs'. The cortège, so long and so slow in movement, eventually passed by and the crowd broke up. My family and I, who had seen it in Hyde Park, walked slowly along Piccadilly, where everyone was in his darkest clothes. I had photographed all I saw on my memory and I wanted a tangible memory as well. We came to Devonshire House on the north side. Its long wall was draped with festoons of laurels and with material of royal purple. There was a man looking over that wall, maybe a servant. I called up to him, very politely and asked if I might have some of that laurel as a keepsake of the day. He nodded and smiled. I pulled off some of the laurel and he suddenly stripped off a small length of the purple material and threw it down to me. I kept those two relics of the passing of the Victorian Age for many years. And they were symbolic too, perhaps, of the passing of Devonshire House itself. But I think those relics were the more precious because they came from that great house in Piccadilly.

6

Edwardian Gold but Piccadilly Changes

When the Old Queen passed—and I received that memory of her passing from the walls of Devonshire House—I doubt if anyone realised how great the change was to be. A new face on stamps and coins—'God Save the King' instead of 'God Save the Queen', 'King's Counsel' instead of 'Queen's Counsel', a man at the head of affairs instead of an old lady living the life of a recluse but holding the love, affection and veneration of over one-fifth of the globe directly and holding the respect of every nation, allied or foreign.

This new King, Edward VII, came to the throne backed by immense popularity. He was gay, he was a mixer, he was 'known about town'. He was pre-eminently a sportsman and if indeed he was also a lover of ladies—well, the Victorians and the new Edwardians were discreet and nobody thought the less of him for that. Rather the more—for Charles II had been a most popular monarch. This new King was no longer young (he had stood in the shadow of his great mother for years) but everyone knew he had exercised considerable influence on the affairs of the nation and that he had a statesman's brain. He was married to a beautiful woman who was the nation's idol, Queen Alexandra, and there was a good family to see that the succession was safe. Two great elements of popularity were Edward's addiction to sport—and more especially horse racing—and his known dislike of Germany and especially his near relative the Kaiser, the belligerent man with the comic semi-fierce turned up moustache whom neither the general inhabitants of this country nor the habitués of Piccadilly trusted at all. It was well known to all British people that the Kaiser wanted to take over the British Empire and make us a subject race. Naturally they did not believe that was possible. But in the clubs in and around Piccadilly the King's dictum about the Kaiser, 'He is no gentleman', was repeated with much satisfaction. To be 'no gentleman' put one right outside the pale, not only in Piccadilly. Piccadilly also highly approved King Edward's friendliness with the French. Not that basically they thought much of the French (England's hereditary enemies) but they preferred them to the Germans. Berlin held no place in their thoughts—Paris was still a city of romance and naughtiness.

With the breaking of the old shackles of stiff and tight Victorian convention there came a quickening in the tempo of life in keeping with the new monarch—a man who was perhaps speed minded, for he had won the Derby and was one of the earliest pioneers of motoring. Those Victorian conventions were not shattered in Edwardian days but they were slightly relaxed, and it may well be that some of the relaxation was not all to the good. But all the same, the general code of manners and behaviour held fast and Society was still Society, although by degrees riches were able to open doors previously closed to them unless accompanied by blood. The great divisions of the classes held—the upper and governing class, the middle class and the working class. People did not mix much but kept to their own way of life.

The chief disturbing element of this period, although it was not regarded with anything but interest and pleasure, was an invention which was to revolutionise the world. The internal combustion engine came into general use. When King Edward VII became a motorist, the accelerator went down heavily and remained down. In early Edwardian days of course the horse was still the main means of transport. But the motor car was in the race and the horse was to lose it, completely and hopelessly. You would see, slipping along amidst the broughams and other carriages which were known to the slightly envious but admiring non-residents of Piccadilly as 'smart turn-outs', a curious sort of vehicle—something like a compressed brougham crossed with a hansom-cab with the shafts sawn off, driven by a man who was not a coachman and had not yet come to be called a 'chauffeur', who sat perched on the front and seemed to make the whole thing look top heavy and liable to pitch forward at any moment. It went along quite noiselessly and made no fuss, explosion or smell, for it was known as an 'electric brougham'. It looked very smart and it was steered by a kind of tiller.

Motors of all kinds increased and 'chauffeurs' were added to domestic staffs. The wealth of this country was still staggering. People of means lived in enormous houses and had huge domestic staffs. Their descendants today have no staff at all and pay a high rental for living in quarters which once servants inhabited—rent free. It is a sign of the times. The Stately Homes of England—famous in song and story—are in many cases still there. They were called show places once, and they are actually show places today, shown to the general public by their impoverished owners at 2/6d. a time. Thus far has something which was once the pride of England descended. Felicia Dorothea Hemans wrote:

> 'The Stately Homes of England
> How beautiful they stand
> Amidst their tall ancestral trees
> O'er all the pleasant land.'

Those which are not tourist resorts, apart from the very few which are still in private hands, mostly house the new aristocracy —the men and women who work on the numerous boards which now administer our freedom and who have replaced the squire and his relations. But when Piccadilly was Edwardian, it was from the lawns and the drawing rooms of those great houses that

England was ruled, and not ruled so badly, through the Establishment, which was always as mysterious in form as our own unwritten Constitution. The great families who today show their homes and treasures for pieces of silver—which is nickel—and maybe make a bit out of catering too would probably make an even better job of it if they had the assistance of a real butler. People who are grateful today for a lady who comes for a couple of hours twice a week may question the story which is to follow, but it is absolutely authentic as a domestic interior of the period. This is what it says:

'In those early days of the present century I first entered private service and met my first butler. They were great men in those days and I wondered if you would like to hear about Mr B. Yes, he was "Mr" and when we of the staff spoke to him, he was addressed as "Sir". I was fourth chauffeur of four and very small fry compared with him. His Lordship had the greatest respect for him and consulted him about every lunch or dinner regarding the wines, cups and old brandies—we had some 1804 and although I was not a connoisseur, I loved its perfume. Mr B. was head of a staff of 28—valet, three footmen, odd man, pantry boy, housekeeper, six housemaids, three scullery maids, two lady's maids and four chauffeurs. I have known over 40 sit down to meals in the servants' hall. When I say meals, I should have said that the full staff (less kitchen) only sat down together for first courses at lunch and the heads (pugs we called them) then left us lesser mortals for the housekeeper's room (pugs' parlour) to enjoy their dessert and coffee. In those days a nine course dinner was most ordinary. I have known eighteen and twenty-two courses on special occasions. Mr B. was always drunk by dinner time yet could still carve and serve wine—and woe betide any footman who thought he was too drunk—he missed nothing. At large parties, we, the chauffeurs, would volunteer to help in the pantry (there wasn't much else to do) and when we reported to the pantry before dinner, Mr B's first order to the oddman was, "Fetch a jug of whisky and two large jugs of beer for these gentlemen." His

Lordship's birthday was on the 30th September and thirty gentlemen sat down to dinner. Ladies staying in the house had their dinner in the Upper Hall, which adjoined the dining room. When the non-staying guests left for home, there was half-a-sovereign for Mr B., from every one of them. If my memory serves me well. Mr B. had only about £50 per annum as salary. I have often opened the cellar in the morning for Mr B. (he could not get the key in the hole) and he would have a bedroom beaker full of whisky at one draught. He must be dead now, but I'll bet his body never rots. Mr Macqueen-Pope, if any of these details are of any use to you, please use them with my blessing. Yours sincerely, James McHallam.'

And my blessings too on Mr McHallam for the vivid and detailed picture of Edwardian days. You will note there were four chauffeurs, so it was probably between 1906 and 1910. I thank him—a faithful fan whom I have never met.

My own encounters with butlers were quite a few. The first I ever met was one who held sway over a wonderful old house in Yorkshire, where my family visited and sometimes took me along, as a small boy. I loved it. I was a good deal scared of the butler when I first met him, for we did not run to butlers at home, and I am sure I showed it. But under his terrific dignity he was a very kind man and he liked little boys. I became his constant companion and got all sorts of treats and tit-bits which the others never saw—notably some perfectly marvellous hot house grapes from the house's own vine. I have since realised that this butler was also never sober after lunch, but that it never impaired his dignity or efficiency, indeed it enhanced both. Butlers were amazing men. I adored him, but the footmen, of whom I think there were three or four, went in mortal terror of him.

Dickens knew all about butlers and gives us some wonderful sketches of them. There is Mr Towlinson in *Dombey and Son*—who, after Mr Dombey's smash-up and reverse of fortune, married the housemaid and set up in business in Oxford Market in the general greengrocery and herb and leech line. He has a magnificent specimen too in *Our Mutual Friend* who is butler for the Veneerings and who is described as an analytical chemist—who when he approves of a guest, concedes him a little more wine than the others and who views the world with general misgivings. H. G. Wells knew them, too, and has a rich and fruity specimen in *Bealby*, Mr Mergleson, who brews his own beer, by the way, which goes to show what butlers are, or perhaps were.

And had not old Kipps—Art's Uncle—been a butler? He had indeed. But he ran a toyshop—an unusual line for such a man. And F. Anstey has a grand butler in his play *The Man From Blankley's*. The family for whom this butler works are, alas, parvenu and live on the wrong side of the Park. He has known better days and better service but his judgment of people has not been impaired. He tells the parlourmaid, who is assisting him at dinner, to 'Serve Miss Seaton first'. The pert maid retorts that Miss Seaton is only the governess, to which the butler replies, 'Governess or not, she is the only lady present and you will do as I tell you'. That was very much of the time. And although those butlers had their 'perks' from tradespeople, if inferior goods were supplied the custom went elsewhere. No good reporting it to the employer; this was tradition, this commission basis and there was freemasonry amongst butlers. Any complaint would have meant that the tradesman making it would have been ostracised. So the vendors of goods did their best and the butler saw to it that quality was upheld. Butlers never got the sack—they had to be real criminals to be so treated. Whilst these lines were being written, there was a story in the newspapers concerning a butler who got the sack for not being too sober. Indeed, times have changed, but maybe butlers have changed too.

Those butlers who let furnished chambers off Piccadilly looked after their 'gentlemen' as they had looked after their families, and sometimes a young man, having had a bad time on the turf or at cards, could borrow some money from his landlord and find it lent gladly. Those young men would beggar themselves to repay.

Piccadilly in Edwardian times reflected all the glory of those days. In its great mansions wonderful receptions were held. Often there was a dinner party first for anything from forty to sixty people, all special guests of course and there not so much because they were friends of the family but because they were what are now known as V.I.P's. Many of these dinner parties and receptions were given with a political motive. The two great parties strove to outdo each other and to impress the nation. Down Piccadilly they came, these guests in the full glory of their carriages and later their limousines. They were the great ones: dukes and duchesses, earls and countesses, and even baronets and knights, with commoners of great distinction. Amongst the guests was a good sprinkling of men from the constituencies, with their wives, invited because of their good service to the party, and now basking in social splendour and feeling more loyal than ever. Around them were men and women whose faces they saw in illustrated papers, whose names they read in newspapers, ambassadors and the Corps Diplomatique were there—ribbons and stars glowed and glistened—noblemen in knee breeches stood alongside provincials in evening dress. Great ladies who were almost incandescent with diamonds and jewels, tiaras shining and silk and satin dresses lisping and rustling, were gazed at in awe by good middle-class housewives whose husbands meant something in some constituency and who would now be able to tell their friends the wonders amongst which they had moved. Up the stairs they went—a wonderful staircase was a feature of every great house—to where the host and the hostess stood to receive them; a handshake, a few words, and then the guests went off into the great corridors and vast rooms, where there was the best possible food, the best possible wines and the best possible orchestra dispensed discreet music. Sometimes Royalty itself would attend for a little while, and in those ceremonious days that was a sight indeed. No words can really paint those occasions. Noel Coward staged one in his great play *Cavalcade*, which could show even at Drury Lane only a segment of the tremendous meeting of power and wealth. And outside in Piccadilly and its neighbourhood, the ordinary people stood on the pavement and watched the great ones come and go.

Yet it was in the golden Edwardian Days that Piccadilly underwent a great change, not in spirit and in atmosphere but in appearance. These waves of destruction and renovation afflict London periodically and wipe out the old, replacing it with the new. Georgian and Victorian Piccadilly faded away to a large extent when the decision was made, in 1902, that the street must be widened to cope with what was considered to be the amazing flow of traffic which passed along it. Traffic has destroyed more of London than enemy bombs. The need to cope with traffic has wiped out treasures which would have enriched London in the days now come upon us when part of our national income must be derived from the tourist industry. Yet still they try to widen the streets, still they try to knock down buildings with atmosphere and story and replace them with semi-skyscrapers, of the dwarfish, stunted London sort, which have no individuality whatever. But, although they changed Piccadilly in the early 19th century, they could not destroy it.

Before the destruction got really under way, there was a catering revolution in that famous street. The firm of J. Lyons and Co. Ltd, opened their Popular Café. This was quite a new departure. It was for the visitors to Piccadilly, of course, not the residents. Indeed many of those residents were leaving pretty quickly because of the noise, and destructive alterations. But at the Popular, which lived up to its name, you got luxurious surroundings, excellent service and a remarkably good table d'hôte dinner for 2/6d, with a first class orchestra thrown in. The dishes were as good and varied, and well cooked as anyone could wish for. Those who could not afford to dine at the Prince's, could nevertheless dine in Piccadilly—at the Pop. For it soon achieved a nickname, an abbreviation which always in this country means success. Teas were marvellous at the Pop—you made a wonderful meal for a shilling, with a tremendous selection of cakes, and always an orchestra. A feature was that there were NO tips. I think that was more honoured in the breach than in the observance. But that was the rule. People from the suburbs and from the provinces flocked to the Pop. They wore their best clothes and got a tremendous thrill out of refreshing themselves in a marble hall in sacred Piccadilly. What better after a tiring afternoon at the Royal Academy in Burlington House than to pop into the Pop and get rid of that headache the Academy always caused. The Pop was a great example of business psychology. Corner Houses were all right in less distinguished surroundings, but for Piccadilly it had to be the Pop. It was built on a site previously occupied by the Geological Museum. Nobody went to that. Everybody went to the Pop. In the 1900's Piccadilly did indeed alter. In 1904 down went Walsingham House Hotel and the Bath Hotel, which stood between Arlington Street and the Green Park. The Walsingham Hotel was a large red brick building which was opened in 1887 and had been a block of flats; before that the site had held one of the largest mansions in Piccadilly. The Bath Hotel was much older, and here, previous to that, had been the famous White Horse Cellars, where the coaches started from. The Ritz Hotel went up in 1906 and stands there today. It has a colonnade over the pavement, which, to some, recalls the rue de Rivoli in Paris but makes others think of that Quadrant which graced Regent Street and which the Londoners would not have at any price.

In 1905 the Egyptian Hall was demolished and a modern building arose for all to see today called Egyptian House. All along that southern side many things altered shape but some remained and carried on. There are arcades, banks, restaurants, what you will. But some of the old names cling on and prosper.

On the opposite side of the road even more changes took place. Away went the St James's Hall and the St James's Restaurant. In their place there arose the gigantic Piccadilly Hotel, which was finished in 1908. It owed its inception to a financial genius named Mallaby-Deeley, who had amassed a fortune by selling men's suits at a most reasonable price; in those days you got a really well cut made to measure suit for £2.2.0d. The Piccadilly Hotel, when opened, was one of the sights of London at the time and also a centre of controversy. The younger generation thought it grand but the older generation did not like it. It has a majesty and it dominates the entrance to that magic mile in fine style. Its classic colonnade on the first floor was believed to be intended as a roof garden but it created no excitement as such. And at the very beginning of this street, setting the rhythm as it were, is one of the most famous shops in the world, which has a long frontage in Piccadilly, and a similar one in Regent Street, but whose front faces on to the magnetic pole of Piccadilly Circus. It is of course, Swan and Edgar's—the great emporium, the place where people make appointments to meet, for everybody knows Swan and Edgar's.

In the 1900's the whole aspect of Piccadilly was changed, but it was not all done without difficulty and the alterations were spread over a long period. In 1912 a row of fine old houses situated between the Savile Club and the Junior Athenaeum Club, were demolished. The site was acquired by a Mr Hawarth, who controlled the Curzon Hotel in Curzon Street and who wanted that site on which to build another hotel in Piccadilly, to be called the Park Lane Hotel. He badly wanted the Savile Club, too, to give necessary size to his new hotel. But the members of the Savile flatly refused to sell, no matter how attractive the offer. They were of the bulldog breed. This was their club, they were of Piccadilly and they were stopping there. Mr Hawarth was a man of equal determination. He began to demolish the buildings on the site which he owned. The members of the Savile sat grimly in the club amidst the roar and racket of the housebreakers and watched their walls crack. But no surrender. However, Mr Hawarth did not succeed in Operation Demolition. The First World War broke out and he was interned as a German. Later, he died. Victory was with the Savile. For many years the Park Lane Hotel remained a skeleton steel structure, like a grim bag of bones, getting rustier and rustier and ever the more unsightly. It marred the vista of Piccadilly. To keep it in some sort of repair so as to allow building to commence later cost about £3000 a year. It was regarded as Piccadilly's Folly. A new company acquired it in 1925 and got to work. They opened the Park Lane Hotel in 1927, fourteen years after the first work on it had begun, and the Savile Club sold their premises to the new company to make room for a ballroom. Perhaps the die-hard spirit had been sapped in the First World War or perhaps the money was welcome, for the same reason. Another club was absorbed by a hotel: the Green Park, which was remodelled out of the Isthmian Club. The change from clubs into hotels marked also the spirit of the times. But the greatest and the most startling change was the disappearance of Devonshire House, the greatest ducal house in Piccadilly. That story belongs to a later period between the two world wars and will be dealt with when that is reached.

Despite the changes, Piccadilly still shone and was the centre of the world. You saw wonderful things happen there and events which stayed in one's memory. I remember with joy the sight of a very lovely and gracious lady who seemed able to defeat time riding down Piccadilly in an open carriage on a summer's day in June in what appeared to be a mist of wild roses. Everybody seemed to be wearing one and Piccadilly had developed a pink flush. We all cheered that Lady of the Roses for she was the beloved and beautiful Queen Alexandra who had come for a ride through London to greet the day of hospital charity which she sponsored, of which her favourite flower was the emblem and to see how the very first Rose Day was prospering. Piccadilly seemed the ideal setting for that pretty picture.

What of the people who went up and down the Magic Mile? Well, maybe they had not changed very much but the Edwardian type had emerged, erasing to a large extent the Victorian type and worthy of study. There were more changes in the road traffic than that on the pavement. The motor was surely gaining superiority—especially as regards the buses—and the old horse buses were surrendering. These smaller vehicles, with their upholstery rather like carpets, their little flights of stairs from mounting platform to top, their brass rails between the seats, their curious and characteristic smell of rather dusty material and their 'stick on' advertisements on the windows—were fading away. The conductor with his number plate, his bowler hat and his cash satchel, his packet of tickets and his hand punch, rather like a somewhat swollen pair of pliers, was giving way to uniformed officialdom. He started and stopped his bus by pulling a thin cord, by stamping on the floor and just by calling out. But he was as human and almost as cheerful as his driver. The motorbus had challenged the horse in 1899 and had failed. There were single-decker buses along Piccadilly from Hammersmith in 1904. It was a Clarkson type and driven by steam. It had fourteen seats and one each side of the driver. It chugged along enveloped in clouds of steam and sometimes flames as well. It came in for quite a bit of derision. There were references to roast chestnuts. It ran from October 1904 to June 1905 and lost money.

But 1905 was the critical year and the tide began to turn. In January 1905 twenty motor buses were plying for hire; by the end of that year they had grown to 200. By the beginning of 1908 they had increased to 1000. In 1905, too, the firm of Thomas Tilling took the decision to buy no more horse buses. Yet they still had 1418 horse buses and carried 217,012,090 people. By 1913 there were 3000 motorbuses in London. In 1907 the *Railway Gazette* said there was too much traffic accommodation in London and that conditions were chaotic, leading to racing and greater speeds than the legal 12 m.p.h.—and that not sufficient time was allowed for maintenance. Nevertheless, the triumph of the motor bus was sure, if slow. When the roads—and Piccadilly amongst them—had both sorts of buses plying for hire, it was amusing to note the expressions of the passengers. Where a choice was offered, it was the younger people who boarded the motor bus, the more mature stuck to the horse bus. They watched each other stealthily—at least the 'outside' passengers did—as they went along, sometimes side by side. The motor bus would do its best to pass the horse bus and frequently succeeded. The horse bus scored through its driver, who had, nine times out of ten, real Cockney wit which he showered on the mechanic who crouched over the wheel of the thing which many regarded as Juggernaut and thought likely to blow up at any moment. There were old ladies who called them 'infernal machines', that being an early name for bombs before those things came into general use for destruction and were reserved for anarchists, nihilists, wild gentry from Russia and sometimes equally wild men known as Fenians. What every passenger on a horse bus hoped for was to find a motor bus broken down. That was joy and triumph. Sometimes the horse vehicle would sweep by whilst the driver flourished his whip and cheered and was joined in the cheering by his conductor and sometimes even by his 'outsides' who supported his type of progress. Sometimes the driver would actually pull up his steeds and offer to lend the sweating and furious driver of the motorbus his whip, wherewith to encourage the engine. Breakdowns were fairly frequent too. The worst that could happen to a horse bus was for the horses, or one of them, to fall down, which only happened when the roads were in a very bad state. Sometimes the triumphant horse bus driver would pretend to mistake the broken down mechanical monster for some kind of a piano organ. 'Give us a tune out of the old thing, mate' he would ask, with great friendliness. Hansom cab drivers rejoiced too and added their quota of chaff. But the drivers of four-wheelers, called 'growlers', just drove by, their dark and often inflamed sullen faces unmoved although there may have been a little flash of light in the usually lack-lustre eye. Drivers of four-wheelers were a race apart—misanthropes to a man. The cab drivers were to have their own bogy—the taxicab which conquered them sooner than the motor bus conquered the horse drawn variety.

The buses, the cabs, the carriages and the riding horses went up and down Piccadilly and on the pavements the men and women went by as well. The mature gentlemen of Piccadilly did not worry much about motor buses or horse buses either. They seldom

used them. Naturally, they disapproved of motor buses as something new and therefore smacking of radicalism and change. They
disliked the noise and the smell, both of which they regarded as
plebeian. When they wanted public conveyance they hailed a
hansom. The more elderly men deplored the changing face of
Piccadilly, which destroyed their set ideas and their background.
It has been shown how they clung to their club when the walls
were cracking on all sides. They were not so heavily dressed as
before; gradually the morning coat was displacing the frock coat,
some of them began to wear lounge suits and bowlers which were
regarded as being 'comme il faut'. There were not so many
beards and whiskers but most men wore moustaches. If you saw
a clean shaven young man he was either an actor, and therefore
not respectable and quite outside the pale, or a barrister. But there
were barristers and learned judges as well who wore moustaches
and even whiskers.

There still remained, in the early nineteen hundreds, even up
to the First World War, some figures of the early and middle
Victorian period, men who would not change and did not accept
change in any way. They looked like figures out of old prints as
they progressed slowly along Piccadilly to their clubs. And in
those days no man of means and standing ever hurried. That was
vulgar—leisure was the thing, and dignity. I remember how,
round about the 1910 period, I would see a tall figure, just a
little bowed as to the neck, wearing perfect clothes of a bygone
fashion but looking perfectly right in them; a man who was like
the illustrations of statesmen that one meets in well illustrated
history books, but in this case thoroughly patrician. His face was
cut like a cameo, it had the fine strain of a perfect thoroughbred, it
was serene and calm and nothing, one thinks, would have shaken
him. He was indeed a patrician and was to be seen at times in
Piccadilly—Lord Ribblesdale. He was generally called 'The
Aristocrat'. The last time I saw him was on a September morning.
There was just the suspicion of a nip in the air and he had a shawl
across his shoulders. He looked what he was—the very epitome of

an English gentleman. I raised my hat and he responded courteously and with a grave smile. He passed on leaning a little on an ivory handled walking stick.

But one thing did not change. As evening came and night fell, that continuous procession passed along Piccadilly, from the Circus down as far as Bond Street, with a slight overspill as far as Dover Street, but never farther, and almost entirely on the northern side—moving slowly with a curiously characteristic gait, something like a wild animal stalking its prey, something like a parade which desired to be examined and appraised—the Ladies of the Town still walked what they called 'The Dilly'.

7

The Pride of Piccadilly

Until the golden days were blown to pieces by the guns of 1914, the male youth of England might have been seen in its power and its glory in and around Piccadilly. Let it be understood that there is no suggestion that just as many excellent young men did not exist in what were then the middle and working classes—there were indeed. But this book is about Piccadilly.

Those guns destroyed the old world, the old order. They blew down class barriers which were never erected again. That may or may not have been a good thing. Piccadilly prior to 1914 and up to the beginning of that war was extremely class conscious, and although any free Briton (only they called them Englishmen then) could of course walk up and down that great street, its own pride was in the young men who were the scions of the aristocracy, the landed gentry and the Establishment in general. They were typical of the time when the British Empire dominated the world, and down the years they had played no small part in maintaining it.

The generation of them which passed with the First World War was the last of the old school—the last of the Englishmen who were always called 'Milor' by sycophantic foreign hoteliers and shopkeepers, who may have disliked them heartily, but who wanted those good, bright honest golden sovereigns which were in their pockets—which for value and stability could not be matched in the world.

For these young gentlemen, Piccadilly was their High Street, to which they turned naturally as their ancestors had dcne. Their clubs were in the streets which were tributaries of Piccadilly and some were in Piccadilly itself. In those side streets were their tailors, bootmakers, their hosiers, their hatters—their barbers, their tobacconists, their gunsmiths—the immediate neighbourhood of Piccadilly supplied them with all their needs, as it had done their fathers, grandfathers and previous generations. To them Piccadilly was London and the centre of the world. They appreciated its quality and they lived up to it—unless perhaps it was the other way round. They represented a phase of our race which will never come again. The First World War wiped them out as it did another stratum of society—that which made the English music hall what it was. The young men of Piccadilly were well born, at a time when birth and ancestry mattered. They were well educated—well, they had been to the best public schools, to Oxford, Cambridge, Sandhurst or Dartmouth. Not that they worried much about education. It played a very small part in their lives—the School mattered far more than what it taught them.

These young men worshipped good form. That was their criterion. Transgressors against that were outside the pale. They had their code, their manners and their way of life, which was much the same for all of them. They saw to it that the status quo was maintained. They differed in membership of clubs, but so long as you belonged to a good club you were all right, you were 'a good egg' in their slang. Club rules had slightly relaxed in Edwardian days from the time when they were so strict about visitors that two brothers who belonged to two different clubs situated opposite each other had to meet in a teashop to talk. Neither could go into the other's club. Most of these young men followed on in their father's club, put down for membership when they were born. And still the club was their haven—a man's stronghold, where he could read his paper in silence and be as unsocial in his social club as he liked.

They were all immaculately dressed. Fashion ruled them not quite so tyrannically as it ruled women, but with much power. The cut and length of a coat, the width of the lapel, the number of buttons on a sleeve, the width of the trousers, the depth of the waistcoat opening, a vent or no vent at the back of the coat, all these were of great importance. The Regency buck died hard in them, but owing to the stabilising effect of Victorian times, they no longer indulged in the excesses of the Regency period.

They kept entirely within a pattern, there was no flamboyancy, no high colours. Their great horror was to appear conspicuous. That was bad form. They were perfectly dressed by perfect tailors and everything they wore was of the best quality. They all looked very much alike. They wore, for the most part, lounge suits, in quiet materials and hues: dark blue, and various shades of grey. Brown suits came in about 1903 or 1904 but were not regarded as quite the thing for Piccadilly. Round about the early 1900's it became fashionable not to fasten the bottom button of the waistcoat. That endured. Always the pattern of the material was quiet; some men affected stripes or checks, but they were mostly of a sporting turn of mind.

The youth of Piccadilly wore morning coats for ceremonial occasions, when ladies were to be present, but seldom if spending the day in the ordinary way. And shirts with morning coats must be white. For some time they had stiff, starched fronts and cuffs. For some time later it was all right to wear a white shirt with a soft front—but the cuffs must be starched. Collars with morning coats were always of white linen. They varied in style. Some in the early period wore the straight-up 'choker', some wore the 'butterfly', or winged type and it was also quite all right to wear the stiff linen 'double fold' when that became popular. What varied was the height of the collar. There was a time when all collars had to be very high, just as for a very short time, very tight trousers were worn. Those tight trousers did not last long.

Stewart's at the corner of Bond Street; now QANTAS Empire Airways

Fortnum and Mason, 1837

John Hatchard

'This day, by the grace of God, the goodwill of my friends and £5 in my pocket, I have opened my bookshop in Piccadilly, 30th June, 1797.'   *His Diary*

They got baggy at the knees and that was anathema. Ties with morning coats must not be coloured. They could be black and white, with stripes or spots, and all shades of grey, patterned or plain. Some men wore the Ascot tie which was very smart indeed but needed some skill in tying properly. There was also the 'four-in-hand', which could be worn readymade, a curious cross over sort of thing, not greatly affected by young men, which demanded a tie pin in the middle. But most men wore tie pins. They could be jewelled, they could be of plain gold, or they could have a single pearl as their head. No jewel was barred. A plain gold pin with a gold knob was most effective. but tie pins were very decorative indeed. Sporting characters wore gold horse-shoes, horses' heads, foxes, hunting horns, all sorts of devices. Some devil-may-care and Bohemian types had pins shaped like a girl's leg. Nobody wore bow ties with a frock coat, but they were permissible with morning coats and lounge suits. But not very many Piccadilly types wore them—they had a faintly theatrical touch—and although these young men took their fashions from the stage, as displayed by Sir George Alexander, George Gros-smith and Seymour Hicks they would have hated to look like an actor. Actors then were not quite respectable. But many wearers of a morning coat wore also a vest slip. This was a slip made of piqué which fitted just above the opening of the waistcoat, looked very smart, and threw up the tie to perfection. It was a bit of a job sometimes to adjust it, but it was worth while.

Hats were various. It had to be a tall hat of course, with a frock or morning coat, but a topper was never worn with a lounge suit. Not in Piccadilly. Members of the Stock Exchange on business could do it but not 'Up West'. The shape of the topper varied. The point was to get one to suit your face. Sometimes they were higher than before, sometimes lower, sometimes they had curly brims, sometimes flattish; sometimes the hat itself had something of a bell shape and sometimes it was almost straight. Even the bands on them varied. These were sometimes narrow and made of corded silk, sometimes quite deep and made of black crêpe.

One must also register the grey frock coat and grey morning coat, such as were worn at Ascot. One could wear a black topper with these but it was not quite right. The grey felt topper was the thing, and you see it at weddings and even investitures today. In Edwardian days the black coat and topper were *de rigueur* for such events. Grey was mostly for open air functions.

Soft coloured shirts came in quite early in the 1900's but not with collars to match—one mostly wore a white silk double soft collar. But the first soft fronted shirts with colour were of flannel and so were the soft collars introduced by Sir George Alexander. These were only for country wear, never for Piccadilly. But the soft fronted coloured shirt with matching collar followed swiftly. The soft collar was kept tidy and its ends together by means of a gold safety pin. Seymour Hicks set a fashion in the soft shirt and collar line by wearing a collar and shirt of pink with a black satin tie. It was considered smart but only very advanced young men followed it, in Town at any rate.

Ordinary hats were the bowler, and the straw hat. Bowlers were in many shapes and here again it was a matter of getting one to suit your shape of face. It changed in the shape of its brim and the height of its crown. It was never an easy hat; it is not flexible at all. Bowlers have recently come back into popularity and are regarded essentially as City hats, but once they were quite general. It is not any easier today to get one to suit you. Bowlers were mostly black with the bow at the side. It was possible however to wear a brown one—though unusual in town—or a grey one and that with a blue suit could look quite smart. Horsy types wore bowlers which had rather capacious crowns and very narrow flat brims. They needed large round faces to carry them off, and preferably weatherbeaten complexions. The straw hat was the general summer wear. Although light and to some extent shady, this was not an easy hat either. It was not so hard to get one to suit your face and fit on your head but it was another matter to get it to stay there. They were very easily blown off by the wind. There was nothing so undignified or embarrassing as to chase a straw hat down the road. Plenty of people tried to help you usually with disastrous results to the hat. So you wore a hat-guard. That was a long black cord, which fastened into the lapel buttonhole, went once round the crown of the hat and was fastened by a little screw through the brim of the hat being screwed into a little black metal cup. Some men wore those little cups on the backs of their bowlers, without the guard. This was to give the impression that they were horsemen—maybe given to huntin'—when it was necessary to secure one's headgear. These types also wore the bow at the back of the bowler. But all straw hats needed a guard. In fine, still weather it could be worn fastened round the base of the crown and merged into the black band, to be adjusted if needed. The usual band for a straw hat was black with the bow at the side. One could also wear club colours—and that applied to ties too— but only in lounge suits. For a long time the brim of the straw was serrated. Then they became smooth which was much better because the teeth of the serrated edge were liable to get broken and then the hat could not be worn. Clergymen and elderly gentlemen often wore black and white speckled straw hats and some parsons wore all black ones. Nobody dreamed of wearing one before May or after 1st September. And in Edwardian days, when they were in their prime, nobody called them boaters— although they were the usual wear on the river. Panamas were never popular with young men, although they were very sensible hats indeed. In the country—but never in Town—oh, never—the young man of Piccadilly could and did wear a cap. It was usually made to measure and of the same material as one's tweed country suit. They were of variable shapes but never so voluminous as the 'Cup Tie' cap of the North, which so many Americans still think to be the traditional headwear of the English. It is no such thing. If there is a traditional English hat it is the bowler—which Americans call the Derby and pronounce 'Durby'. Nobody in Piccadilly would have done that. Good King Edward VII came as a boon and a blessing to men when he popularised the homburg hat, now the usual wear. He introduced it in green velour with the bow at the back, and it was universally adopted. They were all right for town and country. If you wanted to be really smart you wore a little tuft of feathers—eagle's for preference—at the back. The shape came and conquered. It went later into felt but it remained green. Then it went into all sorts of shades and the bow got to the side until the black hat now worn so universally, and popularised by Sir Anthony Eden, swept the board. But two other men wore these hats even before Mr Eden—the present writer and his friend Mr Hannen Swaffer. There had been a kind of soft hat of somewhat similar shape used before, but it was large, floppy and Bohemian and called the Trilby because that classic character 'Svengali', created in picture and literary form by George Du Maurier and in life on the stage by Sir Herbert Tree, wore it. But it was not at Piccadilly. And you might have looked for years and never seen a deerstalker, although there is an impression today that Edwardians and Victorians wore them. So they did—in the Highlands. But never in Piccadilly. That would have labelled them as outsiders, or imitators of Sherlock Holmes trying to make an exhibition of themselves.

Gloves were always worn—they were *de rigueur*. A real Piccadilly man would have felt naked had he walked down that road with his hand uncovered. You took off the right hand glove to shake hands. There were gloves of all sorts suitable to what sort of attire was being worn, from washleather, and doeskin, to kid. And everybody who was anybody carried either a walking stick or an umbrella. The young men did not go in for umbrellas if they could help it, but when they did carry one it had to be immaculately rolled. They preferred to jump into a hansom if it rained rather than disarrange their umbrella. Walking sticks had fashions too—there was quite a craze of green ones at one time—and malaccas, partridge canes and rattans were always popular.

Boots in town were nearly always black. They could be of glacé kid, ordinary leather, box calf or patent leather. Some men wore boots of patent leather with light uppers of glacé, white, yellow and brown kid. The brown uppers were mostly worn with lounge suits, the others with frock coats or morning coats. Boots were either laced or buttoned. In the latter case, a button hook had to be handy and it was a catastrophe if a button came off. Very few men wore shoes, except in the country, and they were mostly brogues. Trousers, for much of the period, fitted over the boot, and great care had to be taken with the braces to prevent them from concertina-ing. They had to be superbly cut, and they were. Then, in the middle of the early 1900's, the permanent turnup became a boon.

When the young Edwardians wore evening dress they wore stiff shirts and either winged or straight up collars, never double fold. They never wore soft shirts and collars with such attire. Dinner jackets were never worn if ladies were to be present. And no man would have dreamed of wearing a white dinner jacket, soft shirt and collar. He would have felt like a ship's steward. Either patent boots or patent shoes were worn with evening dress and pumps for dancing. A tall hat was essential or a gibus (the collapsible opera hat which now seems extinct). Many men still wore those most picturesque and becoming opera cloaks.

In the winter there was a large variety of top coats. Raincoats such as are worn today were hardly known. You could have a raglan, a chesterfield, all sorts of coats, and for evening dress there was a special kind of black coat fitting in to the waist which with a white muffler and silk topper was most becoming. Men of means had furlined overcoats and some sported astrakhan collars, which looked very good indeed.

Most men wore socks with clocks up the side—little decorative patterns, mostly like a small tree of fern, which came half way up the calf. They could be in any colour and were a hangover from the Georgian silk stockings. Socks were usually black and often of silk, but some men liked patterned socks.

For sports all men wore white flannels, and often sported a club blazer, which lent colour to the scene. They never wore such things in Piccadilly and the amount of blue blazers now seen about, all with elaborate crests on the pockets, would have made them raise their eyebrows. It was permissible in hot summer weather, to wear grey flannel suits in town with brown boots, but not at any sort of function. Middle aged men wore spats; young men never did so. And a great many men wore button holes daily, the stalks of the flowers often fixed into a little glass tube which fitted into the button hole by a metal clip like a bit of fern and which held water. The favourite male buttonhole was Parma violets, so seldom seen today. And most young men wore moustaches.

Most men carried little toothpicks in their waistcoat pockets—the prong of which pushed in and out like a propelling pencil of today. One seldom sees toothpicks anywhere today; once they were on every bar and restaurant table, in quill form.

Watch chains were worn. In the earlier days there were Alberts—after the Prince Consort—which went from one waist-coat pocket to the other. Middle aged men often had a gold coin suspended from them or a seal. In one pocket was the gold watch (a half hunter as a rule) on the other to balance was a sovereign purse, a little silver or gold round box which contained sovereigns, fitted over a spring, and sometimes half sovereigns as well. They held five—a small fortune then. And also possibly a gold match box. Later a lighter chain went across the chest. Most men carried matchboxes then, for the lighter was unheard of. They could be gold, as abovementioned, they could be silver or even gunmetal. They held wax matches, called vestas. They were of white wax and had pink or brown heads. They struck along the bottom of the box, which was grooved with indentations, and the friction lit the match. Sometimes the heads fell off—a thing not unknown in 'safety' matches today. The wax vestas gave way to little matches of pine with pink heads which were far more satisfactory. Safety matches were cheap—you got a dozen boxes for 2½d.

Very few of these young men wore spectacles or even pince-nez. Horn-rimmed glasses had not become fashionable. They came from America. But some of them wore monocles, not always because they needed them, either. They had beautifully cut hair—no such thing as crew-cuts, or the weird effects one sees today—and never, no never, side whiskers. They were smooth shaven, and their hair was never long. Those were the Edwardian young men—not a bit like those who today call themselves Teddy boys. A young Edwardian would have kicked any of them on sight.

They were not demonstrative; they seldom, if ever, appeared to be enthusiastic; to betray strong emotion was not good form. They never appeared to hurry, they seemed to have all the time in the world. It was vulgar to rush about or to speak loudly, and as for shouting. . .

Most of them appeared to have little or nothing to do, and yet they did quite a lot. Some of them had very comfortable allowances, some were heirs to estates, whose future lay clearly before them. Some were in the services—the only trace of which was in their bearing for they got into mufti and out of uniform with all possible speed. Some went into the Law, the Church, the Indian Civil Service or Colonial Administration. Although they did not appear to be overburdened with brains, they were able to administer vast tracts of savage country almost without any show of force save a handful of native soldiers. But they took England, they took Piccadilly with them wherever they went and they carried on their usual custom wherever they might be. They dressed for dinner in jungle and swamp and Arctic circle. It was their tradition. I don't think it did any harm.

Their manners were as impeccable as their clothes. They treated all women with courtesy, for women had not their attained 'equality'. They treated their fathers with great respect. Even if they thought that Pater, or the Governor, was a little old fashioned and pompous, they did not question his authority. Their mothers they worshipped. They had no great opinion of their sisters but they looked after them. They did not regard them as 'girls' and if one of their friends fell in love with a sister of theirs they marvelled at what the silly chump could see in such a little wretch. They had little use for their younger brothers whom they regarded as little 'stinkers' but they stood by them if there was trouble. For the family mattered to a terrific extent. That must never be let down. Ninety-nine per cent of them were sportsmen. They read *The Pink Un, The Sportsman, Sporting Life, Pick Me Up,* and other light and airy journals. They revered *Ruff's Guide to the Turf* and *Wisden*. They looked at the illustrated magazines, the 'glossies'—*The Sketch, The Tatler, The Sphere, The Bystander, The Graphic, The Illustrated London News, The Field, Black and White,* and *The Illustrated Sporting and Dramatic*. They rode to hounds, they shot, they rowed, they played football—mostly rugger— but there were also the Corinthians and the Casuals in the world of soccer. They did not think much of professional soccer, and there were no pools. They sailed at Cowes, they were at Henley, at the race meetings, at Lórds for the Eton and Harrow and the Varsity game and all the tests. They wore their old school ties with pride and never dreamed that a later generation would think this absurd. They did not play much tennis, although it was making ground, but they did play some golf, though nothing like as much as now. They did the social round and they shot game in season, even to deer stalking. Some of them went after big game too.

They had their drinks in the club: gin and It, gin and angostura, gin and bitters (orange or peach) mixed vermouth and a little Fernet Branca, and of course sherry. And they took kindly to cocktails when these came in. Most of them drank beer in tankards and of course Scotch and soda or Scotch and polly. If they dined with friends they always took their hostess a gift of flowers. If they took a lady out to dine or sup, they always gave her flowers. They went to the Empire, the Alhambra, the music halls and the Palace. They did not patronise the Opera—unless it was a special event—and they were no great shakes at concerts. They liked the theatre but they preferred a farce, or, above all, musical comedy. Any show staged by George Edwardes was their affair. They would also flock to those of Frank Curzon and Robert Courtneidge —shows like *Miss Hook of Holland* or *The Arcadians*. But their

The Seventh Earl of Shaftesbury

Crockford's, St James's Street

Gloucester House

special haunts were Daly's and the Gaiety—especially the Gaiety. These were the stage door johnnies and they were not the stupid vapid young men which a mistaken tradition represents them to have been but the salt of young English manhood, liking melody, beauty and especially the tangible beauty of a Gaiety Girl. They might have a rowdy evening and end up at Jimmy's, but that had gone in the early 1900's. As to poetry, Kipling was their man. There was no Empire save the British Empire and Kipling was its prophet.

They would spend their last copper in taking a Gaiety girl out to sup. I know one—alive today—who was at Camberley and often had to ride home on a cart returning from Covent Garden Market. He loved it—and he never got caught. Their morals were no worse than those of young men of any age and better than most. They were discreet and never flaunted a conquest. Such a thing as the public 'necking' which goes on today would have shocked them. They might have *affaires* with young actresses, even chosen barmaids. They would take them down to Skindles on Sunday afternoons and lounge in a punt on the river. And if you saw them at tea on the lawn both of you looked the other way. When they did not live at home, there were 'chambers' in and around Jermyn Street—at 10/- a week!

There was another type too whom you would find on Piccadilly. They had rather full and brick red countenances almost devoid of expression and often they wore monocles which stayed in their eye without the safety cord which was usually attached. There was a kind of horsiness about them and they were men of few words who usually found it very difficult to express themselves. They were sometimes apt to forget themselves in their clubs and clap their hands to get a waiter's or steward's attention, and that was not really done. They would speak of lunch as tiffin and would interlard their conversation, if any, with strange outlandish words. They were officers in the Indian Army, either on leave or retired. Their livers had mostly been ruined and their tempers were not too good, but they always behaved like gentlemen.

Those purple countenances were the result of Indian suns, chutney, curry and all sorts of things, with a generous top dressing of hard liquor. They always appeared to be staring yet such was not really the case. They were the lineal descendants of 'Major Joey Bagstock' whom Dickens drew in *Dombey and Son* and, if you remember, he was always wide awake and staring. But they were the sahibs and their wives were the mem-sahibs who ruled India under the Crown and the Viceroy. They had played polo, and tennis at Simla. They had gone on shikari, they had shot tigers and 'stuck' pigs. They had fought desperately on the North West Frontier against wily, agile, furtive and immensely mobile foes whom they seldom saw. They may not have looked very intelligent, and perhaps many of them were not, but they did their job. They upheld the glory and prestige of the British Raj and gained respect for it. Their men would follow them everywhere and anywhere. They are now a vanished type but they were worth their salt and many pinches of it. They had earned that 'chota peg' for which they clamoured and they never dreamed of the day when the Union Jack would not fly over Poona. You saw many military types in Piccadilly and the observant eye could place them. The cavalry type was entirely different from the infantry. Music Hall had a song about them called 'The Galloping Major'. You would meet long lean men with a rather characteristic stride, who placed their feet firmly on the ground. They had bronzed faces and rather fierce moustaches and their clothes and trousers fitted them rather tightly and you could almost hear the jingle of spurs and clatter of sabre as they walked along. Some of the taller and leaner were undoubtedly Lancers and there was a song about them too:

> 'I'm Jones of the Lancers—haw, haw, haw
> They say I'm the pick of the lot
> A gunner or sapper
> May dazzle a flapper
> But women—the Lancers—eh, what?'

Very true and very Piccadilly. If a song writer wanted to pin point the West End, it was to Piccadilly he turned. Vesta Tilley the incomparable told us of Algy, who was the Piccadilly Johnny with the little glass eye, and that other superb and inimitable male impersonator, Hetty King saying much later, of 'Piccadilly, London's Great White Way', Londoners considered that New York's Broadway had been flattered. Even Ella Shields' penurious gentleman who walked down the Strand had a name taken from Piccadilly—Burlington Bertie.

There were two great songs of Piccadilly, contrasted but both showing the power of that amazing place. Those young men who frequented it had in their times many names applied to them— they had been, down the years 'Heavy Swells', 'Mashers', 'Piccadilly Johnnies', 'Dudes', but in Edwardian times they were known as the 'B'Hoys', or more popularly as the 'K'Nuts'. They were immortalised in song by poor Basil Hallam, who was one of them himself, in a revue at the Palace Theatre, *The Passing Show* in 1914, right at the end of the era. It was composed by Herman Finck and it has become a classic of its kind—'Gilbert the Filbert' (the K'Nut with a K). Nothing has summed up the Edwardian Piccadilly youth better and when Basil Hallam sang it, in his characteristic voice—hardly much more than speaking it to music —with the inimitable Palace Girls behind him, and perfectly dressed as the Pride of Piccadilly should be, that was something to remember. That very year the end of the old world came and the K'Nuts vanished into the mists of war, few ever to return again. Basil Hallam was among them, unfit but fighting and giving his life for his country as indeed became the man who was a Pride of Piccadilly and a Colonel of the K'Nuts thereof.

There was, however, another Piccadilly song which embraced the whole thoroughfare and all who pass along it and did not just concern itself with the Edwardian young men. For this song put that magic mile in true perspective. It showed what that street meant to Londoners in general and to the singer in particular. It was sung by a great comedian of the music halls named J. W. Rickaby, and composed by William Hargreaves, a noted writer of music hall songs. The character it presented was to Piccadilly what Burlington Bertie was to the Strand, but Piccadilly meant far more to him. He was one of those amazing men, of whom in those days there were many, who did no work, did not beg, who were ragged but wore their rags with an air and who were always clean and well brushed—the very lowest dregs of the shabby genteel but full of pride and independence. Nobody knows how they lived or where they slept, that was their dark secret. Yet you would be sure to meet them and if a kindly soul offered them a shilling it was accepted as from one gentleman to another. Alms were never asked. There were plenty of them and I don't believe any had a criminal record of any importance. They might have been run in for sleeping out. You don't see them any more, maybe the Welfare State has eradicated them. The particular seedy gent of this song rejoiced in the name of Silk Hat Tony— he told us he was down and stony—not only broken but bent. But he had the firm belief that Piccadilly had been built especially for him. He informed us that he strolled along at his leisure in correct Bond Street measure, that he'd worn out his feet and that his ankles had senile decay. He told us that he paraded the same beat every day, from Burlington Arcade to the Old Bailey, that destination being probably put in for the necessity of rhyme. He made no secret of his sartorial deficiencies, for the fringe of his trousers were lashing the houses as he strolled along. But what did he care?

> 'Though I haven't a fraction
> I've this satisfaction
> They built Piccadilly for me . . .'

He was sure of that. Everybody knew him, he said, Lord Rothschild, the Duke of Westminster, and even the King, who would get out of his carriage to treat his old friend Silk Hat Tony, who despite his financial difficulties did his best to keep up the Piccadilly tradition, as his name implies. But Tony although broken and bent, envied nobody—not even His Majesty—

the date of the song is 1913 when Piccadilly had altered a lot so the King would be George V—and he confided in us that:

'I said to the King once at tea
They built you a Palace
I bear you no malice
They built Piccadilly for me . . .'

That, I think, exactly fills the picture. The tune was leisurely, stately and 'correct Bond Street measure'. It was, it is, the perfect picture of what Piccadilly means to so many—even though it has changed so much—the ducal mansions gone, commerce in almost entire charge; yet if you really appreciate it, you will feel with Silk Hat Tony that indeed they built Piccadilly for you—and maybe you will not be far wrong, either.

8

They Said Goodbye to Piccadilly

At that fateful moment on 4th August 1914, when the First World War smote civilisation, that wise statesman Sir Edward Grey, said, 'The lights are going out all over the world.' He spoke the epitaph of the Old Order—things were never to be the same. That little world within a world, the world of Piccadilly, changed too. It had undergone a structural metamorphosis, and was still undergoing it. That stopped, for War put an end to building operations like that. But although Piccadilly itself came through the conflict, the life which flowed through it changed very much indeed.

Naturally, being Piccadilly, it got itself into the War, by means of one of the great songs of that upheaval—a song which will always be the symbol of 1914–1918, and which stirs the hearts of the veterans of that long drawn-out grapple as nothing else can do. The Second World War produced nothing so vivid or lasting. And, of course, as it was a war song of the British, it was not about War, heroism, or patriotism at all. It was called 'Tipperary'. It had been published long before hostilities broke out but had not been a success, although because it was about Ireland it had some popularity. For the extraordinary thing is that the hatred of England and the English in Ireland is matched by the affection for

Ireland and the Irish in England. This difference is racial and will never be altered. The Irish adore a grievance and will nurture it for centuries. An Irishman told me that another son of Erin whom we were discussing was no good at all. 'He's a b . . . Dane,' he declared. 'His ancestors fought on the wrong side at the Battle of Clontarf,' which I believe took place in 1014. Few young Englishmen know or care if their grandfathers fought in the First World War! The Irish, too, have some capacity for hate. The English have none. If they have a grievance they see to it that it is removed and forget all about it. They will fight an enemy to the bitter end and then be his friend. That leads to a lot of trouble—because other nations do not understand it and do not respond. It was one of the causes of the Second World War. But it does not seem possible to eradicate it from the British mind—at least, so far, but the race seems to be changing.

So when England went to war, that music hall song with the Irish flavour became popular. They sang it as they marched. They did not sing about their country being great above all others, they did not exhort their comrades to march because the day of glory had arrived. They did not have much belief in days of glory, anyway. They sang a song which had a good marching rhythm and said, 'It's a long way to Tipperary'.

Very few even knew where Tipperary was, except that it was in Ireland, but they roared out the lines which bade Goodbye to Piccadilly and Farewell to Leicester Square. They knew all about them. Actually the popularity of that song was made by a correspondent of *The Times*, writing under the nom-de-plume of 'Eye Witness', who heard some soldiers singing it when they landed in France and sent this fact back in his story. Then the song became really famous and in general use. Piccadilly had seen the first fruits of war before the actual declaration came. It saw small bodies of Frenchmen marching to the station singing the 'Marseillaise', waving tricolour flags. It watched them with kindly eyes and some people cheered them. It watched rather more grimly small bodies of young men, with stiff backs and strangely

stiff legs, who did not sing but looked fierce and determined—
Germans returning to their Fatherland to rejoin the colours. It was
the first time most English people had seen conscripts. They were
soon to know more about that. And then, in the topsy turvy
English way, when the actual Declaration came, the people made
holiday. Union Jacks appeared everywhere—the streets were
crowded with excited masses, singing and laughing; soldiers and
sailors in uniform were cheered too—they were few, for mobilisa-
tion was not complete. They were treated in the pubs, they rode
free on public transport, they were given free entrée to theatres
and music halls. But at Buckingham Palace and the Horse Guards
the Guard was mounted in its traditional dignity and grandeur.
That is another difference between the Irish and the English.
The former love tradition and make a tradition of people. The
English make tradition of things.

There was an immediate man-shortage in many restaurants and
in almost every barber's and hairdresser's. So many waiters and
barbers were German. They had always been regarded, half
jokingly, as spies. But the British did not really believe in spies—
how could they harm an invincible nation? And the British
firmly believed they were invincible. That first night of war saw
Piccadilly packed with people, many of whom were coming
from or going to Buckingham Palace, where they acclaimed their
Sovereign. The pubs did a roaring trade. The girls on the Dilly
were busy too. Many of those frail ladies were Germans. But
they immediately became Belgians, and so were very popular.

The K'Nut vanished as if a blind had been pulled down. The
Pride of Piccadilly just faded away. The K'Nuts had gone to join
the Forces. Many of them were already in the services, many were
Territorials, and the rest joined up. They came back sporadically
on short leave to their old resorts. The K'Nut made the best and
smartest officer in the world—and there was no smarter uniform
than that of the British officer in the First World War, with its
Sam Browne belt, and the sword was still worn. It seemed in
Piccadilly as if almost every man was in uniform.

A new world was opening before English eyes, for up to then they had not seen many soldiers except a few on leave, in processions or in the military tournament and reviews. Civilians grew learned as regards military badges of rank, and the coloured tabs of the Staff filled them with admiration. The 'brass hats' of the Higher Command impressed them deeply. It was a world in khaki. This country had not been involved in a European War, or fought against a European race, since the Crimea, in 1854.

In the Clubs the older men got together and talked. Old soldiers gave their opinion as to how the war was to be won. The younger men held their tongues as the seniors spoke. There was universal satisfaction that Lord Kitchener had taken charge of the War Office. Some wondered if 'Bobs' would come back, forgetting his advanced age. But French was in command and he had proved himself in South Africa.

And London—especially Piccadilly—had already had some shocks. There had been a moratorium—and the streets were partially blacked out. That was the strangest thing. The lights of London had been turned down—Sir Edward Grey had spoken truly. The black-out was nothing like so severe as that of the Second War but bad enough for those used to the full lights of the city. Then the golden sovereigns disappeared and were replaced by paper. That shook them somewhat. The golden sovereign was part of themselves and these bits of paper looked pretty poor. But in the English way, they made jokes about them. Printed in a hurry and perhaps without too much care, it said upon them that they were good for any amount. So comic fellows ordered—for a joke—goods worth £100—and then solemnly tendered a £1 note. Instantly of course they got nicknames. They were called 'Bradbury's', because of the signature of Bradbury upon them.

Piccadilly was a little worried, but not scared. These Germans could not do us any harm. There was the Royal Navy. Zeppelins —the new weapon of power? Well, take a look at the guns near Hyde Park Corner! And every evening at dusk, in the failing light of the summer twilight and beautiful weather, a small Royal

Naval airship went up—the White Ensign flying—and sailed around the West End. It gave immense confidence.

But the war was going against us. There was the German rush through Belgium, the Allied retreat, the clash between British and Germans at Mons, and then the story of the Angels at Mons, which many people believed. And suddenly the Germans were nearly in Paris. 'I say, you know, this won't do,' said the men of Piccadilly. They were not scared in the slightest but they were very annoyed. It had been confidently expected by so many that the war would be over by Christmas. Not, however, by Lord Kitchener—who asked for 100,000 men, to sign for three years— or the duration. He got those men, on the magic of his name and that most effective recruiting poster which showed him pointing directly at you—which had its origin in a theatre poster advertising *The Chocolate Soldier*. There he was, his piercing eyes upon you, his finger pointing straight at you. 'Your King and Country Want You', he said. He got that 100,000 at the double.

Then came the victories of the Marne and the Aisne. Von Kluck was defeated—the Germans did not get to Paris—they were thrown back. Was victory in sight? Would the war be over by Christmas after all? Had there been a million British at the Marne it might well have been. But that Contemptible Little Army, as the Kaiser called it, more than did its bit. And had he known it, that insulting phrase of his did more to harm him than anything he ever said.

England at war settled down to the job. The partial black-out did not interfere much. A new kind of life began and Piccadilly became almost its old self again, fitting itself into the conditions of the times. The public wanted to be entertained and take their minds off the war. They wanted the fighting men to have a good time. The restaurants boomed. The K'Nuts in khaki, now mostly 2nd lieutenants—one pippers, they were called—dined out when they could and frequented their clubs, terribly self-conscious in their uniforms and with little moustaches on their upper lips, not unlike the hirsute lip adornment of a curious little English

comedian who had become a great star of American silent films—
a man called Charlie Chaplin. These K'Nuts in uniform did not
say much. Trench warfare had started and the life of the average
one pipper was about three weeks. The K'Nuts knew that, but
they took their fences just the same. It was their job. The stage
doors knew them again during their short leaves, but they grew
fewer and fewer. Those stage door Johnnies, the youth of
Piccadilly, went to their end in the mud and hell of Flanders, many
of them whistling Gaiety tunes. They had said Goodbye to
Piccadilly, Farewell to Leicester Square . . .

The war dragged on and the casualties were enormous.
Wounded men became an everyday sight in their blue hospital
clothes and red ties. It was amazing how London assimilated all
the changes but it did, even that conservative Piccadilly, although
maybe the recent structural changes had prepared the way in some
subtle manner. Uniforms of all kinds thronged the pavements.
There were the men from overseas—the Australians in their
smasher hats, bronzed, truculent, hard bitten, and with plenty of
money to spend—determined to prove to the world that they
were the salt of the earth. They proved their valour over and over
again, apart from Gallipoli, but they had not much regard for
discipline as they flocked to Piccadilly, into the pubs and the
restaurants. The New Zealanders were quieter and seemed very
much at home in Piccadilly. There were Canadians in their
rather short tunics and tightish uniforms, men from South Africa
and from all over the world. And Allied forces too—there were
the Portuguese in grey uniforms and long cloaks, looking rather
like a comic opera army, plenty of French, some Belgians, and an
odd Russian now and again—although the Russian Steam Roller
had mostly acted in reverse. Piccadilly saw them all, and they
all wanted to see Piccadilly.

But even the throngs from overseas could not fill that constantly
deepening hole of death into which the British Expeditionary
Force hurled itself via the stench and horror of the bloody, rat-
ridden, lice-infested trenches. Those who fought in the Second

World War have little idea of what those men endured—men who such a short time before had been on the land, down mines, in factories, in offices, behind shop counters, and now fought, with only a few weeks' training, as dourly and grimly as veterans—men who had served in the shops in and around Piccadilly amongst them. And those one-time K'Nuts, still perfectly calm and self-possessed, trying to keep their uniforms as smart and well pressed as their peace-time suits, did more than their 'bit' maybe. They had those little moustaches on their upper lips, they had a 'batman' instead of a valet, and they sat in their dug-outs trying to sleep in their rest time thinking of Prince's Restaurant, Hatchett's bar—the Empire Promenade, Daly's and the Gaiety stage door, and hoping that they might get another 'leave' before they 'stopped one with their name on it'. They had pictures in their dug-outs—the original pin-ups. Some were photos of their own families, their fiancées, of girls they knew, of actresses, but some were just pictures of girls—glamorous girls drawn and painted by a man named Kirchner, which reminded them of joyous exciting evenings spent in times of peace, of the Thames at Cookham and Maidenhead, of home and of Piccadilly. The men —'other ranks'—had their pin-ups, too. They dreamed and longed for those brief snatches of Heaven, when for a very few days they could tread those well remembered streets, see *The Bing Boys* at the Alhambra, *The Maid of the Mountains* at Daly's—with Josie Collins—or *Tonight's the Night* at the Gaiety. Never mind about chronology—all those things sustained them as the years went by. They sent home their 'Field Service' postcards, with their short, rather naive and printed sentences on them, treasured by recipients despite their official air. They wrote their letters knowing the power of the censor and as they wrote very likely they hummed 'Goodbye, Piccadilly, Farewell Leicester Square', words which had become so horribly prophetic. They all tried to make the best of it, and to improvise, in the good old British way; they groused, which was the age old privilege of the Army but they made their jokes. Portions of the trenches were given names—

names which were officially accepted—and naturally there was a very popular stretch, if such a phrase can be allowed, called 'Piccadilly'. And those ex-K'Nuts, when the time came, looked at their wrist watches as they stood on the trench firing platform, glanced along the line of men on either side, and then at Zero Hour went over the top—it might well be 'Goodbye, Piccadilly' then. What everyone hoped for was a 'Blighty'—a wound bad enough to get one home to a hospital in England. Not that such a thing was likely to land a frequenter of Piccadilly anywhere near his favourite spot. Wounded Londoners found themselves in Manchester, Liverpool or maybe Newcastle. Wounded Scots found themselves in London—it worked in that perverse way. But there would be leave at the end of it. Another name for these 'K'Nuts' had been 'The Lads of the Village'. George Lashwood, great singer of songs and the Beau Brummell of Music Hall, drew attention to their absence . . .

'Where are the Lads of the Village tonight?
What has become of the Boys?
Search Piccadilly and Leicester Square,
They're not there—they're not there . . .'

The K'Nuts went almost as one man—the only test being physical fitness. It was their tradition. But a lot of men did not want to fight, and as they came to know more about conditions overseas, their reluctance was the greater. Patriotism had run riot in the early days and had been misguided. Rather hysterical women dashed about town asking young men in civilian clothes, 'Why aren't you in khaki!'—and presenting them with a white feather. It was such an action which drove Basil Hallam, the Pride of Piccadilly, into the Army despite physical unfitness. As the recruiting drives became more and more intense, the tricks of evasion grew and grew. There were conscientious objectors— many of whom were genuine—but there were a great number who just bluntly did not want to go. Alfred Lester, the famous gloomy comedian, poked fun at them at the Alhambra.

'Send out the boys of the Old Brigade
Who made Old England Free.
Send out my Mother,
My sister and my brother
But for Gawd's sake, don't send me.'

Despite the desperate need for manpower, this country was still trying to cling to its old tradition of Voluntary Service—which reached its last gasp in the Derby Plan—and the shadow of conscription loomed nearer and nearer.

There was great ingenuity displayed in evading military service, and there were those who saw the chance of profit in their country's need and did not hesitate to take it. There was a recruiting office in Piccadilly itself. And one regrets to say that for a time, it was an H.Q. of evasion, when conscription finally descended on the country. Everybody had to register, as in the Second World War. Your dossier, if of military age, went to the recruiting office of the district in which you resided and in due course the Call Up followed. In that Piccadilly recruiting office was a clerk who, before getting that job, had been unemployed for some time, and was then in receipt of £2.15.0d per week, as wages. With ingenuity worthy of a better cause—but with excellent financial results to him, he worked out a scheme of evasion. By various means he put this about amongst interested parties. All you had to do was to take a room in the Piccadilly district and your papers went there, on re-registration, from your previous residential district. This man, who had advised the client of this course, looked out for the arrival of the papers, collared them, and quietly put them in the dustbin with the waste paper. They were removed and destroyed of course. He had a scale of charges for this based on the means of his clients. For a while this trick succeeded, getting by on account of its simplicity. But the authorities in charge of recruiting were not entirely asleep. There was a section whose job it was to deal with what was known as E.M.S. (Evasion of Military Service). It became apparent that quite a few people who should be in were still out. They had registered but nothing could be done until a call up was issued and their documents were missing. All they had to do was to keep clear of the frequent round-ups when everybody so detained had to produce exemption papers. A member of this special department, who knew Piccadilly well, got the job of testing out the district and the office. He mingled, he was simple, he was cunning and 'wide' according to need, and he spent a long time in the bars in and around Piccadilly. Finally he discovered that this clerk, who had been on the rocks so shortly before, now had three banking accounts and another in his wife's name. Also he and she had bought some weekly rental property. This seemed rather steep on a salary of £2.15.0d per week. The investigator believed he had discovered the system. He got acquainted with the clerk in a pub bar. He produced a man anxious for exemption. The sum fixed was £200. The man did as he was told. His papers arrived in due course and the Department swooped on the dustbins as they were being removed. Not only that man's papers but quite a few more were there. The clerk, who did not know this, went round to the pub to receive payment. It was The Yorkshire Grey in Piccadilly, now renamed The Yorker. He was paid, in marked notes. As he left the bar he was arrested. One hastens to say that the proprietors and managers, etc. of The Yorkshire Grey knew nothing about this.

Life was changing fast. It had become hectic. 'Eat, drink and be merry, for Tomorrow we die' was the motto. Men on leave either from the front or training centres came to the West End and lived up to that slogan. The pubs, the restaurants, the theatres and music halls were full. The partial black-out stopped nobody. The dancing craze which pervaded the 1920's had begun. The old conventions were going and with them the old code of morality. These night clubs which sprang up all over the place—and the smaller hotels—could tell a story or two. Women began to do men's jobs and to wear trousers in public. They cleaned windows, conducted buses, worked on munitions, and went into the

women's services, which grew and grew. Pretty young dispatch-
riders in breeches riding fast motor bikes looked very attractive.
Women drove generals in official cars, not always to the general's
delight and approval. Women smoked in public—the great
emancipation had begun. The older men looked on at this changing world with amazement, and not with much satisfaction. Those
who were too old for service, and especially the elderly men of
Piccadilly, joined as special constables or enlisted in the Home
Defence Force, which was the forerunner of the Second World
War's Home Guard. Retired officers of both services found
themselves wanted again and got back into uniform with joy.
The Blimps were created, but many of them were not so stupid as
those gloriously comic creations of Low implied. But they
found life hard to understand and it was not easy for them to adjust
themselves. They resented the disappearance of the golden
sovereign. They did not like these newfangled £1 and 10/- notes
which necessitated the carrying of a wallet specially designed.

Never again could a miracle happen in Piccadilly as had occurred
in 1912—such a short time before. That came about in this way.
There was at the Lyric Theatre a most successful musical comedy
called *The Girl in the Taxi*, the first big success made by the late
beloved Yvonne Arnaud. The manager of the theatre, one Tom
Pitt, was a man of most conservative habit. He did everything the
same way at the same time. Life had really stopped for him at the
end of the run of the phenomenal *The Sign of the Cross* at his
theatre in 1896. What came after that he thought little about.
The theatre's bank was in Piccadilly and naturally he paid in his
takings every day. He never carried the money in a bag, as
most people did in those easy days when smash and grab and
coshes were unknown. He donned an old ulster, which reached
almost to his feet. He put the gold in a canvas bag, the silver in
another and the copper in a third, and these he placed in the ulster
pockets which were deep and roomy. The £5 notes, cheques and
postal orders he put in his inside jacket pocket. One Monday
morning he went to the bank, shoved his paying-in book across

The Quadrant, Regent Street

The Egyptian Hall

The Italian Opera House

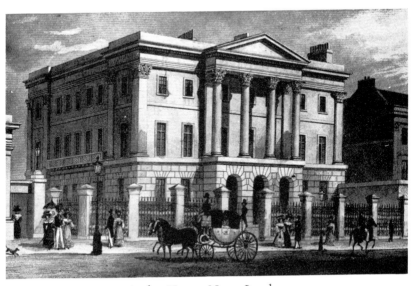

Apsley House, No 1, London

the counter with the money and waited to get it back signed. The cashier counted and checked. Then he looked across at Mr Pitt. 'Where's the gold, Mr Pitt? he asked. 'Isn't it there?' queried the manager, and was told it was not. 'Stupid of me,' he said, 'I haven't taken it out of my pocket,' and he plunged in his hand. He felt around, he went a bit pale. He felt in all the other pockets. No jingling bag of sovereigns. In a state of frenzy he rushed back to the theatre—he must have left it in the safe—and yet he distinctly remembered pocketing it as usual. The safe proved as empty as Mother Hubbard's cupboard. Pitt was now almost beside himself. There had been a lot of gold—two bumper performances on the Saturday and a big advance booking. A dreadful thought struck him. He felt again in that ulster pocket—and horror of horrors, there was a hole in the bottom. Almost beside himself he dashed to Vine Street Police Station, just off Piccadilly. He was well known there as were all theatrical managers who were always on good terms with the police. He demanded to see the inspector at once. He was told the inspector was engaged. He raged, he stormed, it was a matter of life and death, and because they knew him they let him in. There sat the Inspector at his desk counting out golden sovereigns and making them into little piles. Before him stood a gentleman resplendently· dressed—complaining bitterly that he was due at a wedding at St James's, Piccadilly, and reception to follow at Princes. He had kicked a bag as he went along Piccadilly and it gave a ringing sound. He picked it up, saw it contained sovereigns—and brought it straight to the station. Why must he be further detained, he wanted to know. It was Pitt's money. He almost embraced that man and showered thanks on him. The gentleman went off to his wedding, still rather ruffled—after all he had only done the right thing—and so Pitt got all his money back. He never used that ulster again. Henceforth a bag, and his linkman went with him. But that happened in Piccadilly and was a sign of the integrity of the times.

The more elderly men watched the prices rise with apprehension. Taxes as well. They became poorer and poorer. Yet some people grew richer and richer as a result of the war. Those men did not like the ration books which made their appearance, for food was scarce and getting scarcer. To have to juggle with horrible little bits of paper, to work out what they could get for half a coupon, they who had fed so well, really brought home the horrors of war. In the land in general wangling and scrounging arose and were skilfully practised. It became a kind of sport to see how much you could get without giving up a coupon. The time came when even potatoes were scarce and many restaurants served roast kid. Drinks were difficult too. There was an acute whisky shortage, which hit Piccadilly and the clubs. No more did a bottle of Scotch cost 3/6d—it soared to 10/6d, if you could get it. Even the well stocked cellars of the clubs became depleted of stocks. The committees and the waiters had a tough time from old die-hard members. Pubs closed early and remained open for only short periods. The No Treating Order was treated with scorn by the Old Brigade and everybody else. That attempt to curtail the ancient laws of hospitality under the guise of D.O.R.A. did not succeed. Policemen grew scarce—more and more specials took over and some of the clubmen of Piccadilly, as specials found themselves directing the traffic.

Standards changed with the altered ways of living. The customers of those old established shops in Burlington Arcade and elsewhere found that shortages were hitting them, too. But by and large this district and all within it strove hard to maintain old standards. Men had empty cigar cases nowadays and, through the troops, came a recession from the once almost universal Turkish and Egyptian cigarettes to the cheaper and more popular Virginian brands—the Gaspers—foremost amongst which, in that war, were Gold Flake and Woodbines. Ultra patriotic old gentlemen smoked Woodbines who would previously have perished at the thought and who had consumed the best oriental tobacco and the best Havana cigars. 'If they are good enough for the boys over there, they are good enough for me' they said. Those Woodbines—and their pre-war price had been five for a penny—

became immensely popular. A big Russian battleship which had five funnels had at once been christened 'Packet of Woodbines'. Life changed in many ways.

Air raids failed to shake them in Piccadilly. The Zeppelins created far more interest than fear. I remember seeing one caught in the searchlights—which seemed to be flying straight along Piccadilly. The maroons had been sounded, the police had dashed around on bicycles blowing whistles, and bearing cards worded 'Take Cover', but the crowds flocked into the streets to watch the Zepp and on that occasion no bombs were dropped. The Germans missed a wonderful chance in the early days of the war; they could have done immense damage for there was very little defence against them. Among the popular night sights were the searchlights. London watched the long silvery beams probing the skies. They grew accustomed to them—they became a sight of London. If they did not lace the skies with silver, most people reckoned a raid was expected. And in watching those searchlights Piccadilly residents and passers by became aware of the stars in the heavens. They could be seen because the lights of London were so dimmed. So many people in Town had never noticed them before. Eventually the Zeppelins were conquered and the Taubes and Fokkers came, often by daylight. But London and Piccadilly carried on. And whilst a raid was in progress at night one could stand by the Green Park and see the sky dotted with little points of light—suddenly appearing, suddenly gone—the heavy shell fire of the barrage. Piccadilly had never expected to see that.

The Americans came in hordes. They came with the idea that they were conquering heroes and the saviours of civilization. They were extremely clean, extremely smart and had white gaiters which twinkled along Piccadilly in the semi-blackout. They all made for Piccadilly of course. The ladies of the Dilly, the crooks, the 'con' men, the criminal side of the West End reaped a rich harvest from the Yankees—full of dollars—who learnt many lessons, one being that Europe was not quite so dull and effete as they had been told. The Higher Command was glad to

see this huge army and vast potential manpower. The British
looked a bit askance at these smart young men, some of them
regarding the Americans rather in the light of guests who were
late for dinner. Although American plays, American music and
dance bands, and American films were flooding the land, the
First War Yanks did not dominate affairs as did those of the
Second World War. Still the war went on. There were many
upheavals. Many people lost their fortunes and their incomes—
others made new ones. A little illiterate Jewish play impresario,
named Joe Sacks, who could neither read nor write, was staying
at the Piccadilly Hotel and was to leave for America in the
morning. He was having dinner with a business associate when a
third man joined them, whom Sacks did not know. Sacks talked
of his plans. The newcomer, who was a stockbroker, was impressed. He told Joe Sacks he would like to invest £1,000 with
him. For once in his life Sacks did not really need the money.
But the man insisted and the other friend backed him up. The
stockbroker gave Sacks a cheque for £1,000—remember he had
never met him before! A short agreement was drawn up on a
menu card—and was signed and witnessed—Joe making his
mark. That £1,000 invested during that war-time night in the
restaurant of the Piccadilly Hotel turned itself into £35,000. And
most of it during the war, too.

One of the greatest signs of the upheaval of the times was the
fact that the man who now led Britain was a man whom Piccadilly had, in pre-war days, reviled and hated. His name was
Lloyd George. The gentry who looked upon Piccadilly as their
preserve regarded this man as the devil, out to ruin them. Now
he was leading England to victory. That brought things home.
And all the Piccadillians were doing war work of some kind, men
and women together; the ladies of the Peerage and the Landed
Gentry and the Establishment putting up a fine show with hospitals, charity, and Red Cross at home and abroad.

But what I think myself brought the war home more forcibly
to the elders of Piccadilly was a day in their club when they got

a terrible shock. For because of the manpower shortage which was acute, suddenly there were women waitresses! Women waitresses in those all-male strongholds into which women were not allowed to enter at all. Or had not been before this wretched war began. The old gentlemen were horrified, but nothing could be done. Indeed, indeed, the world had changed.

But other things were happening. The Germans were breaking —the war was opening out, the end was in sight, and then, suddenly, at 11 a.m. on the morning of 11th November 1918— Peace came with a bang. It had been expected for a few days before but after more than four years of war it hardly seemed possible. The maroons crashed and as the guns of 1914 had blown Peace to smithereens, so the maroons of 1918 blew War away. London, the whole country, downed tools. They went mad, they surged into the streets, they made for the important centres; in London they made for the Mansion House, for Trafalgar Square —and for Piccadilly Circus. Incredible sights were witnessed. Strangers might have been dear old pals, the pubs were stormed and very soon the short supplies of all kinds of drinks gave out. The cheering was almost continuous. Piccadilly was packed with people and the dear old gentlemen in the clubs even smiled at the unwelcome waitresses. Peace, peace and now the old world could come back and happiness would reign. There would be no more war. They really believed that. London was one gigantic carnival, and Piccadilly was en fête. It was Mafeking Night all over again on a bigger scale. The tubes and buses began to bring crowds into the centre of London—soldiers, sailors, Royal Flying Corps men, soldiers of every Allied Nation were carried shoulder high, for everybody wanted to treat them. There is a tailpiece which lingers joyously in my memory and it happened in Piccadilly. A Staff Officer of high rank was walking along, obviously en route for his club. He was a real specimen of the old-fashioned professional regular officer, immaculate and shining, resplendent with red tabs and brass hat, his grey hair and moustache beautifully trimmed and brushed; a genuine Blimp. He was a figure of dignity, not to say pomposity, for there was a suggestion about his whole carriage that seemed to say, 'This is very largely my work; this victory.' It is very doubtful if he ever reached his club. For a crowd of girls got him, kissed and embraced him, two or three at a time, and despite his struggles and even his appeals to passers-by they got him on their shoulders and bore him away in triumph. Never has such anger, such shame, embarrassment and agony been depicted all at once and so vividly on one purple countenance. In Piccadilly too . . . if he was seen by a friend or acquaintance he would never live it down. There was at least one man in London who bitterly regretted that Armistice Day had come to Piccadilly.

9

Between the Wars

The First World War changed the entire world—and Piccadilly, an important part of the British world, mirrored every facet of that change. Its habitués, the people who lived around it, dealt at its shops and belonged to its clubs, were the hardest hit. The people who had combined riches with quality were faced with problems of which they had never dreamed. Heavy taxation, although then a mere shadow of what it is today, increased the cost of living, problems of the upkeep of houses and estates, even of domestic staffs, seemed impossible to solve. The elderly and middle aged men of Piccadilly were seldom seen, and even the clubs were not finding things too easy. Yet the country was still very rich, as compared with modern standards. It owed heavy debts—and did not like it. It owed a debt to America in dollars, but it hugged to its heart the belief that it would get reparations from defeated Germany. That dream was a mere vision. However, the British Empire was intact and even greater than before. Millions of square miles had been added, in the form of previous German colonies.

So many sons of families were missing; the cream of Britain's young manhood lay under the mud of Flanders, the sands of the desert, in 'Mespot', in Palestine, some even in Russia and under the waves of the oceans of the world. That was a deprivation worse than financial loss. Young men who had gone into the Army and Navy as mere boys, were now coming out to face civilian life in a world of which they knew little. There were no more K'Nuts in Piccadilly—the Lads of the Village had gone. They were never to be replaced. Gradually it dawned upon the governing and upper classes that things were never going to be the same again. Those town houses and country houses—they could no longer afford them. They had won a great war, but they still did not realise the price paid.

A different texture had come into the life in the West End, People had gone dancing mad. They danced everywhere and all the time, and jazz bands from America, or playing in American rhythm, were the order of the day. Restaurants whose pride had been their restful atmosphere, their silent expert service, found that they had to provide dancing or shut down. That mattered more than food. Couples left delectable dishes to grow cold whilst they struggled round on a small space of floor cleared in the middle of the dining room, in a mass which could hardly move, let alone dance as it had been understood. Vintage wines of beautiful quality were neglected for whisky and soda—easier and quicker to drink. Dancing mattered more than food.

The first year or so of the post-war period were hectic in the chase for gaiety. It was only natural to a nation which had for four years and a quarter lived under the shadow of slaughter, with war right on its doorstep, to want to relax. Let the people rejoice in their achievement of victory over the German monster. They had broken that up. The Kaiser had fled, his power was broken and Prussianism and the jackboot were things of the past. That hymn of hate directed against England had never frightened them; they had replied with shouted demands to know who was downhearted—with the statement that whoever might be missing 'Here We Are Again'—with sentimental songs about a world containing only a boy and a girl—and about a long, long trail which went winding into the land of their dreams. And those songs had smashed the hymn of hate. The mighty German Navy, built

The Old Haymarket Theatre

Sackville Street

Hyde Park Corner, about 1900

Piccadilly, 1900

expressly to exterminate them, had been forced to surrender after only one real trial of strength with the Royal Navy and now lay under the grey waters of Scapa Flow, self scuttled in shame. They had something to rejoice over, on the surface. And rejoice they did, but not in the old way.

A new freedom had come about. The war had mixed up the sexes and they never got untangled again. The old conventions had gone, the old strict rules of morality had slackened. Women claimed equality and got it. Maybe it was for their good, maybe not. They now smoked in public, invaded bars, and made-up faces became general. That had once been the outward and visible sign of a Lady of the Town, a Lady on the Dilly. Women went to night clubs, they went about singly at all hours of the day and night. They invaded the old male preserves of Piccadilly; there were Ladies' Nights in clubs and many of the old regulations went by the board. The die-hards were horrified. In pre-War days women seldom walked about the West End alone for they were liable to molestation if they did so by men under the impression they were 'no better than they should be'. Nobody cared about that now, and the social or moral status of women was harder to detect. The horse had almost gone and the internal combustion engine ruled. Everybody wanted to own a car and more and more people did so. What had been mews became garages—machinery was becoming dominant.

In 1919 Piccadilly and the rest of London saw a marvellous Peace Procession of fighting men herald the new world. Detachments from all Allied nations passed through London. The King and Queen attended Ascot in semi-state. And that conquest of the air, which had been really won in the war enabled Captain Ross Smith to fly from England to Australia. Truly the age of marvels had begun. But in the same year, just to show the power of peace, there was a great railway strike which almost paralysed the nation. Piccadilly saw strange sights, including great milk floats trundling and throbbing down it to the milk depot established in Hyde Park. Grand Parade, which might have taken its name from Piccadilly, won the Derby. And maybe many people forget that there was a police strike that year, too.

Following in quick succession in those inter-war years came the League of Nations in which many devoutly believed but many more doubted. There was continued industrial unrest and there was still a chance for pageantry, as when the Princess Royal married the Earl of Harewood. On and on went the march of science and machinery. Gramophones boomed—and in 1922 a new force entered the world; radio had arrived. Despite the League of Nations, there was little peace and there arose in Italy a body known as Fascists, with a young man named Benito Mussolini at its head. Piccadilly recked little of that, but it grieved with the rest of the nation when Marie Lloyd died—the greatest queen of music hall—who had been truly billed on her last appearance at Edmonton Empire in October 1922—as 'Queen of All Comediennes'.

In 1923 a man who was to live in Piccadilly got married. He was H.R.H. the Duke of York and he married a lady who was not of royal blood but of very ancient lineage: Lady Elizabeth Bowes-Lyon, daughter of the 14th Earl and Countess of Strathmore. Horse carriages, not cars, took them to and from that wedding.

But the men of Piccadilly got a shock over those reparations which they thought would pay their war bills. For the finances of Germany crashed. In November 1923 the English pound was worth 18,400,000,000,000 marks. What hopes for reparations?

There were some outstanding and intimate signs of the changing of the old order in Piccadilly itself. Devonshire House vanished— the last but one of its great ducal mansions. This had been acquired in 1918 by Messrs Holland, Hannen and Cubitts for about £1,000,000. The site was up for development—for building—for business premises. There were several prospective buyers but nothing transpired. One proposal was to erect a monster cinema, facing Piccadilly. But none of these ideas or negotiations matured. It was not until 1924, six years after demolition, that building was begun—for so long had this amazing site, the richest and best in London, gone a-begging. That was a sign of the times, too. But eventually the new Devonshire House went up—a fine modern building of nine stories. According to the ideas then prevalent, and one presumes still held, this was a grand place and so of its kind it is. But it is just the sort of building one meets in every great city in the world. There is nothing of the true Piccadilly atmosphere about it. But probably that is of no importance today. The Piccadilly frontage houses big salesrooms for cars, and banks, flats and restaurants, and forms an island site. But on the rest of the site, once the grounds, are many offices, a new street named Mayfair Place and another luxury hotel, the Mayfair, in a continuation of Stratton Street. If the site had hung fire at first when it did start it got going pretty quickly, in accordance with the days of speed which it represented. The car mostly ruled in the commerce which invaded it. It was all covered, built and let in two years.

But a portion of Devonshire House still hangs on, across the street on the other side of Piccadilly. For there, on the edge of the Green Park stand the old gates, very beautifully made of wrought iron. Those gates had come to Piccadilly in 1897, being brought from the Duke of Devonshire's house at Chiswick. They are a well loved landmark of an older time.

In 1925 another landmark of Piccadilly vanished, when the house of the late Baroness Burdett Coutts at the corner of Piccadilly and Stratton Street was pulled down. Old Piccadillians greatly regretted its passing. More and more commerce invaded Piccadilly, but somehow the standard of the magic mile survived and still does so. It works upon those who come into it and gives its own atmosphere of quality.

That derelict steel structure which had been an eyesore now became another hotel—the Park Lane Hotel, so called, in that delightful London way, because it is not in Park Lane—just as the Piccadilly Theatre is not in Piccadilly. The new hotel opened in 1927. A very fine comedian—who was a typical Yorkshire lad, went to live there with his wife. It was decided that now he had become famous he must become West End. What could be more West End than Piccadilly? So, much against his inclinations, into the Park Lane Hotel he went. His name was Sidney Howard and he was a dear, good fellow of simple tastes who was always a bit surprised at his own success; but it was due to his real shining talent, his simplicity of approach, his genuine sense of humour and perhaps above all his quite remarkable hands, which seemed to dominate all he did, and yet were always under control and spoke as clearly as his face or his tongue what was passing in his mind. His heart was still in Yeadon, near Leeds, where he was born and where today a memorial stands to him in the local chapel in which he had worshipped. He was dead scared of that hotel, its liveried attendants, its imposing and to him quite meaningless menus and food, and what he called its 'poshness and lah-di-dah'. He was a friend of mine and I used to visit him. We would, to his joy, sneak out of the place and go to a little homely teashop in a back street not far away where he could have his cup of tea and the bun or tea-cake, which he adored, and in season what he still referred to as pikelets, which we call crumpets. In that little shop he was at home. He was a star of stage and screen. I still cherish happy memories of one film of his in which he was supposed to be 'broke'. He read in a scrap of newspaper about a man who had been left a lot of money because he had helped an old lady to cross the road. This seemed to him to be a good chance. He tried it on. But he did not understand the newly installed traffic lights and when they said Stop he stopped, and when they said Go he and his elderly charge—who was resentful of his help anyway—were plunged into dire danger from the hurtling traffic, which was quite right in its interpretation of the lights. And in that same film, with just sixpence in his pocket, he gazed into the window of a cookshop in which were displayed sausages and pies. He could not make up his mind which to buy but he was famished. He decided to toss up for it. Just to make it right, he decided, 'Heads, sausages—tails pies'—and he murmured, 'I do hope it's tails'. He tossed up, he missed the sixpence as it fell and it went down a grating, gone from him forever. The sight of Sidney's despair was a comic tragedy of supreme quality. He respected Piccadilly, but he did not like living in it.

For some reason today, the 1920's are labelled as being gay. They were no such thing. There was just a scum of hectic gaiety on the surface and even that faded as the period advanced. True, we had the Bright Young Things, who made much noise, got much publicity, but did not amount to much after all. Many of them were of the Piccadilly tradition, but they cast it off. True, there was the Charleston craze but that made little or no impact on life in general and lasted such a short time. The Age of Gracious Living had passed and in its place there was the Age of Speed, and to many people, the Age of Ugliness dawned. Women's fashions had never been more terrible than in a portion of the inter-war years, with those very short skirts and dresses, that display of knees which in so many cases would have been better hidden from sight, and the cloche hats which destroyed individuality. Individuality was one of the things well on the way out; it had previously been a hallmark of Piccadilly. Piccadilly was selling cars and as flying became more and more general, as it did right through the period, the airlines opened depots in Piccadilly and remain there today. But still some of the old strongholds carried on; there were still the great shops which have been mentioned and still Burlington Arcade quality. Still that little stuffed dog sat outside its shop therein, deceiving so many people and even other dogs, carefully put on leads.

The older men realised the changes more and more. The younger men, released from army life which had relieved them from the necessity of taking much thought of their own affairs, found a new world which they did not know confronting them. The authority with which their commissions invested them had gone. They became just part of the crowd. Those who had survived from pre-war days—a pitiful few—found their old haunts and manner of life changed completely. They tried to go into business.

They had their gratuities on demobilisation and that in many cases represented their entire capital or expectation, for their fathers were now impoverished. They tried to find a niche in this new world. They rushed into the growing motor industry, they became bookmakers and many of them lost all they had. Those who could do so, went abroad to what had been the colonies but were now becoming Dominions. The open air life drew them. They were lost to a country which needed them.

And the older generation saw new wonders. They saw a Labour Government come to power—a thing they had scarcely believed possible. And they saw, in 1926, a General Strike—the nearest thing to a revolution which this country had seen since the Civil War in the reign of Charles I. The men of Piccadilly— of all ages—ranged themselves on the side of Law and Order, along with the greater portion of the general public and the middle classes and between them they beat that strike in a most decisive manner. It should however be remembered that in that same year unemployment reached the amazing total of 1,638,000. This was apparently the Land Fit for Heroes which had been promised. Piccadilly had its lighter moments, though. It was the scene of some famous practical jokes. Some men arrived, dressed as workmen, complete with ropes, red lanterns, poles, stands and all the paraphernalia which go with road repairs. They roped off a piece of Piccadilly and gave it out that there was a job to be done. Nobody interfered with them. Indeed, authority gave them every assistance. It was such a common sight in that city which a wag described as 'London, where the roads are always up and consols are always down'. They roped off their site, they did a lot of damage with pickaxes—and departed, to return no more. After a while enquiries were made. It was still nothing unusual even in Piccadilly where the water authorities would come, tear up the street, do a job, cover it up and depart, to be followed at a very short interval by the gas people, the electric light concerns and so on. There never seemed any co-ordination. But at long last it was discovered that this was a joke, and perhaps there were some red faces amongst those in authority when it was shown how easy it was to outwit them. But also, perhaps not. A much simpler and more profitable joke was carried out by one individual for a bet. He made a wager that he would lie down flat on his back in the middle of Piccadilly for an hour during the busiest traffic hour and come to no harm at all. His bet was taken, with derision. He proceeded to carry out his boast. He drove his car into the middle of Piccadilly, stalled the engine, stopped it, got out and laid on his back under it. Kindly policemen offered help. He replied he was all right. At the end of the time, he got up, restarted his car and drove away—the winner.

The whole British way of life was changing. Insularity, once its backbone, was going fast. The war had broken it down. The stiffness had gone out of the collars and cuffs too and out of life, which was far more free and easy. Fewer and fewer people put on their best clothes when walking down Piccadilly. Fewer and fewer had the leisure to stroll there. There was a much stronger American element in England now, brought about by the cinema which had now begun to speak; the language it spoke was predominantly American.

More and more people went abroad for holidays—more and more people took longer and longer weekends. Almost every week new air records were made. Distance was being annihilated and speed reigned. Radio became part of everyday life, people became celebrities merely by their voices. Motors roared down Piccadilly and almost the only horse vehicles were those run by old established tradesmen whose smart equipages were really for publicity. If you saw a discreet brougham with a pair of horses, it was likely that it was a royal carriage out for exercise. The older people regretted the passing of the carriage and pair. The younger welcomed the motor.

But in many ways that war fought for freedom left freedom much curtailed. Wartime restrictions were slow to go. All was not well with the world. And there were plenty of wars going on all over the place. But there had been some sort of a social revolution at home and in this country they take place almost overnight and without bloodshed. The election of the first Labour Government was one. Women had got the vote—in pursuit of which they had smashed the windows of Fortnum and Mason's—and were indeed in Parliament. Ireland had Home Rule. The old order on which Piccadilly was based was changing beyond recognition. More and more of the colonies were getting dominion status and in reality independence. India wanted to throw off the British Raj. A man called Gandhi challenged the whole might of Britain. He did not look like a hero, this odd, froglike little man in a white linen wrap and loincloth. The British found him funny and he became a national joke—just as the Kaiser had been. In 1921 he or his followers had set fire to a heap of imported clothing in Bombay. That was the beginning of a fire which was to embrace all India and sever the bond which bound it to the Empire. Gandhi was always in and out of prison. Nothing could keep him down and eventually his policy of passive resistance and his indomitable will gained his country that freedom it desired. He was one of the world's great men, but it remains to be seen if indeed his policy was the right one.

Russia had liquidated its Tsar and Royal Family—kings were becoming scarce in the world. But one came to visit this country in the 1920's. His name was Amanullah, and he was King of Afghanistan, a place which had cost the British dearly in terms of blood and money for many years. He came to visit us, however, and he stayed, for the duration of that visit, in the Ritz, in Piccadilly. He was a very strange man. His passion for publicity was a godsend to hard working reporters, who never failed to go and see him, were always received and never came away without a story. He brought his wife with him, a handsome lady who perhaps looked better when seated than when standing up. There was one reporter who before the first official press reception claimed that he could speak the Afghan language but either he spoke a patois or the King did not know his own tongue, for not much came of that. But the King knew a little English and with interpreters for difficult bits had no trouble in making himself understood. He answered questions almost before they were asked. He had a real passion for having his photograph taken. He had bought lots of new clothes and had a big supply of elaborate uniforms. He wanted the Press photographers to take his picture in them all. After a while they got fed up with it but he besought just one more. He would not keep them waiting more than a few moments, he promised. He rushed away to change and the Press consoled itself with the very lavish refreshments. Then the King came charging back in the most showy uniform yet displayed. He rushed headlong into the room, he trod on a mat which slid on the polished floor. He crossed that room like lightning striving wildly to maintain his balance but he collapsed into a sitting position with a good hard bump before he reached the end of the apartment. That was the most popular picture of the lot, although it was never published. His addiction to certain customs of this country brought about King Amanullah's downfall. He became obsessed with the glory of the bowler hat. To him this was the last word in headgear. He imported thousands into Afghanistan and tried to make his subjects wear them. Very sensibly they revolted and he lost his throne. It may well be that his addiction to bowlers can be traced to the influence of Piccadilly.

And then the nation suffered a great loss in the death of a most beloved monarch, King George V. This sailor king had been overshadowed in his youth not only by the tremendous power of his grandmother, Queen Victoria, but by the immense popularity of his father, King Edward VII. When he came to the throne there were those who wished it could have been his uncle, the Duke of Connaught. But by dint of talent, real patriotism and his immense sense of duty he became one of our most beloved kings, and his wife, that great and gracious lady Queen Mary shared his life and his work with him. She too had been overshadowed by Queen Alexandra but the British public discovered her true worth. When George V died, into his place as Edward VIII stepped his eldest son, the most popular young man in the Empire—save perhaps in

India—if not in the world. He was well in touch with the affairs of his country, had served in the war, and travelled the world. He was a sportsman and well known in Piccadilly, if it came to that. High hopes centred around. What followed is too well known to need repetition here. There was a tremendous upheaval, a short but bitter struggle. Church and State, in the persons of the Archbishop of Canterbury and Mr Stanley Baldwin, then Prime Minister, set their faces against what others regarded as a romance. The young man said goodbye to his kingship and his people over the air, by means of radio and slipped quietly away—out of the country, out of his birthright—no longer a King-Emperor, but just a Duke.

So there was a new king and that king was at that moment living in Piccadilly with his Scottish wife, whose charm and smile had already endeared her to the people. They had the last of the Piccadilly dukes as neighbour, the Duke of Wellington, at No. 1 London, Apsley House. George VI, whose children spent their childhood in Piccadilly and whose eldest daughter became our present Queen, had not expected to rule, did not want to do so. But in him was that sense of duty which had carried this country through so many crises and dangers in its age old history. Not strong physically and with a disability which was a terrible hindrance in his exalted position he stepped into the breach. He became King of England, of the British Dominions beyond the sea, and Emperor of India. When his life closed so tragically and suddenly he had proved himself one of the best and most gallant wearers of the ancient crown of this realm. He had left the monarchy as strong and powerful as it had been in the days of Queen Victoria, his great-grandmother. His reign included the greatest war the world had ever seen—total war in all respects—he ruled when this land faced its moment of greatest peril from which it emerged into victory once more. And on the scroll of English kings and queens the name of George VI will be written in letters of shining gold. And he had lived in Piccadilly.

The crowds which surged along Piccadilly were not so well

dressed as of yore and far more cosmopolitan and easy going. Life had shed so many conventions. The girls on the Dilly no longer worked only under the shadow of night but now flaunted themselves in full day. The great clubs found things difficult; the night clubs were no improvement on the older form of night life, those cafes which were open to the public and to constant police patrol. Yet still odd things could happen in Piccadilly.

There used to be a coffee stall there in those days outside the Green Park; yes, a coffee stall in Piccadilly. I remember once seeing a big theatrical deal clinched at that stall; it had been under discussion all day and night and it was then 2 a.m. The deal was done and a cheque for £2,000 changed hands over a cup of 'mahogany' at that coffee stall in Piccadilly.

But abroad things were happening which were challenging that rather dubious peace and security which had replaced, since 1918, the previous peace and security of this land. Mussolini in Italy had grown in power—his Black Shirts, the Fascists, now were supreme and through them he ruled Italy. He had done a good deal for his country but he grew drunk with the lust for power. He was endangering the peace of the world and had already conquered Abyssinia. This country had made but a feeble attempt to stop him. Bolshevism ruled in Russia and was a menace too. The men in the Piccadilly clubs could not distinguish this Bolshevism from Mussolini's Fascism. But a new and greater danger arose. This came in the form of the man Schickelgrueber—who called himself Hitler. He was actually an Austrian and had been a house painter. He had fought in the First World War. He had dreamed dreams, and had put them in a book called *Mein Kampf*. He put his followers into brown shirts. Ruthless, dominant, relentless, with a voice like a circular saw but with an immense power and belief in himself he raised a defeated nation from the dust, gave it new heart, new aspirations. He saw a world outside Germany torn by dissension—a Britain unarmed and unprepared, a France which was unstable to a degree, and America determined to keep out of war at any cost. He tore up treaties, he defied the world, he made links with his brother dictator Mussolini. He called himself the Fuhrer—the Leader. He gave and took the old Roman salute. And suddenly Armageddon threatened again. A British Prime Minister tried to stave off the evil day with appeasement. All he gained was a short breathing space—but a valuable one for a totally unprepared country. Life still flowed along Piccadilly but menace was in the air. Men and women joined the Forces, conscription came again. They joined the new civil force called Air Raid Precautions. They listened to the Satanic voice of Hitler as it came over the air and the tempest of cheers which it drew forth. And they waited in silence. And then one Sunday morning, in September 1939, the sad voice of the British Prime Minister told them they were at war again, and almost at once the air raid sirens wailed . . .

For many, many more it was Goodbye Piccadilly again.

10

Black Out and Lights Up

Just a couple of days before the Second World War—on the Friday preceding the Declaration, I was going down Piccadilly in a taxi, to collect something I had bought in a shop at the other end of Knightsbridge. As we passed Hyde Park Corner, there were the anti-aircraft guns again, as they had been in the First War—only larger and more deadly looking guns and on the ground instead of on top of the arch at the Corner. The taximan looked at them, and turned his head to me, 'Reckon that 'Itler means it, guvnor?' he asked. 'I'm afraid so,' I replied. He thought for a moment. 'Well, I shall put me wallflowers in just the same,' he said. ''E's not going to rob me o' them'—and that appeared to content him. That was the typical English point of view as regards war. It could not have been better expressed.

All around us, as we drove along, sandbags were being laid down around buildings, wire netting erections were going up to divert bombs (much good they would have been) and in the Park itself, they were digging trenches. There was a curious sense of unreality over everything—a sense that this familiar London scene was a mirage which might at any moment vanish away. And it seemed that it might. We had been warned that attack from the air, instant, mighty and deadly, would be our lot. We had already

173

got our gas-masks, for a gas attack was seriously expected. Some of us had got tin hats. I was amongst them. And quite a lot of us, who were over military age, and some who were not, of course, had joined this new service—the Air Raid Precautions—A.R.P. We were wardens—and the name had a romantic sound. It took us back a bit; there had been the Warden of the Marches and there was the warden of the Cinque Ports. We had been to classes and learnt our jobs. There were many other services and some specially for women, like the Women's Voluntary Service—the W.V.S.—which did magnificent work. And as I drove down Piccadilly, I gazed about me and tried to fix it all into my memory for it might well be that a raid, a shower of bombs, would bring Goodbye to the Piccadilly I had known so long. We did not then know what the power of attack would be.

All around, too, shop windows were being protected from blast, wire netting was going over them—in some cases long strips of material to prevent splintering—basements were covered with sandbags; it was a busy scene. And on that Friday the barrage balloons went up and the Lights of London went down, down to a very minimum, making the first war blackout seem like the illuminations at Blackpool. London groped its way about. Piccadilly was a long, dark ravine, which seemed to have no beginning or end. The lights of the vehicles were dimmed and shaded and the traffic lights were also shaded so as to be invisible from above. When the darkness really fell, the sudden flicker on and off of a pedestrian's torch, or the lighting of a cigarette was like a flash of lightning—or a beacon. It was September and beautiful weather, but night came all the same, and in Piccadilly, as elsewhere, one heard the shout of the alert Warden, 'Put that light out'. Caught once more unprepared and scantily armed, Britain was falling gack on her genius for improvisation.

It was a rather breathless, hurrying Piccadilly by day with everybody trying to get their work or their business done and be home before the blackout. In those early days, all theatres,

cinemas and places of amusement had been closed by order.
The restaurants kept open—people had to eat but except for the
hotel residents there was hardly any custom. People stayed at
home, listened to the radio and were ready to duck into the many
shelters when the bombs began to fall. Piccadilly has of course,
its own Tube railway which runs its whole length, which had been
there since 1906. It has a station all of its own—quite apart from
the great junction of Piccadilly Circus station. The station in
Piccadilly is that of Green Park. That was a potential air raid
shelter.

But Piccadilly was not entirely devoid of passers-by at nights.
The ladies of the Dilly did not desert it. They walked their
historic beats despite the blackout, despite war. They were there
in the day time too. What seemed incongruous to me was the
fact that all these so-called daughters of joy carried gas masks
slung around them. To the ordinary man who did not trade with
them, these women had always seemed a little unreal—not quite
human—something apart from ordinary humanity but having
their place in the scheme of things. And that gas mask seemed to
add a touch of grimness to the arch smile, the questioning eye, and
the murmured 'Hello dearie—want a little love?' It was like the
skeleton at the old Roman feast. These women were of course
entitled to gas masks and the same protection as everybody else,
but it seemed strange. The ladies of the Dilly stuck to Piccadilly
through thick and thin. And in the Ritz Hotel, almost immediately after the outbreak of war—there came some remarkable
women, superbly dressed, who looked and moved with grace,
wonder and charm. They were the super cocottes from Paris,
come to take refuge quite naturally in Piccadilly. No wonder
James Agate, the famous dramatic critic and wit, said at the sight
of them 'How are the Fallen mighty'.

To the middle aged and elderly man or woman passing along
Piccadilly—it seemed as if the inter-war years had never been at
all—that the First World War was still going on. Here again
were the crowds of men in khaki. The style of the uniform had

changed—the modern battledress was probably very efficient but not very smart. The style of saluting was not so magnificently mechanical nor was saluting so meticulously observed. But otherwise—save for the sandbags and the anti-blast precautions, it was much the same. Indeed one met and saw men one knew—back in khaki again, which heightened the illusion.

Those threatened air raids did not materialise. Piccadilly began to come into its own again, after nightfall. Although the buses went along like faintly luminous fabulous monsters through the dark, taxis hummed by like moths with no lights showing inside and only a pin-point outside, and private cars were almost unheard as well as unseen, the people began to come back to the West End again. The theatres and cinemas re-opened—but closed early—the restaurants recovered—night life began again. Soldiers arrived from overseas, and like those of the First World War, they made straight for Piccadilly. More and more it seemed that the same War was still on.

Then, after months of what was called 'The Phoney War'—which followed an autumn of surpassing loveliness—came the spring—following a winter which had been hard and cold and most uncomfortable for all concerned. And with the spring came those aerial attacks so long withheld—came the Blitz. Real, total war—aimed against civilians as well as military, against domestic and business targets as well as those of military importance. The Germans were once again relying on frightfulness. During its centuries, Piccadilly had sent its men out to fight battles overseas. They had fought under Marlborough, Clive, Nelson, Wellington—and all those men had lived either in or around Piccadilly, too—they had fought against innumerable warring tribes all over the globe—against the Russians in the Crimea, the Indians in the Mutiny, against the Afghans, the Chinese, the Dervishes, and in South Africa against the Boers. They had been poured into the cauldron of the 1914–1918 slaughter. But now the War came to Piccadilly.

Few people had ever anticipated that; but it happened.

It came in the form of that long delayed aerial attack. First the Germans smote us tentatively by night—then came the all-out attack—day and night—the Battle of Britain which those young airmen of ours, now forever known as 'The Few', won with decision. They were the counterpart, in many ways, of the Old Contemptibles—but they fought their battles in an English sky and over the English countryside. Then, having discovered the danger of day time, the vast bulky Goering gave orders for the night attacks. It was safer.

Dunkirk had been the greatest defeat our arms had ever known, retrieved amazingly from an absolute holocaust. Once again there was a miracle as the little boats fetched those soldiers of ours from the sea, into which they had waded when driven from the beaches and mercilessly bombed by the Germans. Piccadilly saw battered, tattered men in khaki, with eyes so weary that they seemed age-old and eternal, wandering down its pavements, still bemused at the idea of being home and alive; their weapons gone, their equipment gone, all gone save hope and a fixed determination to win. And still the blitz went on and on through that second autumn and winter of war.

A new night life came to Piccadilly. It was not the gay pleasure seeking life of old. It was grim and strange. It was real and earnest. Nothing like this night life had ever been seen before and those who took part in it had never dreamed that they would do so. They were the men and women of Piccadilly, who worked there during the day and now stayed there at night, taking their turns to protect it from the enemy. They were in every building; groups of men and women, the men mostly middle aged or elderly, the women of all ages, from young girls just out in the world to women of maturity. They were the Fire Guards, whose job it was to fight the bombs which were showered on London, irrespective of district or special target in an attempt to wipe out the greatest city in the world, to beat to their knees the people of London, to smash the capital and so break the mainspring of the war effort of the land. Paris had surrendered with hardly a blow struck. A matter of days had sufficed to bring France, once so famous for its military glory, to its knees. But London was a different matter. That British quality of tenacity was still there, unimpaired. So those groups of men and women, working on a rota after their day's work, took their spell of duty to defeat the Germans. Most business places and shops closed a bit early, to enable their workers to get home. Traffic was difficult. The tubes were overtaxed, and there were crowds down there sheltering from the raids. It was pretty awful in the early days but organisation got it right and, all things considered, very speedily. The buses were jammed and had to take devious routes because of roads being closed by bomb damage. These routes often varied every day and the journeys took longer than usual. Everyone wanted to get home before dusk, if humanly possible.

There was no suggestion of panic anywhere but there certainly was a great desire to get home. For as dusk fell, the sirens wailed—what a detestable sound that was—and within a few moments there was the sound of death droning overhead. But the population of London took it calmly. Although it did not happen in Piccadilly, the following instance will illustrate the mood of the Londoners. I had to go home by bus because my tube was for the moment dislocated by enemy action. I went down to Victoria Station whence my bus started and joined a long, long queue. It was raining quite heavily. People stood waiting and reading their papers. The sirens had already sounded. What mattered to everyone was when the bus would arrive and whether they would be able to get on the first one. Suddenly, right overhead, was the sound of a German plane—one knew the note of the engine so well—and from under the low cloud swooped a German bomber. I was trying to read my evening paper. In front of me a man nudged his neighbour, who was also reading, and motioned with his thumb. The reader glanced skywards, too, nodded and resumed his reading. Nobody moved out of that queue. And then, not far away, in fact well within a qurater of a mile, a bomb fell. But nobody fell out of that bus queue. What mattered to them was the coming of the bus and at that moment it hove in sight. At once the crowd brightened up. This was what mattered—to hell with the bombs. It was quite typical. On another occasion, in my capacity of Chief Warden I was working at an Incident—as the chaos and death caused by a falling bomb was·called in the understatement so beloved by the British. A row of cottages had been hit and were well ablaze. There was one which the flames had not yet reached and I told the old lady who lived there that I was afraid she must come out. 'Wot, me?' she said, 'leave me 'ouse for 'Itler? Not me. He ain't my landlord—I don't pay the Duke of Kent to 'im'! And it was quite a job to get her out. She was a real old Cockney, bless her, and by 'Duke of Kent' she meant the rent—it was old-fashioned rhyming slang. Being something of an expert in it I spoke to her in that medium myself. I don't believe she would have left her house otherwise.

The Fire Guards of Piccadilly—and everywhere else—had the same spirit. Night after night they spent in the premises where they worked by day. They got to know each other amazingly well. Men who were heads of departments and may be feared by their staffs became human beings and friends. They sat there the night through; they played cards, they knitted, they wrote letters and told stories, they debated all sorts of things, and characters came through which had been entirely unsuspected. It was a tremendous human revelation, that Fire Watching. They would call it Fire Watching, although their job was not to watch fires but to extinguish them if need be. They read books, everything on which they could lay their hands. Literature boomed if other things slumped. Many and many a man and woman had his or her first introduction to the classics in those nightly vigils. The blitz actually did a great deal for culture. They ate their food, which they brought with them, and food was heavily rationed. They shared with each other and enjoyed it as a picnic. They smoked a colossal amount of tobacco and drank whatever they could. Gallons and gallons of tea were consumed—to say nothing of coffee and cocoa. A cup of tea was something from heaven on those weary nights spent in close companionship with the prospect of what is sometimes called 'liquidation'. They had A.R.P. expert guidance. They had their stirrup pumps, their shovels and their spades, which were their weapons, all in readiness, and of course their gas masks were to hand—in case. Later on each group had a quota of steel helmets. They got some fitful sleep, taking it in turns, and of course sleeping in their clothes; some firms provided beds for the Guard. But they always had an eye and an ear open, at the ready. The worst thing about all those nights spent under the blitz was not the danger—that had exhilaration—but the boredom and lack of sleep. They listened to the radio too and sometimes they heard the voice of Winston Churchill, which acted like a powerful tonic. And they also heard J. B. Priestley, who was really talking about them, and those wartime broadcasts of his were amongst the best things of the war effort and the finest this great author has ever done. I have a vivid recollection of one I heard when lying helpless in bed with pneumonia in a West End hospital, unable to do anything about it if a bomb had made a direct hit. Priestley talked of the working girls of London—he was not very complimentary as to their looks, if I remember, and gave the impression of girls skinny and undernourished, living mainly on cups of tea and buns, he said, who day by day and night by night defied the bombs and struggled to and from their work under unbelievable difficulties. It did me a power of good.

The Fire Guards kept up a ceaseless vigilance and, if and when bombs fell, they were out at once. The incendiary bombs were their main objectives and a fall of these acted on the weary watchers like a shower of rain on a parched bed of flowers. They met it with almost eager delight, it was a break with boredom, an exciting justification of their purpose. They even competed for bombs. I remember once seeing a woman attacking an incendiary which was just getting really going. But she knew what to do. Another woman approached to help. 'Go away, I tell you,' said the attacker. 'This is my bomb. I saw it first.' One of the worst things about being a Fire Guard was the uncertainty of what was happening at your home. Were your family all right? Were they under direct attack? That was worrying and phone calls were not encouraged. One just had to wait and hope. From dusk to dawn it went on, and if you had the radio on, you knew when raiders were approaching because the volume lessened.

And then, as before, America came into the War. It had been a friendly neutral; there was a thing called 'Lease, Lend' and all sorts of material assistance. But one day, without any warning, the Japanese attacked Pearl Harbour and did enormous damage to the unsuspecting American Navy. So America declared war on Japan—Germany's allies—and on that same day Britain declared war on Japan, too, against whom it had not been fighting. That should not be forgotten when our side of the war is under consideration. The Americans poured into this country, the only free ground in Europe to fight from. And the American soldiers flocked to Piccadilly, which to them, was London. Their fathers had done so in the First War, the waves of visitors had come back from England full of Piccadilly, and many of the soldiers who now came to fight had been there in peacetime. So they could not wait to go there again.

This time it was different. They came to a country which had been and still was suffering great privation, which had lived with death for a considerable time, where money now was very scarce, for everything had been thrown into the melting pot of war, where such things as new clothes were so scarce as to be almost unobtainable. Rationing was fierce and everything was rationed. These Americans, very smart, and many of them bemedalled, which was a little difficult to understand, seemed to the younger generation of Londoners like people from another planet. Their uniforms were trim and clean, they had what seemed to the poor Londoners oceans of money and a complete confidence in what they were going to do to Hitler. They found London quaint and they got their first taste of war not on a foreign battlefield but in London and often in Piccadilly. They did not quite take it all in. They did not realise, many of them, that for a whole year this small island had stood foursquare and unbeaten against the full might of Germanic power. Had it not done so, America might have become a battlefield, but once again the land of the Stars and Stripes was saved from that. They made a tremendous impact on London, did these sons of the States. Children followed them about, begging chewing gum, and the ladies of the Dilly, who were still there, blitz or no blitz, reaped a rich harvest.

But the worst sight of all was provided by an outbreak of terrible, satanic and ghastly young girls, who invaded the West End and Piccadilly to prey upon the American troops. Where they came from has never been discovered—their like had never been seen before—although the behaviour and total lack of discipline and decent living which they displayed has alas not yet been eradicated. These perfectly horrible girls, many of them only just in their teens, came to town in swarms. Perfectly uninhibited, they hunted in couples and in droves. They fastened like lice on those wretched Americans—on looking back one deplores the taste of those G.I. men, many of whom were of course very young, very inexperienced, coming from the deep and wide rural districts of the States—who fell for these little horrors and suffered therefrom. One can only imagine these shocking creatures, who disgraced their sex, came out of the sewers and eventually returned there. They were hated by the professional prostitutes, for whom one really felt sympathy.

The Americans were out for a good time and got as near to it as they could. They were all sorts and in great numbers. Decent people did their best to make them welcome and invited them to their homes. But the majority of them reached the West End and Piccadilly. They thronged the bars and the restaurants and many people exploited them. Taximen discovered extraordinary and devious routes from one place to another—the shortest distance became quite a long ride—and the Yanks of course knew no better. They loved taxis and would crowd in six at a time. The average Londoner had a small chance of getting a taxi when the

Yanks were in town in force. There was a great deal of profiteer-
ing out of the Americans, who once again were fleeced by crooks
of all sorts. Some of them behaved like supermen who looked
upon the wretched British as a struggling semi-defeated people
whom they had come to save, and they paid for that. That American swarm over the West End and over so many places continued
the Americanisation of London which the First World War had
begun, and which the American films and plays had steadily
carried on. Young Londoners began to acquire a phoney American
accent, which was superimposed on the native Cockney and which
has grown stronger ever since.

Those newly arrived Americans would rush out to watch a
raid. Many of them thus tasted the efficiency of London hospitals.
That first wave of Americans in Piccadilly saw some amazing
sights—not all of which are printable. That war gave me a
sight of Piccadilly the like of which I shall never see again.

I did much broadcasting during the Second World War. Much
of it was for overseas programmes. There was one programme on
which I worked which went out from the Criterion Theatre
which is underground, at 3 a.m. one morning every week. It was
aimed to reach New York at 10 p.m.—peak listening time—the
previous night, allowing for the difference in time. We were a
small band but we represented London. There was an orchestra,
there were vocalists and instrumentalists who sang songs and
played music of London and I, who can neither sing nor play,
would give little descriptions of London Town before and during
the blitz and tell London stories. It was a very popular programme
in America and we had shoals of letters. We gathered at the
Criterion at midnight and we rehearsed. I would come from
Drury Lane Theatre, where I was also Chief Warden. Outside
that theatre the guns roared and bombs screamed down, often
very close at hand, but we carried on. When it was over many of
the participants would sleep in the theatre but I, who had to make
an early start at work, wanted a little more rest than that would
provide and had a bedroom at the Piccadilly Hotel, a few hundred

yards away. There I got a few hours' sleep—about three or three-and-a-half—a bath and a breakfast and could start moderately refreshed. I remember coming out of that stage door of the Criterion one morning in spring at about 4 a.m., turning into Lower Regent Street and then into Piccadilly Circus. I could see almost the whole of Piccadilly before me. There was not a soul in sight—not even a stray cat—nothing but the double row of buildings which constitutes Piccadilly, stretching away down towards Hyde Park Corner and entirely deserted, looking unreal and amazingly aloof, with something naked and primeval in its utter loneliness. Not even a policeman to be seen in one of the busiest places on earth. It looked very clean and newly washed under that bright spring sun from a blue sky. I did not see so much as a pigeon or a sparrow as I walked along the pavement, my footsteps seeming to echo, although the strange effect made me walk on tiptoe to avoid disturbing that absolutely noiseless place. Such a sight can hardly ever be seen in London. I might have been the last man left alive, alone in Piccadilly, as much alone as if I had been stranded on a tiny atoll in the tropic seas—more lonely even than Alexander Selkirk. I think the ghosts of Piccadilly surveyed me.

And there was a very different sight in Piccadilly in which I played a leading part though not by any means as the only performer. Much was done to make the lot of the fighting men and women of the services bright and happy. New York had a famous place called the Stage Door Canteen. It was decided that London should have one too. It was not a very easy matter to establish this—there was much red tape and wartime difficulty to overcome—but a quite small and most energetic committee, of which I was privileged to be a member, consisting mostly of men and women concerned with the theatre, eventually carried it through although by that time the war, unknown to us, was entering its last phase. Naturally the only place for such a thing as Stage Door Canteen was the centre of London, and that meant Piccadilly. That famous restaurant of Messrs Lyons was taken over—the Popular Café. It was just the place. Nobody worked harder than two famous ladies of the stage, Beatrice Lillie and Dorothy Dickson, who was born an American. At length all was ready for the opening. That was a night I shall never forget. As soon as the doors opened a mob of service men and women poured in and filled the place. The refreshment bars sold out over and over again and the assistants worked like slaves. There did not seem a particle of room left yet more and more squeezed in. Well known entertainers gave their services—all sorts and conditions of them. Bea Lillie and Dorothy Dickson worked wonders. They helped us to get order—to get the 'boys and girls' in the front facing the little stage to sit down so that those at the back could see and hear. The galleries were thronged. Joan Hammond's wonderful voice rang out in operatic arias and cheers rent the air. The full committee was in attendance but was lost in the mob. The civilian portion—and I use that word here meaning those who were not in the entertainment industry—were a bit out of their depth, but we who were, knew how to handle crowds, especially a good-tempered one like this. There was no fixed programme; the entertainers came along as they could and performed straight away. When night fell there was a huge mob outside striving to gain admission. Some of course left and made room, but many just stayed on. And as the evening advanced the entertainment, quite rightly, got starrier and starrier. Jack Buchanan came down. This wonderful artist—who was the West End personified—had never been in better form. The Service audience adored him and many of the Americans knew him from his New York triumphs. The audience revelled and he was on that stage for about an hour.

Then word came to me that something extra was about to happen, if I could get the people in. I went out to the front of the building by devious routes which I had discovered and there were Bing Crosby and Fred Astaire, and with them Cecil Madden of the BBC, Percy Hoskins of the *Daily Express*, and John Harding, who was running a similar sort of place, very successfully, at what had been the Prince Edward Theatre and is now the home of Cinerama—the Casino in Old Compton Street, Soho. In this venture there was a link with Piccadilly, for his partner was the Marquis of Queensbury, descended from Old Q of Piccadilly fame. I had to get those people in across the roof to the artists' room at the back. Bing Crosby was marvellous. He sang, he sang and he sang, to enraptured audiences. Nothing was too much trouble. He and Jack Buchanan did a spontaneous show, gagging at each other for almost an hour. The men and women would not let them go. Bing mixed with the crowd, chatting and laughing. He gave autographs and he signed his name in large letters, as a memento, on the wall of Stage Door Canteen. He was magnificent and so was our own Jack Buchanan. It was all a great success.

And whilst that show was going on I bethought me of the special opener, Mr Anthony Eden, as he was then. I reckoned that the Committee would have overlooked the necessity of meeting him and I made my way as fast as I could to the front entrance —just in time, for Eden and his wife were just getting out of their car. The doormen fought off the crowd and I took the couple in hand. I could not ask them to clamber over the roof, so I fought a way through that packed hall almost by brute force. Pictures in the Press the next morning showed me doing this with the Edens almost crouched behind me. I am afraid I hogged that publicity— but unwillingly. Mr Eden made a delightful speech, put everybody in a good humour, and 'mixed' to a degree. I was now alarmed at the condition of the balconies, which were so overcrowded that I feared at any moment they might collapse. But they held. We got the Edens out, spirited Bing Crosby and his party away once more across the roof, and the show went on. My wife remembers that evening as the first and only time she was 'on the tiles' in Piccadilly. The show went on. It was a wonderful night in Piccadilly and nobody inside cared what went on outside—there had of course been a raid. Even if things were a bit chaotic—and they were—that was the usual condition of the

British war effort. And victory was gained, anyway. Kings, queens and great people from lands overseas which had been overrun by the Nazi hordes, came for safety and shelter to the haven of England. Many of them lived at the Ritz, in Piccadilly.

Of course the bombs took toll. Burlington Arcade was bombed, at the end farthest from Piccadilly, but carried on and is itself again today. The Naval and Military Club, which, it will be remembered, had once been the home of the Duke of Cambridge, suffered too, but is open again and shows its famous 'In' and 'Out' signs which give its nickname. There was other damage but perhaps the worst blow was the bombing of St James's, Piccadilly —the church in the magic mile. Wren had a hand in its building, so had Grinling Gibbons. It was badly hit and it lost its tower. It is now rebuilt and part of its churchyard was made into a charming garden in which those who were weary but still alive could get some rest. This was done as a tribute to the citizens of London for what they had endured during the blitz. I think it is the only tribute they ever received.

The war went on, phase succeeding phase, through the flying bombs and the V2 rockets, but still life passed up and down Piccadilly. Then at long last, Germany surrendered. There came what was called VE—Victory in Europe—Day. Again London rejoiced and cheering throngs crowded Piccadilly. I do not think there was quite the same excitement as the 11th November 1918 had brought about, but the people were war weary to a degree, and had been in the war as much as the fighting men. There was enormous relief. The memory of that day which I treasure most was a man I saw kicking his gas mask along the gutter outside Simpson's. Most of us had long abandoned ours, but he probably had some special hate. It was very human. VJ Day, which marked the collapse of Japan and the end of a more distant war came almost as an anti-climax.

And so the life of Piccadilly as seen today emerged from the debris of war—a very different life from the old days, a very different life from that of the inter-war period. Standards have changed—

everything has changed. People dress with an informality which would have made them ostracised in the Piccadilly before 1914. Commerce holds firm sway and except for flats the street is hardly residential. But the great airways of the world have their offices there and you can book an air ticket to any land from the very centre of things, Piccadilly, which once was the centre for the stage coaches. Britain has ceased to be an island, London and Piccadilly have become more and more cosmopolitan. An old timer would be astonished and not a little appalled at the number of coloured faces he would see, and the variety of foreign attire. But despite it all, Piccadilly remains Piccadilly, and the people flock from overseas and revel in walking along it. They feel they walk on magic soil and do not know the reason. Yet the reason is there, some of it still to be seen, some of it to be realised when known. They walk along a street which is essentially English. They walk amongst the great names of England—Burlington, Devonshire, Bruton, Cavendish, Clarendon, Albemarle, Stratton, Berkeley, Bond, Clarges, all of which have remained as landmarks. They tread where monarchs have trodden, they pass by where monarchs have lived, and underneath their feet lie relics of the days which have passed since that tailor gentleman, Mr Robert Baker, gave this place its strange name from his Pickadils. Few of them, I fear, observe a relic of a much older Piccadilly which still survives above ground. For right at the far end—near Hyde Park Corner, outside the Green Park Railings and against the kerb—stands a curious raised platform of iron, placed there many years ago by someone, now unknown, who had observed that porters carrying their loads towards the West were very tired after tackling that little hill and so provided them with this resting place for their burdens before they continued with their toil. Its use has long since gone, but one feels gratitude that so far this delightful link with older and more leisured days is still preserved —though few people even notice it or know what it was for. May it stand forever as a tribute to that man—or woman—who had a thought for those who were heavily laden.

But, for the time being at any rate, the ladies of the Dilly have forsaken it, driven therefrom by laws of social reform. It may be of course that this is for the good of the community, but Piccadilly lacks a very old feature without them. There is something about this amazing street which one finds in no other thoroughfare in this vast metropolis—a sort of feeling of personal possession which Tony of the Silk Hat felt so strongly when he sang 'They Built Piccadilly for me'.

11

The Charm of Piccadilly

For a great portion of its length on its southern side, Piccadilly runs along an area of green grass and trees, separated therefrom by railings. This is the Green Park, which also gives its name to Piccadilly's own railway station. But this place is more than a mere Park, Royal Park though it be, at least to the mind of the observant passer-by. For here, displayed to view and open to the sky, is the actual soil of London, so seldom seen. Here there have never been more than a handful of buildings mostly of a temporary nature; here is that actual Piccadilly when it was the 'Way to Reading' or 'Colbroke', where the viper's bugloss bloomed in the dry ditches and where those old time thieves and harlots sheltered, to the detriment of the King's subjects. Here is still, although tamed and regimented by man, a bit of the old country-side which hemmed in that small city of London in the days gone by. And in some nooks and corners it still retains its rural aspect. It is a royal park, as stated, but it has never been formally laid out or planned like Hyde Park and other open spaces. It has been left, very largely, except for paths and drainage, as an open space to delight eyes tired of the seemingly eternal bricks and mortar.

You pass the massive Ritz Hotel, which even dominates the pavement, and you feel the winds of heaven upon you—you see the verdure of the herbage and the trees, the blossom in Spring, the sky with clouds driving across it like galleons—and you have what in any other city than this would be one of the finest boulevards. That does not operate in London. But this sudden disappearance of buildings, this sudden glimpse of the natural earth, is the source of much of the charm of Piccadilly.

For the soil you see has been the stage of exciting events romances, disasters, violence and robbery, and was at one time an actual field of battle. For that amazing place, Piccadilly, thanks to the Green Park, can actually claim a battlefield in its history. Its story as a park dates only from the Restoration but it had seen stirring events prior to that.

It was in the beginning just a piece of the countryside—waste land so far as the Town was concerned, or better still, perhaps, a kind of vast meadow, uncultivated and rough. It was intersected by ditches and there were willow trees along the banks. It was a very quiet and somewhat lonely spot—where cattle and sheep grazed and where, in its bushes maybe the children from the Royal Farm at St James's—from whence Bluff King Hal drew his eggs, butter and cream, and of which a wall still exists tucked away off St James's Street—went birdnesting in the clumps of brambles and the masses of bracken which abounded. A quiet, solitary place, little dreaming of future glory. But on 5th February 1554, that solitude was banished and armed men crowded the field. Heavy guns were dragged across it to the not considerable but still commanding height of what is now Constitution Hill, and a regiment of cavalry lined what is now Piccadilly, stationed we learn, 'above the new bridge over against St James's'. That little bridge spanned the Tyburn which flowed across Piccadilly. There was rebellion in the land and the malcontents were marching on London under the leadership of Sir Thomas Wyatt, who had roused the men of Kent to come to the capital and prevent Queen Mary from marrying a Spaniard, Philip of Spain. Her Majesty had summoned the Earl of Pembroke to her defence. He came hot foot and deployed his men—the guns on Constitution

Hill, the cavalry in Piccadilly and the infantry at what is now
Charing Cross. Stow, the great chronicler of London, who was
alive when these events took place, puts on record: 'Wyatt and
his company planted his ordnance upon a hill beyond St James's,
almost over against the Park corner (it is almost certain that this
must have been Hay Hill), and himself, after a few words spoken
to his soldiers, came down the old lane on foot, hard by the Court
Gate of St James's, with four or five ancients (officers), his men
marching in good order.'

Apparently he was going to attack the infantry. The Earl of
Pembroke was a better strategist than Wyatt. He let the main body
of the rebels pass, then cut them in two and attacked the rear. The
guns began to roar across Piccadilly. Those of Wyatt's on Hay
Hill fired harmlessly over the heads of Pembroke's horsemen—and
the main body of the rebels marched on leaving the rearguard to
shift for itself. If Wyatt's artillery did no damage the Pembroke
guns were better aimed. One cannon ball, at any rate, mowed
down a whole file of Wyatt's men and then buried itself in the
wall nearby. The cavalry cut up the unmounted rebels. Wyatt
went on to besiege the Tower and lost his cause—and his life. His
head was displayed on a pole on Hay Hill, from which his guns
had been so ineffective in battle. Such was the Battle of the Green
Park—or of Piccadilly.

Then what is now the park sank back again into its peacefulness
for almost one hundred years until again it awakened to war.
Again the people of England were in arms against their monarch,
this time Charles I. In 1643 the Parliamentarians surrounded
London with a circle of forts and defensive field works. A
redoubt and a battery were erected on Constitution Hill. The
people of London helped to build it. And in so doing they swarmed
over what is now Green Park, fetching earth therefrom to build
the defences. An eye-witness has recorded a note of this—'It was
wonderful to see how the women and children and vast numbers
of people, would come and work about digging of earth and
making their new fortifications.' Yet it is improbable that any of

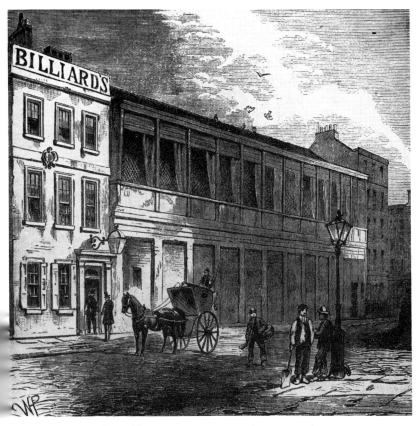

The Old Tennis Court near the Haymarket

Regent Street from Piccadilly Circus, 1828

those Fire Guards who defended Piccadilly in the Second World War knew anything about those who had helped in its defence almost three centuries before. Those forts and redoubts did not stand for long. After four years they were demolished, under an act of Parliament.

It was Charles II who was responsible for the making of the Green Park. He did much for St James's Park and there is a record that in or about 1667, he bought thirty-six acres of land to add thereto. These acres were never actually placed within the boundaries of St. James's Park—and are described as 'several fields, which ran up to the road, and as far as Hyde Park and are now enclosed with a brick wall'. The road was Piccadilly. Already it was only possible to extend the open space west and north for the rest formed part of the Court of St James's and its gardens. The wall cost £2400 to erect, and this new enclosure was given the name of Upper St James's Park.

The first building went up on its soil somewhere about 1660. It was the first refrigerator this country had ever seen. It was described as 'A snow-house and an ice-house, as the mode is in some parts of France and Italy, and other hot countries, for to cool wine and drinks for the summer season.' Waller, the poet, mentions it and describes it, correct in custom maybe but incorrectly in locality—although it was still called Upper St James's Park:

'Yonder the harvest of cold months laid up
Gives a fresh coolness to the royal cup;
There ice, like crystal firm and never lost,
Tempers hot July with December's frost.'

This father of all British fridges stood almost in the centre of Green Park. Its foundations were traceable in the early 1800's. At the western extremity Charles II established a deer-harbour, but otherwise little was done to alter its original meadowlike appearance. In 1681 a strip at its eastern end was granted to the Earl of Arlington, who was part of that famous Cabal. His name survives in Arlington Street, built upon this piece of ground.

Green Park had its uses to the nobility and gentry of the Piccadilly neighbourhood. It became a favourite place for the gentlemanly habit of duelling. On Saturday night, 11th January 1696 Sir Henry Colt and Beau Fielding measured swords there. Fielding wanted this venue so that his prowess could be watched by his notorious inamorata the Duchess of Cleveland—behind whose house, later Bridgewater House—the combat took place. One wonders if she did indeed watch and if so, what she thought of the sporting spirit of her champion. For it is recorded that Fielding, who was no hero, ran Sir Henry through the body before that worthy had the time to draw his sword. But despite this the much more gallant baronet continued the fight and disarmed Fielding, which brought the combat to an end. In 1730 there was another duel which made a good deal of noise at the time. This was between William Pulteney, afterwards Earl of Bath, and Lord John Hervey, whom Alexander Pope dismissed as:

> '. . . That thing of silk,
> Sporus, that mere white curd of asses' milk.'

The duel had a political cause, and the contestants met on Monday, 25th January 1730 between three and four in the afternoon (which shows how lonely the spot was even then). Both of the duellists were slightly wounded, though at one time, if his foot had not slipped, Pulteney could have run the lord through the body. So the seconds intervened. Pulteney embraced Lord John, but his lordship made him no answer but a bow and walked away. Another duel which made news in its time was fought in the Green Park between Edward, Viscount Ligonier and Count Vittorio Alfieri. The Viscount discovered a liaison between the Italian and his wife. He immediately went in search of the Count, ran him to earth in a box at the opera, and asked him to step outside and fight it out. Vittorio, despite a damaged shoulder and with his arm in a sling, accepted the challenge. The two men then—without seconds—repaired to the Green Park and fought in the last glimmerings of twilight. Alfieri was wounded in the arm. Ligonier considered this enough to appease his honour—he evidently did not think much of his wife and left the field in triumph while Alfieri went back to the opera. That opera was being performed in the Haymarket, where Her Majesty's Theatre now stands, convenient to the duelling ground. Eventually there was a ranger appointed to the Green Park who had a pleasant lodge in which to live.

It was Queen Caroline who made the place a royal park. She appears to have been very fond of it. She had a private walk laid out along its eastern extremity, which was known as Queen's Walk and is still there, so that she and the royal family, 'could divert themselves in the Spring'. She wanted to build herself a house therein but it never got further than the erection of a sort of Pavilion, which was called 'The Queen's Library'. It caused her death. On 9th November 1737, she walked there to breakfast, caught a severe cold, took to her bed and died within ten days. . .

For a long time there was no water in the Green Park, although the dank dismal pool in St James's Park, known as 'Rosamond's Pond' adjoined it. This was a favourite place for suicides, especially by women. But in Queen Caroline's time, a small reservoir was constructed there to supply water to Chelsea. It held 1,500,000 gallons of water. When, in 1735, Rosamond's Pool was cleaned out by a Welsh engineer named Hugh Robarts, a wag posted a notice on an adjoining tree advising those desirous of ending their lives by drowning to patronise the more modern and extensive means provided by the reservoir in the Green Park. And, believe it or not, there were those who did so—amongst them Harriet Westbrook, Shelley's first wife, and several others. They could not have read that notice because their deaths occurred much later, but evidently the lure of the Green Park for suicide was pretty great. The reservoir was filled in in 1856.

George II, husband of Queen Caroline, was often in the Park. He was a soldier and a gallant one, the last king of England to lead his troops in actual battle. Soldiers indeed accompanied him everywhere, not so much for security reasons as because he liked to be amongst them. A troop of horse even went with him when he hunted. He used the Green Park as a convenient parade ground for military reviews. On 24th January 1747 His Majesty attended by the Prince of Wales and accompanied by the Duke of Cumberland, the Duke of Richmond, Lord Harcourt, Lord Cadogan and several other noblemen, reviewed Sir Robert Riches' Dragoons near the Queen's Library. There was a sight for the public—a whole regalia of royalty—if the collective description can be accepted. The regiment was at full strength, except for twenty-four men whose names were on the roster but who were either dead or ill. But they were on parade before their King, too, by deputy. Their horses were in the ranks with boots hanging from the saddle, the boots of the sick men pointing towards the horses' heads as they would have done if the riders had been in them, and those of the dead men pointing to the tails. His Royal Highness The Prince of Wales rode through the ranks, accompanied by the Duke of Queensbury—a local link—and His Majesty was greatly pleased. And on the following Saturday were reviewed the Duke of Cumberland's Dragoons, which had been formed from a body of men enlisted by the Duke of Kingston during the 1745 Rebellion—the first body of light horse used in this country. Known as the Duke of Cumberlands Own Regiment of Light Dragoons, they carried short carbines, slung to their side by a movable swivel, pistols, and a curved sword. This was their first appearance in public and great crowds wanted to see them. To prevent overcrowding all the gates and avenues into the Park were closed and guarded, but many climbed the wall and got in, with broken arms and legs amongst them. One unlucky man fell amongst the troops and got trampled by the horses. The Green Park was a very military place then, for a permanent park of artillery was kept there, surrounded by a chevaux-de-frise. Four companies of the artillery were reviewed on 19th April 1749 by the Prince of Wales and the Duke of Cumberland—'Butcher' Cumberland of the hideous purple face but a fine soldier—and infantry lined the chevaux-de-frise to keep the public back. Still, accidents occurred as seems to have been usual then, but this time it was amongst the military and not the onlookers. A wretched bombardier had his arm torn right off because his gun was fired before the rammer had been removed.

The Green Park does not seem to have been a lucky place for celebrations at all. Great national rejoicings were announced when peace was signed at Aix-la-Chapelle in 1748. The festivities were to begin in the April of 1749. The nation was on tiptoe with excitement, for the proceedings had been publicised.

A great pavilion was erected in the Green Park on the lines of a Doric Temple. It was 114 ft high, 410 ft long and was extremely decorative—covered with gilt, artificial flowers, inscriptions and allegorical pictures and twenty-three statues of colossal size. And on the pediment was a picture 28 ft by 10 ft, showing the King giving peace to Britannia. On the top was a gigantic sun, which was to burn for four hours. The Londoners reckoned it was one of the wonders of the world. Nor was this all, for there was to be a terrific display of fireworks with illuminations, transparencies and set pieces. It was going to be wonderful. But ill luck seems to have dogged it from the start. The original scheme was drawn up by a famous Italian architect, Servandoni, who fell ill before it was completed and handed it over to the Chevalier de Casali to complete. But the Chevalier came in for the hoodoo as well—he was badly hurt by a large piece of timber which fell on him.

On the Sunday before the display, half London went to inspect the marvels. The crowd was enormous, the crush frightening, and the light-fingered gentry of the period reaped a reward. Women lost the trains of their skirts, to say nothing of hats and bonnets, gentlemen lost their silver-hilted swords and even the gold embroidered tails of their coats. On the Monday some experimental fireworks were let off. Lieutenant Desaguliers, R.E., in charge, was seriously wounded. Thursday, 27th April was the day appointed for the glory. All the entrances to the Green Park were opened, and a breach fifty feet long was made in the wall along Piccadilly to give the crowds a chance. A special stand was erected for the Privy Council, both Houses of Parliament, the Lord Mayor and Corporation, and members of the City Companies. The guns were removed and the Horse Guards paraded the streets all night to keep order. His Majesty King George held a review of the Foot Guards in the morning, and at seven p.m. went to a special pavilion erected for him, expressed his entire satisfaction with the arrangements and presented purses full of guineas to the various workmen. The Prince of Wales, on bad terms with his father, kept aloof and saw the show from the house of the Earl of Middlesex in Arlington Street. The actual performance began with a grand military overture composed for the occasion by Handel. The orchestra consisted of 40 trumpets, 20 French horns, 16 hautboys, 16 bassoons, 8 kettle drums, 12 side drums and a bunch of fifes, besides 100 discharges by the guns, in time with the music. A salute of 101 guns followed. At half-past eight two rockets whizzed aloft to announce the fireworks, and the fireworks started in earnest—in more than earnest because the Doric temple caught fire and blazed gloriously. Inside it were 100 lbs of gunpowder. By luck this was got out in time or nobody can have had much chance of escaping injury. After a considerable portion of the building had been destroyed the firemen got control. The King sent presents to the men who had so distinguished themselves. But the discharge of fireworks had continued all the time and so their effect was considerably spoilt. At eleven o'clock what was left of the ruined building was illuminated and so remained until 3 a.m. The King, however, went home at midnight.

Accidents and trouble were rife. A large rocket dived into a stand, struck a Miss Harriott Sear, broke her arm and burned her severely. A boy fell from a tree and broke his neck. A drunken cobbler fell into Rosamond's Pool and was drowned, a painter engaged on the fireworks fell from the top of the building and dashed his brains out. The Chevalier de Servandoni, who had come to see his own work, fell foul of a Mr Frederick and drew his sword. That was a heinous offence in a Royal Park and he was arrested. He was locked up and in the morning hauled before the

Board of Green Cloth and bound over to keep the peace. And on the next day a carpenter, working on the demolition of the half burnt temple, fell on the spikes of a gate and demolished himself. The whole unfortunate affair is said to have cost £90,000.

The Green Park had also an unenviable reputation as a place for robberies. And soldiers of the Foot Guards were not blameless in this respect. The soldiery then were pretty rough specimens and did not live in barracks but in billets, so could roam about at night. They roamed the Green Park at night to the great peril of pedestrians. Most impudent and barefaced robberies were committed and sometimes the victims lost their lives. One evening a gentleman and three ladies were coming out of a private door near the reservoir, which led into Piccadilly. They saw two men endeavouring to open it as they approached but apparently their key would not work. The gentleman politely proffered his. Directly they had the key the two men drew their pistols, rifled the gentleman and his lady friends, taking all their valuables, pushed them through the door into Piccadilly, shut it and vanished into the darkness of the Park. There are countless stories of robbery with violence in the annals of the park. There were no regular police and it would seem that in the Green Park at least crime was a paying concern.

In August 1760 some workmen digging a drain discovered, six feet below the surface, a coffin which contained a skeleton. The bones were complete except for a hole in the skull. It was reckoned to have been there for some twenty years but who it was has never been discovered.

In 1761 King George III bought Buckingham House and turned it into Buckingham Palace. He cut off a good slice of the Green Park and incorporated it into the grounds of his new home. In the following year the wall which had separated St James's Park from Green Park was taken down and railings were substituted. Another lodge was built there too, in addition to that of the Ranger. A small grove of trees, near the new lodge, was glorified by the name of the Wilderness.

In that reign, the Green Park was very popular for evening promenades. It was still a place for duels, and for robberies, however. In 1773 the old lodge was rebuilt, and it is said that the King himself was the architect and indeed he had a gift for it. This new lodge was his *chef d'œuvre*. Lord Orford, the Ranger, had it in his gift and it carried the title of Deputy Ranger for its tenant. Everybody wanted it and it would seem that bribery and corruption were not absent. George Selwyn got it and the Ranger had a financial profit. In 1778 Lord William Gordon, brother to the Duke of that name and also to the gentleman who caused the riots, was in possession. But its maintenance cost him a pretty penny.

In 1780, St James's Park, owing to a turn of fashion, lost its social pre-eminence as a parading place of celebrity and fashion and the Green Park took over. The parade of 'haut ton' on summer evenings was amazing. Houses at the back of Arlington Street with windows looking on to the Park fetched high prices. The ladies and gentlemen of title and of Society walked there after dinner in full evening costume, and strolled around the reservoir which had a fountain. It must be remembered that the air was clean and fresh—it was open country to the south and south-west and the view was first rate. There was a sensation in the summer of 1790, when ladies appeared veiled. The gentlemen were very annoyed, for the popular pastime was quizzing the ladies as they passed by.

But improvements were being made all around. The wall between the Park and Piccadilly was removed, and replaced by railings, and flower beds were laid out inside them. The contemporary Press was full of praise—it was said to be charmingly inviting and to provide a public walk unequalled in any other land. The Green Park was crowded nightly by everybody who was anybody and a great number who were not.

During the Napoleonic threat to these shores, the Volunteer movement flourished and the Prince of Wales' Association was several times reviewed in the Green Park. They carried out martial evolutions to the full satisfaction of the Earl of Harrington and masses of spectators. During the day the park was not greatly frequented but in the evenings and on Sundays it was the centre of fashionable society.

A comet made its appearance in the heavens in October 1807 and there was a prediction that it might collide with the earth. This gave it a fearful interest and crowds flocked to the Green Park every night to see what could be seen. Many had telescopes and ladies gazed through them at the disturbing aerial visitor. Feminine interest in astronomy received a great fillip. But it should be recorded that not all the ladies who visited the Park went there to see the comet. Some preferred mortal men to heavenly bodies, and they reaped a good harvest.

In 1809 there was a very splendid display of flowers and people thronged the park until midnight. It must have been a picturesque sight for the clothes were gay and highly coloured, there was a good sprinkling of fine uniforms and all around the green of the park and the trees, with the rooks winging homeward to the rookery behind Carlton House. And those evening promenades led to a *cause célèbre*. Lady Charlotte Wellesley, wife of Sir Henry Wellesley, afterwards Lord Cowley, sister-in-law to the Duke of Wellington, eloped with Lord Paget, whilst her carriage and servants waited for her at the entrance to the Park. One can imagine that meeting, the stealthy escape from the crowd and the hurried flight in another carriage. There was a great uproar. Colonel Cadogan, the lady's brother, challenged Lord Paget, who declined the honour. He married his eloping lady after a divorce had been obtained. Although he had declined the duel he was no coward for as the Marquis of Anglesey, it was his leg which was buried with military honours on the field of Waterloo, under a monument and a weeping willow, whilst the solitary boot was preserved as a relic.

The Green Park saw another firework display in 1814, to celebrate the centenary of the accession of the House of Hanover. In the July there began the erection of a great, but temporary

G*

building which occupied almost a third of the Park. It was to be covered with allegorical pictures and called the Temple of Concord. About a week before the celebrations were due to commence a lengthy programme was issued, telling of wonders to come. It was to be transformed in an instant, like a scene in a pantomime, from a Gothic castle, there would be a spirited battle and siege and then the Temple would materialise in a blaze of pyrotechnics. Anyway it all sounded marvellous to the Londoners never averse to a free show.

The fête was to take place on 1st August and the day started with lowering clouds and threat of rain—but just as happened later on the occasion of Queen Victoria's Diamond Jubilee, the sun broke through. The Green Park was thronged all day. No amusement had been laid on for the daytime. The people sat about eating, drinking, making their own fun and probably wondering what it was all about. They had been told that at one time a great bridge would spring into view on which would be the Royal Family. They hoped for the best. The weather had now turned very hot indeed. At six p.m. a Mr Sadler—'an intrepid aeronaut'—went up in a balloon and floated gently in the direction of Kent. At nine o'clock the royal bridge was made visible—but only just—by a meagre display of Chinese lanterns. It was seen to be emblazoned with the names of naval and military heroes. At 10 p.m. there was a terrific bombardment by artillery firing blanks, which lasted for twenty minutes and this was the signal for the fireworks and the siege. Rockets went soaring up and then the temple itself was disclosed, but the excitement of a siege was totally absent. The temple itself was not so bad and lit with lanterns in pretty good taste but many people left to watch the pagoda in St James's Park burn down, which rockets had set on fire. No glimpse of the Royal Family was vouchsafed. They were all too busy at a sumptuous supper to bother about fireworks. The thing itself had been a damp squib.

The next day told its story. The Green Park which had lived up to its name so nobly was nothing but a brown waste. Every blade of grass had been trodden down. This caused a comic advertisement to be inserted in one of the papers. 'Lost, on Monday night, the beautiful Green Park which used to extend from St James's Park to Piccadilly. It is supposed to have been removed by Mr John Bull who was seen there last night with a pretty numerous company, and who has left a Brown Park in exchange of no value to the Ranger. Information on this subject will be thankfully received by the two stags over the lodge in Piccadilly.' Those stags now decorate the Albert Gate of Hyde Park.

As a place of spectacle and public amusement the Green Park never seems to have succeeded. There were riotous scenes there when George III celebrated his Jubilee and a fair was held in Hyde Park and another in St James's Park. The railings and walls of Green Park were removed to allow the public access to and from, but mobs trampled all over the place and every sort of vehicle used it as a short cut irrespective of paths or public safety, which made much confusion.

The Temple of Concord still stood there. On 12th August of that year, the Prince Regent celebrated his birthday. No announcement had been made of any form of entertainment at all, yet the public flocked to the park expecting fireworks at the least. They stared at the Temple of Concord hoping for illuminations, rockets and whatnot. When nothing transpired, a leaven of roughs which had come with the crowd began to uproot the fencing round the building. Sentries tried in vain to stop them. The mob got control, piled the broken fencing into a big heap, threw the sentry boxes on top, tore off branches from the trees for good measure and made a gigantic bonfire. The rumour spread through London that St James's Palace was on fire. The military turned out and dispersed most of the mob, but many remained there all night yelling, milling about and displaying much drunken frenzy.

Although the fire had not destroyed the Temple of Concord, which had caused so much discord, it had blackened and defaced it. It stood for two months longer, and was then sold by auction for £198.6.6d., and pulled down. Rank and fashion deserted the

Green Park in 1817. This was not on account of riots or footpads but because the hour at which the smart people dined had changed from four and five o'clock, to eight or nine. So that full dress after dinner parade was no longer practical, and the fashionables left the Park severely alone. A phase had ended. Nor did they try anything more in the way of great fêtes. When King George IV was crowned all that took place there was a balloon ascent, at one p.m. The balloon had a legend on it—'George IV, Royal Coronation Balloon'. The aeronaut was Mr Green. It rose in a moderate breeze, which evidently freshened higher up. It headed for the north and was visible for nearly half an hour, so clear was the air. It descended in a field near Potters Bar and North Mimms at 1.40 p.m. having travelled upwards of fifty miles, as it blew backwards and forwards in gusts of wind, in about forty minutes. Little did the inhabitants of the then purely rural district know that a German death-dealing airship would fall—years afterwards in flames—on almost the exact spot.

In the spring of 1842 the Rangers' lodges were removed, the appointment having been done away with, and the gardens were merged into the park. The whole place was much improved and Sir Robert Peel, then Prime Minister took the greatest interest in it. He wanted to fill it with fountains, flower beds and statues like an Italian Garden. That never took place. He himself met his death on its verge for he was thrown from his horse on Constitution Hill and died three days later. So the Park became what is seen today and many people like it best that way. It retains much of its rurality and little of sham rusticity. It is a place of grass, trees and good paths. Concrete posts supporting wire netting stand between it and Piccadilly and there stand the Devonshire House gates, opposite Half Moon Street. From these gates a tree-lined avenue runs across Green Park to the Victoria Memorial outside Buckingham Palace. This was intended to be a Broad Walk, like the one in Kensington Gardens, but H.M. Office of Works changed its mind. There was once a scheme too for placing a royal statue in the park.

THE CHARM OF PICCADILLY

So despite the changing years and all sorts of events, despite the
cataract of traffic which now throbs and thunders along Piccadilly,
the Green Park remains a very restful place. Not quite so peaceful
as in Victorian or early Edwardian days when it had the subdued
clatter of horses hooves, the jingle of the hansom and the roll of
wheels as a ground bass, but peaceful enough. On a fine day in
spring, or a warm day in summer, there is no finer walk in
London than along Piccadilly beside the Green Park. The width of
the pavement separates two worlds—a world entirely dominated
by the internal combustion engine, and soil which is the absolute
foundation of London (mostly unbuilt on) facing the sky still as it
has done since our earliest history. There are no crowds promena-
ding, for it does not really lead anywhere; at best it is a short cut
from Piccadilly to the Mall. It has no display of flowers, no
sparkling fountains, no man-made display. But it has its grass and
its shade, given by the trees, and it seems to be the resting place of
many Londoners. For a glance across it on a summer's day might
make you imagine you were looking at a battlefield—and once it
was a battlefield—across which the storm of war had just swept.
All over the grass lie recumbent figures, in all sorts of positions.
But no need to worry—they are not corpses—just Londoners
taking their rest on Mother Earth, with the scent of growing grass
in their nostrils instead of the reek of petrol. Men and women sit
on chairs in the shade, reading, knitting, just staring before them
or watching the passers-by. Dogs go mad as they do when there
is a stretch over which they can dash at speed. One may say this
is not a place of great beauty. It is not, but it is a place of infinite
charm. For spring seems to come to the Green Park before it
reaches other places. The trees burgeon there before less favoured
rivals and one looks upwards through a delicate mist of green and
yellow. There are planes of age and girth, noble elms, oaks,
poplars, limes and chestnuts, and nowhere else does the flourish
of the maytrees seem more red, white or luxuriant.

The Green Park lies below the level of Piccadilly and from the
low, concrete, shrub lined posts and wire netting, the ground

slopes sharply and makes a bank which faces south and traps the sun. There bloom the first of London's daffodils, their green lances piercing the grass very early—and their yellow trumpets do indeed take the winds of March with beauty—and sometimes herald the coming of that month, for as these lines are being written, on the last day of February, a few of them are in flower. They stand amongst the crocuses, which enamel the turf with specks of mauve, gold and white, as if an artist had flicked his brushes there.

The blackbirds love the Green Park and throng there, playing their flutes as if in a country garden; the aldermanic wood pigeon now an urban bird, is there, portly amongst his domesticated cousins who have made it their home too and blue-tits chirr and dip from branch to branch, whilst the London sparrow is everywhere. The Queen's Walk is still a promenade and stately houses gaze at it from one side. But when one reaches the end of the park, by Hyde Park Corner, there one savours the real country. For this is a place of small hills and dells, sheltered and tree-decked, dainty in miniature where maybe still the Little People of London hold nightly revel...

But for me the abiding memory of the Green Park is a remark made by the man who really created it—King Charles II. The Earl of Rochester gave him a witty epitaph:

'Who never said a foolish thing
Or ever did a wise one.'

King Charles made one of his most sage remarks in the Green Park —his brother James, Duke of York, came upon him walking on the Constitutional Hill side, very scantily attended and suggested he might be in danger. 'No kind of danger, James' said Old Rowley 'for I am sure no man will kill me to make you king.' As regards his lack of wise actions—well, he gave us that precious garden of rest, Piccadilly's Green Park.

12

Another Root of Piccadilly

If you walk along Coventry Street today, on the left-hand side, going towards Piccadilly Circus, you will see, just after you have crossed the top of Oxendon Street, a narrow turning on the left again, which runs between restaurants and shops and turns, at its far end, into the Haymarket. Mark the name of that small street. It is Shaver's Place. It shows with what tenacity the old place names of London hold on. It has nothing at all to do with barbers, as its name might suggest—but a great deal to do with a habit which is inherent in the whole human race—the habit of gambling. It also marks the site of another root of Piccadilly.

There is little or no doubt that this curious name derived from Piccadilly Hall, the residence of Robert Baker, the tailor, which stood in what is now Great Windmill Street. But a little later another Piccadilly Hall arose, which has created some confusion. This second building was situated at the top of the Haymarket, on a piece of land between that thoroughfare and what is now Whitcomb Street, which rejoiced in the name of Scavenger's Close—not a very romantic name for the source of such a renowned portion of London. In 1585 it was held by a man named Thomas Wilson. It was about 3½ acres in extent and had on it two buildings—Gunpowder House and Conduit House. But a future lay before it. In 1634 there was some trouble about a famous bowling green in Spring Gardens which led to its being closed down. Bowling was then the national game of England. There was a howl of complaint and so another bowling green was made and this appears to have been on Scavenger's Close, in 1634. In those days the public bowling greens were under the control of the Lord Chamberlain. That office was then held by Philip Herbert, Earl of Pembroke. There were a lot of nice little jobs going in those distant times and one of them consisted in looking after the Bowling Greens. To do this the Earl had appointed a deputy, one Simon Osbaldeston, who was his own gentleman-barber, who no doubt profited thereby. Something had to be done for him when Spring Gardens green closed down and so the Lord Chamberlain gave him a charter dated 8th July 1635 to open another one not too far away. Osbaldeston got to work at once. He built it on Scavenger's Close and with it he built a house for refreshments and for gaming on rather more elaborate and extravagant lines than the bowling green could afford. It became known eventually as Shaver's Hall. There is a comment on this in a letter written by George Garrard to Viscount Conway in 1635. He wrote, 'It is called Shaver's Hall, as other neighbouring places hereabouts are nicknamed Tart Hall, Pickadel etc.' But Shaver's Hall was not so called because its builder was a barber. There was another reason, which will transpire.

Osbaldeston did very well, right from the beginning. He laid out £4,000—a lot of money then, and one wonders from whence he got it—probably from the Earl of Pembroke himself. There were two bowling greens and the building was on sumptuous lines. It became the resort of fashion, and the Lord Chamberlain himself went there to take part in what were described as 'great bowling matches'. High wagers were laid on the results, but the stakes were as nothing compared to those obtaining inside of Shaver's Hall. All the renowned gamblers went there, including Sir John Suckling, the poet, who was there daily. Play was high. It became known that Lord Dunbar had lost £3,000 there in one sitting and word went around town that a certain northern lord 'had been shaved pretty close'. Thereby probably came the name of Shaver's Hall, although it is possible that the fact that its proprietor was a barber lent extra colour to the story. But that name did not last long, as attached to the building. It blossomed out into an 'ordinary' renowned for its excellent fare, and then it was called Piccadilly Hall, maybe after Baker's house, not far away. It was so called in 1641, because there is an account of it extant which says, 'Mr Hyde, going to a place called Piccadilly, which was a fair house for entertainment and gaming, with handsome gravel walks with shade and where were an upper and lower bowling green, whither very many of the nobility and gentry of the best quality resorted both for exercise and conversation, as soon as he came into the garden the Earl of Bedford came to him, who told him he was glad he was come hither for there was a friend of his on the lower ground who needed his counsel.' The place flourished, both as bowling green, gaming house and ordinary. Osbaldeston paid £4 per annum as rent and 18/6d. as rates. That would shake some of the tenants on the spot today. It grew in popularity as time passed by; tennis courts were added —not lawn tennis but the original game—and there was a shady orchard. The house was beautified and enriched, Piccadilly Hall or Shaver's Hall, inside its outer walls, was an oasis of verdure with well gravelled paths, green lawns, shady trees and opportunities for all sorts of amusement. The banqueting hall of the 'ordinary' was said to be very fine. And to the majority of people it was Piccadilly Hall. Its boundaries were the Haymarket, and what are now Coventry, Whitcomb and Panton Streets.

You would search in vain for any trace of verdure there today and the hundreds who work in the offices and shops now covering this once pleasant resort have no idea what it was once like. A man named Geares took over from Osbaldeston and made even more improvements but it would seem that the growing power of the Puritans brought about its end, for soldiers were quartered in Piccadilly Hall and nobody appears to have succeeded Geares as proprietor. But, in 1664, Colonel Thomas Panton purchased the property. No doubt he knew it well for he was an inveterate gambler. He had one enormously lucky scoop which enriched him to such an extent that, like a wise man, he foreswore the tables from then on. He announced that he wanted to build what he called 'a fair street of good buildings between the Haymarket and Hedge Lane'. Some troublesome local rules held him up but the matter was referred to Sir Christopher Wren, who said he thought it a good idea, so Panton got his way. He built his street, which is called Panton Street after him to this day. And at the rear of the premises occupied by L. & H. Nathan, the premier theatrical costumiers of the world, there is a portion of a building which is surely the stabling belonging to the original street, and part of their own building is 17th century, too. Nathan's have every right to be of the Piccadilly People. Their original home was in Titchfield Street and later, in Coventry Street. The firm started in Titchfield Street, now part of Piccadilly Circus, in the latter half of the 18th century and have been within a stone's throw of Piccadilly ever since. They are one of the oldest firms in the Piccadilly neighbourhood and they maintain that quality, too.

Panton got a licence to build from Sir Christopher Wren, a condition of which was 'no brew houses, melting houses or other noisome trades must be allowed'. And Panton Street perpetuates his name—that of a soldier gambler who built well and enriched the neighbourhood. He did not pull down Piccadilly—or Shaver's Hall—although he purchased it. It was occupied then by a famous man, Henry Coventry, who was for a long time Secretary of State for Charles II. He addressed all his letters from Piccadilly Hall, and he bought property around it, so the road in front of his dwelling became Coventry Street as it remains today—one of the principal arteries leading into Piccadilly Circus.

Nobody plays tennis there now, although even that was possible until just before the First World War, nor do they play bowls. On the site of Piccadilly Hall arose shops and flats in one of which lived Paul Rubens, who enriched our musical comedy stage with such delightful scores as *Miss Hook of Holland* and many more. And, in Coventry Street and next door neighbour to that site, is a theatre—The Prince of Wales'. Old customs die hard, and cling to places which have been associated with them for centuries. There are cafés and snack bars on the site today, and the foreigners who serve in them know nothing of Piccadilly Hall, nor for the matter of that do the customers. And as for gaming, well, just across the road there is a Pleasure Arcade, with games of chance, shooting machines and pin tables. It is a mechanised form of gambling to suit a mechanised world. You can ge your photograph taken there for a passport—an impossibility in the days of Henry Coventry. But that place marks what old timers regard as a downward step in London's West End. And for many years another sport could be practised in Coventry Street, right against that old home of games and gaming. For under the Prince of Wales' Theatre was a shooting alley, of considerable antiquity and said to be the one on which Dickens based his description of that run by 'Mr George', in *Bleak House*. It was quite a busy prosperous place and many people found time to keep their eye in with rifle and revolver. I was a regular customer. I happen to be a good shot with gun or pistol. Many of my targets, which showed what are known as 'highest possibles' (every shot in the bullseye), were displayed in the street level window of that range. And although the place was not a source of income to me, it used to bring me extras. I frequented the bar of Challis's Buffet, just across the road, and also the West End Hotel, almost its next door neighbour. My friends liked to make little matches, pitting me against boastful casual customers. When the American Forces came to Town in the First World War, I was back in circulation in the West End—carrying on my own profession and a war job too. The Yanks would be encouraged to talk of their shooting prowess, to boast that they were the best and quickest shots in the world. My pals would make a match and we would all go down to the underground range. You would be surprised how many rounds of drinks—and also lunches—I won from American warriors, who were dumbfounded to find that an effete Limey and a Cockney at that (for so they regarded me) was quicker on the draw and more accurate than any of them. I never lost a match but I doubt if it encouraged good Anglo-American relations. Alas, the shooting gallery vanished years ago.

Panton Street runs parallel with Coventry Street and it follows the line of an ancient footpath. When first built it was described as 'a good open street inhabited by tradesmen'. In George I's reign 'Hickford's Great Room' was situated there—the principal auction room of London. Hickman himself lived there. Oxendon Street runs out of Coventry Street and into Panton Street. It appeared in rate-books as early as 1675 and was said then to be a 'pretty broad and considerable street'. In 1717 the Countess of Newport lived there and so did Brigadier Panton. It still possesses some old houses. Richard Baxter, the great Nonconformist divine, had a chapel in it, against the wall of Coventry's Shaver's Hall estate. But the services he held were badly disturbed by the King's Drums, which Mr Secretary Coventry caused to be beaten under the windows. There was little toleration then for Nonconformity, especially after the Civil War. Baxter only preached there three times and then he gave the drums 'best'. His successor, Seddon, was eventually imprisoned in Westminster.

A tennis court survived the extinction of Shaver's Hall for some years. Its actual location cannot be pinpointed but it may have stood in Panton Street or in what is now Orange Street but was then James Street. Shaver's Hall held on for thirty years and had its epitaph in 1686, from Phil Porter:

> 'Farewell, my dearest Piccadilly
> Notorious for good dinners
> Oh, what a tennis court was there,
> Alas, too good for sinners'

But the tradition of amusement and eating seem to have gone deep into the soil. Although the Piccadilly 'ordinary' vanished, the trade of refreshment went on and goes on today. There is the

Comedy Restaurant in Panton Street, good food at a reasonable price, although it cannot compete in this respect with the old 2/- Ordinary. And there was another celebrated eating house in Panton Street, which London lost by enemy action during the Second World War. This was Stone's—one of the last of the famous chop-houses of London. Founded in the early 18th century, it always maintained its tradition, its atmosphere and the quality of its fare. It had no outside display, only its ancient frontage. Nor was it very spacious and it spent little or nothing on what is now known as 'decor'. But its atmosphere was beyond price. It had been built up by the passing centuries. People would describe it as 'Dickensian' but it was far older than that. It disregarded the passing of time and outside it, right up to the end, stood a couple of buckets of water for the refreshment of the horses, once so numerous but by the time Stone's itself vanished almost extinct in Panton Street and most other places. You could have your food, excellent and splendidly cooked, either at the bar or in the Coffee Room. If you chose the bar, there were a few tables in the window but mostly you sat at the bar itself, on stools, and, because of its numerous customers, packed elbow to elbow. But it was odds-on that you knew your neighbour.

You were served by 'Tommy' who had genuine Titian-colour hair and came from Wales. Nobody ever knew her other name, she was just 'Tommy'. She wore a perpetual smile but she seldom spoke. She took your order in silence, she served you in silence. She hardly ever indulged in a little chat. That smile served and was eloquent—it could express almost every emotion she was called upon to show. It had many variations. She never made a mistake, she never served the wrong dish or drink. Great people of the theatre and music hall, of the law, art, literature, of the world of sport and of Fleet Street, she served them all alike. She had no favourites, but she herself was a great favourite with her customers; perhaps because she seldom talked. If you went into the Coffee Room, that was another matter. That was very quiet as compared with the chatter in the bar and it was not by any means so democratic. For when you ate in the bar, you often sat along-side cabmen, and working men, but nobody minded that. It was all part of the democracy of Stone's. The customers of the Coffee Room were on a higher social level, and again you would find representatives of every art, and of commerce (in the higher ranks), sport and journalism. Actors abounded. But it was a purely masculine place—no lady took refreshment at Stone's. You sat in high-backed oaken pews and you were served by Charles, a waiter in whom that specialist in waiters, Charles Dickens, would have delighted. He was a personification of the English waiter at his very best, tall, dark, good-looking in a Victorian way and very taciturn. Like 'Tommy' (who never penetrated into the Coffee Room) Charles wore a perpetual smile, not nearly so broad or cheerful as that of 'Tommy'—but a half smile which seemed to express amused tolerance for the world and mankind, and was half hidden below his dark moustache. His hair was plentiful and curly, his manner extremely dignified. There was no hurry or bustle about Charles—yet he never kept anyone waiting. He did not so much walk as progress and at a perfectly uniform rate. If you yourself were pressed for time, it was no use trying to hurry him up. You took your turn, as soon as you had given him your order. And he served by rotation. It did not follow however that you got what you had ordered. If you were a 'regular' of whom he approved (and he did not approve of all his 'regulars') he brought you what he thought you ought to have. It was nothing to order roast mutton and onion sauce and to find a plate of crisp fried plaice before you. It was Charles's way of telling you that, in his opinion, the mutton was not so good, but the plaice was excellent. And one must not forget the green peas which Stone's served, in season. They were not frozen or processed, they were genuine garden peas. I have never seen such large ones, nor of such a perfect colour. They were heaven to consume. Nobody ever discovered from whence they came, but you never saw their like elsewhere. Charles moved as if in a dream, in a world of his own. The slight smile was either one of tolerant pity for those who were outside the world in which he lived—or arose from some amusing reverie in which he was wrapped.

In all the years I knew him I only saw him laugh once and that was when my dear old friend Robert Hale, the comedian, egged on by Dr Bulloch, an eminent literary man and habitué of Stone's, gave a wonderful impersonation of a Yorkshire character named Bob Cutting, a specialist in fur and feather, who knew every rabbit and pigeon at shows by sight and all about them. Robert Hale's impersonation was so brilliant that even Charles stopped to watch and listen, and when the show reached a climax he rewarded the performer with a loud laugh. The whole Coffee Room applauded. Charles was in this world but not of it. Stone's maybe was real, but the rest of us were just ghosts. On his way to work, when not in his dress clothes, he affected a straw hat matured by the sun and rain of many seasons and he passed along Panton Street as a thing apart—almost a Procession of One.

All the public rooms of Stone's were spotlessly clean. That essentially masculine domain, was nevertheless run by a manageress, a spinster. Her name was Miss Herbert. She was tall and always dressed in unrelieved black except for a row of incredibly large imitation pearls round her throat. She was very, very pale, with a yellowish tinge like old parchment, and she had big teeth which were very white. She stood no nonsense from anyone—a noisy drunk wilted before her mere look and departed as speedily as he could. To get a smile from her showed that you were a person of importance in her estimation. And she reckoned importance not in terms of social standing or success but entirely in terms of good behaviour. When the First World War broke out and many of her customers joined the Forces, she wrote them long letters of good advice, friendly encouragement and religious admonition. She also sent them cigarettes which were even more acceptable.

Stone's is to rise again, but although doubtless the tradition of good food will endure it won't be possible to find a Charles, a Tommy or a Miss Herbert.

And almost opposite Stone's stands the Comedy Theatre, which dates from 1881. Great plays of all kinds and great performers shone there. Fred Leslie rose to fame as 'Rip Van Winkle', W. S. Penley, Ada Rehan, Arthur Dacre, Arthur Roberts, Kate Rorke, Marie Tempest, Winifred Emery, Cyril Maude, Charles Hawtrey all played there. It was at the Comedy that the great Herbert Beerbohm Tree started his actor-managerial career with *The Red Lamp* in 1887. Gerald Du Maurier played *Raffles* there. And once, when it had struck a bad patch, there came another actor-manager named Lewis Waller who staged a romantic costume play entitled *Monsieur Beaucaire*. This left ineradicable memories in the minds of all who saw it. Lewis Waller was the finest romantic actor the world has ever known—and just as fine a Shakespearean. Naturally he put the Comedy on its feet again, and it plays on today. Its manager in the old days was a great character. His name on the bills was Arthur Chudleigh but was in reality Lillies. He took his stage name from that lovely place Chudleigh in Devon near which he was born. He was a true Devonian, courageous, resourceful, adventurous and invincible. He was in many tight corners but he always came out on top. He was supposed to be deaf, but he always heard what was not intended for his ear. He had a large clean-shaven fresh complexioned face, a perky demeanour and a great sense of humour. When running the Court Theatre he disagreed with his partner over the production of a play but was over-ruled. On the first night, in high dudgeon, he went and stood at the back of the gallery. The gallery booed the play and Chudleigh, delighted to have his judgment endorsed, booed as heartily as any of them. To his friends he was 'Chuddles'. He loved horse racing and would go to meetings with his friend Walter Hackett, the American dramatist, riding in Hackett's big Daimler. He would shout at pedestrians as they scurried to the pavement, 'Get out of the way of the rich.' Yet his worldly wealth was probably an overdraft. Once in that same car he arrived at Honiton in his native county. A great crowd stood staring at a platform and harassed officials dashed about—the man who was to address that meeting had not turned up. Chudleigh arrived in the big Daimler. An official, imagining him to be the tardy speaker, seized him and took him on the platform. Chudleigh was not at a loss. He made a long and impassioned speech—knowing nothing of the subject for which that meeting had been called. He roused his audience into enthusiasm, and then got into the car and drove away, thoroughly satisfied with his morning. There are no characters like that today.

Panton Street also held Wisharts, a famous tobacconist's which made a most delectable pipe mixture and from Whitcomb Street, a tributary, has just departed 'The Lord Belgrave', whose steaks were world famous. You picked your own and you could watch it being cooked. But we must return to Coventry Street, the direct approach to Piccadilly. It is a short street but an important one. It is indeed, almost Piccadilly. In fact a newspaper seller who worked there up to a short time ago was certain that it was Piccadilly. He would say to visitors enquiring the way, 'Piccadilly? Why, you are in it. This is Piccadilly.' He could not be persuaded to the contrary. But Coventry Street links Leicester Square to Piccadilly—which really begins at the top end of the Haymarket and the lower end of Windmill Street. It was—up to the end of the First World War, a smart and 'best dressed street' as became a Piccadilly approach. It contained much in its short space and all of the best. It has a theatre—the Prince of Wales—a hotel which had been a club—The Motor Club and then The Engineers' Club, and Fanum House, the headquarters of the Automobile Association, which stretches into Leicester Square. And there are plenty of places where one can eat, from small snack bars to large cafés and Lyons Corner House. Once the Globe Restaurant stood in Coventry Street until 1911, where the food and wines were excellent and the company often included quite a few ladies of the town. Sometimes the lights failed (quite unaccountably) and there were real fun and games in the temporary darkness and some surprising scenes when the darkness vanished.

On this site was built the present Rialto Cinema, above ground. During the First World War the Rialto was run by a wealthy and patriotic gentleman named Sexton, who displayed great banners across the frontage bearing the device 'Tommy and Jack, God Bless You', and who gave free admission to all Service men in uniform. The basement below the cinema became the most expensive, if not the most exclusive, restaurant in town, called the Café de Paris. Great international stars appeared in its cabarets. A bomb struck it in the Second World War and the casualties were many, including a famous American band leader, but it survived and opened again. It was never quite the same, for the age of extravagant spending was passing but in its later days Noël Coward and the fabulous Liberace have appeared there. It is still open, but not quite on the old and extravagant scale.

The eastern boundary of Coventry Street is Wardour Street, which takes its name from Sir Edward Wardour who built it on a site known as Doghouse Close and for a time it was called Edward Street. It was not completely finished until 1720. The other northern tributary of Coventry Street is Rupert Street, named after that dashing Royalist cavalry leader, Prince Rupert of the Rhine, who also lived thereabouts and who in his advanced years and after a bachelor life fell a victim to the charms of Margaret Hughes, the first actress to appear on the English stage. That lady took all his wealth from him and he died as a result a poor man.

On the corner of Rupert Street there stood another place of refreshment in Victorian and Edwardian days—Challis's Hotel, famous for good food and good company—a kind of informal Bohemian Club for the artistic and theatrical night side of London. It was a delightful resort but it got swallowed up when Lyons Corner House arose. Its name endured even then for in Rupert Street there was a bar—part of the Corner House—which was still called Challis's Buffet. That too became a sort of unofficial club, carrying on the old atmosphere. It was a microcosm of London although most of its customers were 'regulars'. It was a place I knew well. For some happy years it was presided over by two super barmaids called 'Darkie' and 'Brownie' who knew everybody. Its customers were all characters, ranging from really celebrated people to jockeys, bookmakers and their clerks. There were plenty of music hall stars to be seen in Challis's and notable and most regular amongst them was Tom Stuart, a splendid burlesque artist and an Irishman of charm. He suffered from a complaint which he diagnosed as 'Depression' for which the only sure and speedy cure was a very constant succession of 'double Scotches'; he got them in Challis's. He had a great sense of humour and drink was a thing he took seriously, as other people might devote their attention to science or the arts. Another great figure in Challis's was John Humphries, of music hall, revue and pantomime fame. He was known as 'Fat and Artful' and never was a nickname better conferred. He would come into the bar in rather a clumsy manner, and always seemed to bounce off the side of the door. Tom Stuart gave a wonderful impersonation of him. He would then sit at the bar and either Brownie or Darkie gave him his 'usual'—he never had to ask—a double Scotch and small ginger ale. Friends would come in and ask him to 'have one' and John would say, 'Oh, it's very kind of you—just a small one in here'—indicating his glass—and in it would go. That glass never appeared to be empty; even in the whisky shortage of World War One it was like the widow's cruse, and John never appeared the worse. He was a man of gargantuan appetite and he mostly ate at Stone's. Tom Stuart said he ate the bone and all; he certainly had a prodigious appetite which never seemed satisfied. Ted Ransom, London representative for a celebrated brand of whisky, was always in Challis's; he was a little dapper man, Puck personified. He was never happy except when making some sort of mischief—never malicious and always funny—and was one of the most artistic practical jokers of all time. There was another regular whose real name never materialised. He was a tall, dark and rather distinguished looking man—although he had only one eye—well read and well educated at Blundell's School, but in Challis's he was known as 'Mr Usher', because he drank only Usher's Green Stripe whisky. The prices at Challis's would seem fabulously cheap today. Any brand of Scotch was 3d. a go, and a splash of soda was free. I once caused a sensation in there by ordering the most expensive drink they had—a Grand Marnier—which cost me ninepence. The bar was hushed—they regarded me as a millionaire. There was a most popular aperitif sold there known as a 'Cherry Mixture'. This was some concoction of sherry and vermouth I suppose with a cherry in it. I never found out although I drank many of them. It was not unpleasant although there was a lurking suspicion of hair oil in the flavour, but it cost only threepence and was in great demand. It was especially beloved by dear Leslie Henson, that great comedian now passed away. Brownie and Darkie looked after their customers and even when during the First World War whisky was almost unobtainable they managed to supply their regular customers, although they had many battles with John Humphries who always wanted more than his ration. And when the Armistice came on 11th November 1918 most of us made a beeline for Challis's. Such was the demand to celebrate peace that the place ran dry except for some Madeira, and we soon drank that up. And we had Brownie and Darkie dancing on top of the bar, too. That was a real day of celebration.

Challis's did me a very good turn once. The man for whom I worked, who became Sir George Dance, wanted to have a writ served on another big theatrical manager who owed him a lot of money but could not be found. I was ordered to find him. I always got the hard jobs and when you worked for Dance you had to emulate the gallant 600—yours not to reason why, yours but to do or die. The debtor had just been married and the story was that he had gone for a world tour with his bride. Dance did not believe it. I was sent to find him. I spent all of a boiling hot day in August in that search. I employed all sorts of tricks and devices—but I drew blank. This was serious. I got back to Coventry Street about four in the afternoon, worn out, weary and very thirsty. In those good old days the pubs were open all day long. I dropped into Challis's for a cool dock glass of lager, which cost three-halfpence. I sat sipping the liquid and wondering what sort of a reception I should get from Dance when I reported failure. It was not a pleasant prospect. A man I knew came in, looking very sunburnt, We greeted each other and I asked him if he had been away. 'Just up for the day on business, old boy,' he said, 'going back tonight. I am staying at the Felix Hotel, Felixstowe and, by the way, there is a man in your profession there.' I enquired whom this might be and—great heavens—it was the very man of whom I was in search. I thanked my friend, bought him a drink and sped back in triumph to the office in Leicester Square. I did not say where I had got the information, for Mr Dance had a hatred of bars, but the next day the writ was served, and I got the kudos. Challis's has gone now and on its site stands a restaurant known as the Wimpey. I can see it from my office. I watched in sorrow as they took away the old doors which had been there in Challis's day; another link with the gayer past was severed.

The Corner House has spread over a curious little corner of London which was known as Arundell Place, named after Henry, 3rd Lord Arundell of Wardour—so do the names of the old nobility endure. Cabmen were always most meticulous to call it 'Arun-*dell* Place'. It was a strange little backwater, on the Coventry Street corner of which stood a lovely old shop with its original Georgian frontage—Lambert's, the silversmiths—where lovely things were displayed and there was always some remarkable Sheffield plate. Arundell Place was a cul-de-sac but it contained some old Georgian houses, privately inhabited in those days and at the far end there was actually a tennis court (lawn tennis however) which carried on that tennis tradition of Shaver's Place. In that nook you seemed far from Piccadilly. And although small Arundell Place contained three hotels: the Previtali, the Mathis and the West End. The first two catered largely for South American visitors to London, they even supplied guides and interpreters and did very well. The West End was different. The wine was good, the food was good and the company was good, if you were out on a 'binge'. Everybody enjoyed himself in the gay, free and easy atmosphere. There was a strange thing about the West End. You could always pick up—literally— a lady's handbag there; often quite a new one. Outside the hotel was an area with a railing and down that area light-fingered gentry who had snatched handbags and got away with them would throw the bag after rifling it. There was always a large selection. The best part of the West End was the downstairs bar, presided over by 'Bunnie'—one of London's extra-super barmaids and a great character. No matter what went on upstairs she maintained discipline and good order in her bar. She knew everything about everybody but was discretion itself. No secret ever leaked from her. She was most particular whom she served. If she did not like a customer, out he went. I heard her once tell the notorious Horatio Bottomley that she did not want him in her bar—she preferred his room to his company. He went like a lamb. Ladies, even if accompanied by gentlemen, were not served in Bunnie's bar. One day a lady of the town fell downstairs into the bar. The waiter rushed to turn her out. 'No ladies served here', he declared. The fallen lady—in every sense—laughed. 'Lady?' she said, 'What do you think I am? I'm no lady, I'm "on the game" and I want a brandy and soda.' She got it.

There was, in Coventry Street, one of the finest stationers in London, called Mudie's. The goods were superlative and the manager was a man named John Goulden. A quiet man, with a ruddy face, he knew his job and he knew his customers. Smart, slick gentlemen would come in and want to order curious packs of cards or dice which always fell the same way up 'for a new game,' they would explain. Mr Goulden knew all about them and they got no satisfaction. His happiest days were spent fishing and, off duty, he wore a tweed hat with 'flies' hooked in it. He was also a regular at Challis's, where his country complexion and his fair moustache were well known. But there was always a day in his year when he put on his best clothes and went down to see Queen Mary with a selection of Mudie's new and best lines, from which she selected many of her Christmas presents.

On the opposite side of the way is still the Prince of Wales Theatre. It is rebuilt and modern now, but then it was in keeping with Victorian days, with a canopy across the pavement from which hung baskets of flowers and ferns. This was built and opened in 1884 by Edgar Bruce, a great man of the theatre, and it had—and has—a most distinguished and successful career. Beerbohm Tree laid the foundations of his fame there—Mrs Langtry was there, and there that lovely thing *L'Enfant Prodigue* was produced with Jane May and Zanfretta in the cast. It knew Marie Tempest and all the great ones and it staged many famous musical plays including *La Poupée*. It reached its peak under the management of Frank Curzon—a theatrical manager who was a great sportsman and who eventually won the Derby with Call Boy. Curzon produced many musical successes at the Prince of Wales, many composed by Paul Rubens, with Isobel Jay (Mrs Frank Curzon) who could act well, sing like an angel and was a very beautiful woman, as leading lady. Such things as *Miss Hook of Holland, Dear Little Denmark, The King of Cadonia, The Balkan Princess* and others will be remembered gratefully by an older generation. And there too, tall, very handsome and extremely masculine Bertram Wallis set every female heart awhirl—the matinee idol of matinee idols. Later, that great comedian Sid Field burst upon London at the Prince of Wales, and we must be thankful that it is still a theatre today. It was the brother of Frank Curzon, manager of the Prince of Wales—Mr Mallaby Deely—who built the Piccadilly Hotel. The Prince of Wales is Coventry Street's jewel box of memories.

One peculiarity of Coventry Street was, and still is, that no buses run along it. Yet it links Leicester Square with Piccadilly Circus. And Coventry Street was a famous beat for the Ladies of the Town. They started their promenade at Hippodrome Corner —at the other end of Leicester Square, they crossed the Square, they went the length of Coventry Street as far as the London Pavilion and then they turned and went back. They never crossed the Circus or turned into Shaftesbury Avenue. Those places belonged to others of their sisterhood. They never trespassed—it was a tribal law.

Coventry Street in Victorian and Edwardian days was a smart street of Quality—in shops, restaurants and in people. The men were all well dressed and looked happy. They had golden sovereigns in their pockets and they knew nothing of war or bombs. London was an enchanted place and they savoured it to the full. At about eleven, it suddenly was packed with folk in evening dress who came out of the Prince of Wales Theatre. Some walked to their supping place, some rode in their carriages and later in their cars, and some rode in hansoms, or taxis when they took over from the horse cabs. It was however a very English street and essentially West End. The few foreigners were easily placed—either visitors to London or else those employed in the hotels and restaurants about the neighbourhood. Today, you hear more foreign tongues than English. It seems as if the English have been dispossessed. I look at it from my window and I marvel at the change my eyes have seen. I hardly know the place at all, but I summon up my memories and I see it as it was when I knew it and loved it, before the guns of the First World War brought about such a shattering alteration in the whole globe. And I can see, across the road, that sign on the wall which says 'Shaver's Place' and that takes me, rather gratefully, back to the beginnings of Coventry Street. For London has a habit of holding on in odd ways and those who know the signs can gather comfort that, however much it changes outwardly, it is still London underneath.

John Nash

Maskelyne

and Devant

13

Haymarket Highlights

This famous street, one of the most celebrated in London, first appears in the rate books, as such, in 1657. At that time there were about thirty-five houses in it. There is a mention of it, as a street, in 1661, when a Colonel Edward Harley had a horse 'at Mr Baxter's stables in the Haymarket, near Piccadilly'. Evelyn records that in 1662 he sat with the Commissioners about reforming buildings and streets in London and 'we ordered the paving of the Haymarket and about Piquidillo'. But there are references to a market there as far back as the days of Queen Elizabeth I and in 1642, Sir John Suckling wrote:

> 'At Charing Cross, hard by the way
> Where we, thou know'st, do sell our hay.'

In 1660, Robert Kilvert, who lived in Piccadilly, petitioned to be granted the office of weigher of hay and straw at Charing Cross Market. Charing Cross as a district had a wider significance then than is realised now; it embraced all that is now Trafalgar Square and part of Whitehall, and would probably stretch to what is now the Haymarket. But the Haymarket justified the latter end of its title if not the first, in April 1663 when the Earl of St Albans, who owned the land hereabouts, got a grant for a cattle market to be held in the Haymarket twice a week. In 1681 it was recorded that a market had been kept in the Haymarket for many years past, every Tuesday, Thursday and Saturday—that being the high road from the Mews—now the site of the National Gallery —and Piccadilly. According to an Act of Parliament the profits should have gone to repair and upkeep of the roads—but the Act had lapsed or been repealed in some way and the streets had decayed and become wellnigh impassable. Eventually one Edward Warcup got the market grant, on condition that he kept the place paved and in repair.

The wealthy and distinguished residents of the neighbourhood did not like the market at all. Henry Coventry himself opposed the grant. But the market went on and was subject to several Acts of Parliament and in 1697 it was actually paved. The Haymarket was then bounded by Shaver's Hall at its top end and beyond that by land walled in and belonging to the Earl of Suffolk which included what is now Orange Street, Suffolk Street and Suffolk Place. A water supply was laid on in 1665 and by 1682 the Hay-market was practically built.

It was mainly a business street, as might be expected from the market, and it had numerous inns. 'The King's Head' was described in 1675 as 'a large place for stabling and coaches'. On the corner of James Street was Paulet's Ordinary, 'much resorted to by the nobility and gentry'. Those were on the eastern side, whilst on the western side there was a noted hostelry called 'The Phoenix' and also 'The Nag's Head' which stood on the corner of Norris Street. There were also private residents of distinction: the Earl of Lincoln, Lady Fitzhardinge, the Duchess of Devonshire (in 1710), Sir William Wyndham and the Duke of Dorset (in 1716). There were other hostelries and pubs besides those mentioned above. It was in the Waterloo Tavern, which stood on the corner of what is now King Charles II Street, that the fatal malady of the great Dan Leno was first noticed, to be made clear at Her Majesty's Theatre just across the way. But the pubs have lessened as the years increased. 'The Waterloo' is no longer there, nor are

'The White Horse', 'The Black Horse' (a landlord of which was hanged for murder), 'The Cock', mentioned by Pepys, which stood just round the corner in Suffolk Street, 'The Unicorn' and 'The Blue Posts', a most notorious house which Otway mentions in one of his plays and which keeps cropping up in old records because of the constant affrays and fights which took place in it. It was actually at No. 59 Haymarket. The western side was riddled with dark little alleys of ill repute. King Charles II Street was a mere passage then, known as Six Bell Alley. And not all the notable residents of the Haymarket were titled folk. Addison lodged in an attic over a small shop and there he wrote 'The Campaign'. Sir Samuel Garth, the celebrated physician, was a Haymarket man, and Anne Oldfield, the famous actress discovered by George Farquhar in a tavern in what is now Piccadilly Circus, who rose to queen it at Drury Lane and now lies in Westminster Abbey; she lay in state in the Jerusalem Chamber there before burial. And the Haymarket was the birthplace of George Morland, the great artist.

There is a public house today at the corner of Jermyn Street, which covers the site of the old 'Black Horse'. In Edwardian days it had a splendid snack bar unequalled in London. The food was wonderful and you could have anything you wanted, all of the finest quality. There was always a huge china bowl of hard boiled eggs, at 1d. each. This bar was presided over by a master of his trade whose name was Arthur. He had the most famous smile in the whole of London—he won a prize for it from the *Evening News*. It was perfectly natural to him, not assumed for business purposes, and it made the sun shine on the blackest winter day. I am glad to report that he now holds a very responsible position in his calling—and I don't doubt that he still smiles. That snack bar is still there and still as good as ever, although times have altered the prices. Presiding over it is a man whose name is Charles Edward Stuart—namesake of the Young Pretender. He is no pretender— he knows his job, his customers and how to look after them. The way he makes a sandwich gives it an additional flavour. He is not a young man but he keeps alive the Edwardian quality, and so does his cheery assistant Len. The saloon of which that bar is part is now a comfortable lounge and the company who frequent it are all decent people. You will find many ladies there, who are not professionally employed. But in the older days it was a different place. The main bar stood in the middle, in circular form. It was always crowded and the mixture was of the strangest. Good class honest people rubbed shoulders, unwittingly for the most part, with half the crooks in London, from prosperous looking and well dressed 'con' men down to shabby and needy grafters, screevers, mumpers—the lot. There was a man to be found there who would arrange any sort of desperate deed required at statutory charges. There were some 'noses' there too, yet it all looked so respectable and was so quiet. One of the barmaids had her hand-bag stolen and told the police. The Force, being fully aware of the sort of people using the place told her to come to Scotland Yard and look at some photos. She might recognise the man who had robbed her. She went, and was shown the pictures in the Black Museum. She fainted. So many of them were her regular customers. That is all changed today and you could take your Victorian grandmother there.

The Haymarket is very greatly changed and has always been changing. But it is still possible to see what it was like in the 18th century because a piece of that century still lingers there—for our delight. It stands there as the shop of Fribourg and Treyer, the famous cigar, tobacco and snuff firm, which has been there unchanged in quality and surroundings since 1720. Those delightful premises and the house next door keep the old Haymarket alive and to those who have a feeling for the past, Fribourg and Treyer's is the loveliest shop in London. The building next door, a Victorian affair, which now has a restaurant on the ground floor, was once a block of residential flats. For a time Paul Rubens, never moving far from his beloved Prince of Wales Theatre, lived there. One night, he went from there to a dinner. During the meal a melody came into his head. Quickly and surreptitiously he pencilled a few notes on the stiff starched cuff of his dress shirt, to remind him. He then devoted himself to his social duties and forgot all about the tune. But when he awoke next morning, he remembered. He called his valet and wanted the shirt on the cuff of which was the core of the melody. The man's face fell. The laundry had called early and he had sent the shirt. Paul Rubens leapt out of bed. It must be recovered at all costs! The valet sped by cab to the laundry and was able to rescue that music decked shirt just as it was going into the tub. He brought it back, in relief and triumph. Rubens wrote the melody from those rough notes —it was one of his most famous songs and one of the loveliest— 'I Love the Moon'. It may surprise moderns to know that laundries in those times called every day—and returned the wash on the day following. Right into Victorian times the back streets around the Haymarket had a most unsavoury reputation which was well deserved. To a large degree it was a foreign quarter. Dope dens, illicit gambling houses and brothels abounded. It was in one of those dens that the amazing journalist George Augustus Sala received the blow on his nose which spread it all over his face and made it always a bright, shining red. Not that he cared.

The Haymarket has been constantly altering its appearance since 1897. It is now a very handsome and mainly Edwardian street. It went down in sections and it must be admitted that finer buildings arose. But there are some things which are missed: in Edwardian days some of the shops there still followed the fine old custom of having craftsmen at work in the window. There was an expert who stitched saddles in the window of Sowters—a well-known saddlery firm—and across the road in the old windows of Loewe and Co.—perhaps the most celebrated makers of tobacco pipes in the world—a very skilled craftsman named Bloom sat there and practised his art, sending a beaming smile from time to time at the crowd which always found time to watch him. He was an Austrian by birth but had spent almost all his life in this country and it had no more loyal citizen than he. Loewe's is still in the Haymarket but further up towards Piccadilly Circus, in more modern setting but still as famous for the pipes, which were mostly made in a factory in Lexington Street and which went all over the world from that Haymarket show-room.

But the great glory of the Haymarket lay in its three theatres, two of which still fly their flags nobly. It had another theatre later, the Carlton, which became a cinema and as these lines are being written is going back to being a theatre again. Its career as a play-house was very short; maybe times will change again. The other Haymarket cinema has been closed for some time. But the Haymarket is noble theatrical soil. Its first theatre arose on the site of the above-mentioned Phoenix Inn, and was built by no less a person than Sir John Vanbrugh himself, but the address which described it was humble indeed—'The second stable yard on the left going up the Haymarket.' Vanbrugh was backed in his enter-prise by £30,000, subscribed by 300 people at the rate of £100 each of whom had also the right of free entry to any and every performance if he so desired. It was called 'The Queen's Theatre', out of compliment to Queen Anne, and its foundation stone was laid by Lady Sunderland, a very beautiful woman and Marl-borough's daughter. That was in 1703. The theatre actually opened in 1705. Ill luck dogged it from the start. Despite the fact that its leading man was the great Thomas Betterton, it failed as a theatre. It would seem that Vanbrugh had paid too much atten-tion to decoration and not enough to more important things. The acoustics were terrible. Nobody could hear what was said on the stage. After further tribulations it became an Opera House, the first one this country had known. Opera had been performed, of course, but no theatre had been dedicated to it. The operas were not very good, indeed they were crude. Plays came back with no success and then opera reigned again. But in 1708 things got better and there arrived a singer of note, the Italian Nicolini. The very English English of those days had got a bit tired of listening to a language which they did not understand, but Nicolini's voice charmed them. In 1710 a German, who was

Chapel Master to George I in Hanover was invited to England. His name was George Frederick Handel. Aaron Hill, a playwright and also manager of The Queen's Theatre, asked him to write an opera and on 24th February 1711, Handel's first opera, *Rinaldo*, was produced, in the Haymarket. It succeeded and ran fifteen nights. Nicolini sang in it and appears to have been as good an actor as a singer—but still failure dogged the Queen's. The name was changed to the King's Theatre and many of Handel's works were done there. Male soprani—the castrati—were then in great favour. Operatic stars sang and waged war on each other, their admirers taking sides and creating polite riots. Then Heideggar, bandmaster to King George I and said to be the ugliest man in London—held some successful masquerades there. In 1720 a Royal Academy of Music was established at the King's, for which Handel was engaged to compose operas. The whole thing was a ghastly failure and £15,000—a very big sum then—was lost by the end of the year and by 1728 the enterprise closed down having lost £50,000. Yet it was at the King's, in the Haymarket, that the first oratorio ever heard in England was sung—Handel's *Esther*, in 1731, and in the next year, at the same theatre, came his *Acis and Galatea*.

The years went on, great names came and went, but always money was lost. One notable event was the production of Dr Arne's *Artaxerxes* in 1762. Vanbrugh's theatre, which was when first built the second oldest in London, junior only to Drury Lane, was burnt down in 1789 and the loss was estimated at £73,000. It was said that the fire was caused by the leader of the orchestra who had a grudge against the management. Instead of leaving it alone, they built another Opera House—also called the King's—which opened on 26th March 1791 and at first encountered many difficulties. All the great names in opera sang there and all the fashionables attended, but money was always lost. Ballet grew to fame there under Vestris, and his wife, the celebrated Madame Vestris sang there too. Still money was lost. When Queen Victoria came to the throne there was a slight improvement; the greatest singers appeared, and the great composers conducted, Rossini amongst them. Madame Sontag was a great draw. One of the most exciting events however was the London debut of Jenny Lind, the Swedish Nightingale, in 1847. Momentarily the place made a profit. Titiens was another great success. Fire struck again and destroyed the building in 1867, but it was rebuilt, for hope springs eternal in the breast of operatic impresarii. It was now called Her Majesty's Theatre and, alternatively, the Royal Italian Opera. It was a gigantic building which overlapped into Pall Mall and what is now King Charles II Street. Again failure dogged it although one of the earliest troupes of nigger minstrels to visit this country, Haverly's Minstrels, drew royalty there. But even pantomime, the surest bet in the theatre, failed there and the place began to decay and was closed for demolition.

Across the road, at the Haymarket Theatre, a man was watching and at the right moment, he swooped. His name was Herbert Beerbohm Tree. He was then an actor-manager and he dreamed of building a theatre for himself. Here was his chance. He took half that site and the other half was used for the erection of a luxury hotel, to become world famous and named the Carlton—now alas, demolished to make room for Dominion Government buildings. Tree's dream came true. He built Her Majesty's Theatre, which he called so rightly, 'My beautiful theatre', opened it on 28th April 1897, the year of Queen Victoria's Diamond Jubilee, and made it shine like a diamond from its very opening night. He gave that lovely place a soul—his own soul. It was to all intents and purposes his home. In the dome above it he had apartments—which did not seem to be of this world. His own dictum concerning his profession was, 'The whole business of the Theatre is illusion'—and how right he was—for when the Theatre deals in illusion it prospers, when it strays into reality, it fails. That dome was a place of illusion. You were faced by a great door, like that of an ancient castle, and before you entered, you were inspected through a grille. Then you stepped

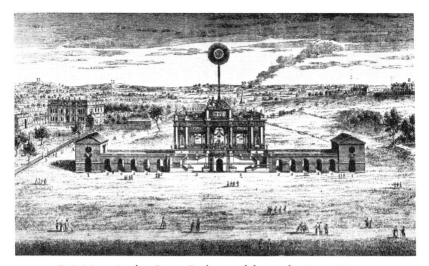

Rejoicings in the Green Park to celebrate the Peace Treaty
of Aix-la-Chapelle, 1748

Mafeking Night in Piccadilly Circus

Richard Corney Grain

into a great baronial hall; you went back in time, and there sat the master of illusion, weaving his plans and making his visions come true. He gave great banquets there in regal splendour and the greatest in the land esteemed it an honour to attend. If he entertained intimate friends, a small table was set in an alcove at the far end. Then, from somewhere behind the arras which lined the walls, would appear Mrs Brown (and nobody could cook as she did) who served a meal fit for the gods. Quails were very often served and one drank the finest burgundy, poured from a solid gold chalice crowned by an amethyst, which had been presented to Tree when he celebrated his twenty-first year as actor-manager. It was magic such as cannot be savoured today. He was one of those people born with the fever of creation in their souls. He must always be pressing on. He abhorred long runs and would take off huge, massive and successful productions to create something new. Money had no place in his mind—achievement was everything. His productions were things of grandeur and glory with magnificent settings and magnificent casts. The first night audiences too shone with brilliance. Everybody who was anybody was there; even General Booth, of the Salvation Army, would attend. When the lights dimmed down and that great dull red velvet curtain swept up, it disclosed a perfect picture such as drew forth gasps of admiration and a burst of applause. Tree's idea of illusion was to show you something which looked absolutely real, but was just painted canvas and properties which his magic touch had brought to life. Such stage pictures as the 'Garden' in *Twelfth Night*, 'The Wood Near Athens', 'The Forum in Rome', 'The Coast of Wales'—scores and scores more, have never been equalled and such things probably never will be seen again. He made his theatre the greatest repertory theatre the world has ever known, because of the number of plays, revivals and the variety of subjects which he presented to an almost bewildered public. In that all too short eighteen years in which he was spared to control his theatre he presented forty-seven new productions, almost innumerable revivals, and every Easter there was a Shakespeare Festival, with four or six of the great plays with what amounted to all star casts. And, as if that were not enough, there was the afternoon theatre at which plays which were then not considered 'box office' were seen—Ibsen and the like—because he thought the public should see them. This is not the place to give details of what he did in that wonderful theatre—which became under his guidance the foremost theatre in Europe if not in the world. He ranged from Shakespeare to light opera, farce and children's plays. Nor is it a suitable place to discuss him as an actor. He could be very bad, but he could also be magnificent. He would often miscast himself but always there was beauty and grandeur. His 'Svengali', 'Fagin', 'Falstaff', 'Malvolio', 'Colonel Newcombe', 'Isodore Isard', 'Zakkuri', 'Richard II', 'King John' and 'Mr Micawber' stand unchallenged today.

It is the man himself, that great personality of the Haymarket on which the limelight must be thrown. Those of us who were privileged to work for him called him 'the Chief', and a chief, or leader, he was, leading his people shoulder to shoulder, not standing aloof like a king. It was said of him that he was a poet who wrote without words, a painter who used no canvas, and that if he captured you you were his willing slave—all of which is true. There were of course pro-Trees and anti-Trees, for a man of his imaginative and almost impish genius was bound to cause controversy, but the pro-Trees won hands down. You could not resist him for long. His charm swept you away, and it was an effortless charm which was an integral part of him, not an assumed brilliance. Leslie Bloom, still, and for many years the President of the Gallery First Nighters' Club, the oldest playgoers' club in this country, will tell you that if he saw Sir Herbert walking down the Haymarket, he would follow him and try and put his feet exactly where those of Tree had trodden. There's richness for you. He was in every way as remarkable a man as he was an actor-manager. He was tall and somewhat stately, with a most characteristic walk, and a habit of bending one knee in upon the other when standing still. His left hand would rest on his hip, his right hand would wander in the air and speak volumes in silence. He was full of mannerisms but we accepted them as being part of himself. His eyes were pale blue and gazed into the future, but he knew everything which was happening around him. He appeared vague and mystic; that had, I think, started as a pose and then become part of him. His voice was flat and a bit guttural at times, but quite unmistakable and you never missed a word he said. At short range, his personality was overwhelming and he was the complete embodiment of the theatre. He was the acknowledged leader of his profession, the mantle of Irving descended upon him and he filled every inch of it. There has been no such leader as Tree since his death. Seymour Hicks might have worn that mantle but he preferred to have fun—and maybe he was right. Not that Tree was averse to fun—quite the contrary. He had a tremendous sense of humour. No day was any good to him unless it contained a first class joke. If one did not materialise on its own, he manufactured it himself. His power of repartee was devastating. His wit had the shine, the swiftness and, when he so desired, the deadliness of a rapier. You could never catch him out. And ninety-nine times out of a hundred, it was perfectly spontaneous. I remember he did not approve of some moonlight effects we showed him. He made us do them over and over again and still remained unsatisfied. Then he said, 'Come outside with me' and we followed him into the street. Overhead was a deep blue sky— and a wonderful silvery moon. 'There,' said the Chief—'that's all I want. Just give me that.' And we followed him back and tried again. There came a loud sigh from the Chief and he said in that most penetrative sotto voce 'aside' voice of his, 'Ah, what do they know of moonlight that only limelight know?' I rather think he had thought that one up beforehand. But mostly it came on the spur of the moment. There are countless stories about him and they are nearly all true. You could never get the better of him in argument. One afternoon between the matinee and evening show he and I walked down the Haymarket; we had been out to tea as he wanted to give me some special instructions. When he reached the theatre he stopped and, literally, swelled with pride, for the House Full boards were out. The house had been entirely sold out at the matinee and was so again for the evening. There were already enough people waiting at the pit and gallery doors to swamp even the standing room. We were playing *Twelfth Night* and it was boiling midsummer weather. Tree was in a state of delight. 'Look, look, look,' he gasped, 'House Full boards everywhere. And Shakespeare at midsummer. It couldn't happen anywhere else in the world. Wonderful, wonderful.' He was ecstatic. Across the road from the Haymarket Theatre came one of the management. Tree grabbed him, 'Look, look, Charlie my boy,' he said, 'House Full boards everywhere—for Shakespeare at midsummer. Nowhere else in the world.' 'You don't look very far, do you Chief,' said the man from the Haymarket. 'Just glance across the road—we've got 'em out too for *Bunty Pulls the Strings.*' Tree looked across. His face fell for the moment, 'Yes, yes, yes,' he murmured, 'You've got them out too. House Full for you—House Full for me. Well, well—you have got House Full boards,' —and he sent a swift glance of appraisal at both theatres—'but you haven't got as many boards as I have'—and he swept through the stage door, the undoubted victor.

His love of mischief often caused us heart throbs and anxiety, but it was impossible to be cross with him. Not only did he behave mischievously himself but he egged others on to do so. I have told many stories of him in other books but there are always fresh ones which come to memory. One night he demanded that a hansom cab be fetched. There was a rank of them down the centre of the Haymarket. That selected by the messenger came bowling round the corner to the stage door and pulled up with a flourish. Tree had demanded that the horse must be fresh, fit and capable of covering a considerable distance at top speed. He surveyed the cab and the cabby who saluted with his whip. 'Is that a good horse?' queried Tree. 'None better in London,' was the reply. 'Can it go very fast?' asked the great actor-manager, 'and for a long way?' 'You try it,' said the proud Jehu, 'why, this 'orse

won many races on the flat, governor.' 'But very fast is what I
want and for a long journey,' said Tree, still apparently in doubt.
'This is your 'orse for the job,' the driver assured him. 'Right,'
said Tree getting into the cab, 'drive like hell—to the Carlton.'
That was next door. He took a cab once but did not like the cab-
man's face. 'Where to, sir,' asked the cabby. 'Why should I tell
you where my beautiful home is situated?' demanded Tree.

I was with him once when he addressed a large assembly of
students who are never respecters of personalities or celebrities,
however great. There was a lot of noise and banter. Tree put up
his hand. 'Gentlemen, gentlemen, a little less noise, if you please.
I still have some pearls to cast.' He beat them. It was his impish
humour which made him, when alighting from the train on his
famous visit to Berlin, call out to Stanley Bell, his chief of staff,
'Stanley, Stanley, what a lot of foreigners.' His rehearsals,
especially his dress rehearsals, seemed to go on forever until he
attained the perfection for which he always strove. We snatched
sleep on the scenery, in corners—as we could. Once, and I think
once only, Stanley Bell revolted. He was starving. 'It's no use,
Chief,' he declared, 'I can't go on and I won't go on. I'm starving.
I must have something to eat. I must have my dinner.' And he
glared defiance. Tree gazed back at him, and then turned to the
company. 'Ladies and gentlemen,' he said, 'Mr Bell is hungry.
He wants his dinner.' Slight pause. 'He shall have it. With me.'
And he took Stanley to dine. We got a welcome break.

He had an amazing habit of vanishing into thin air. You might
be talking to him on the stage, and just glance at somebody.
When you looked back Tree had gone. He did this when things
were hectic and his nerves frayed. Nobody ever saw where he
went, nobody ever saw how he went or what he did whilst he
was away. It was a mystery. And one day we set a trap and made
the discovery. He would shoot through a small door, which
opened from the stage into that perfect relic of Georgian London,
the Royal Opera Arcade. In that arcade was a barber's shop—its
proprietor scorned the word 'Hairdresser'—and into that shop went

Tree. He was a constant customer—he kept hair brushes of his own there. He would sit in his usual chair and the man who always attended on him proceeded to brush his hair upwards from his head—not around it—but upwards. There Tree would sit undergoing this operation which soothed him completely until he felt better able to cope with the difficulties facing him. Then he would return to the theatre like a giant refreshed.

He was polite to everybody. He treated his audiences as his guests and gave them presents, beautiful and artistic souvenirs of the productions which hundreds, probably thousands, treasure today. Cost did not matter. They had to be beautiful. For he worshipped beauty, this great man, and he always achieved it. What he would have thought of some of the productions today —well, it would have been worth hearing. He was probably the greatest man the Haymarket ever knew in all its long history. He was more than a personality, he was a great man and a very great, inspired, creative artist. He had his failures but his successes out-shone them as the sun does a candle. Irving, who did not like him much, although Tree held Sir Henry in great respect, once described him as a 'mummer'. Tree was delighted. He was proud to be a mummer, for that was pure theatre and with him the theatre came first of all things. I am often asked which wa. the greater of the two—Irving or Tree. It is not possible to coms pare two such very different men or two such diverse characters- Irving lifted the theatre almost from the gutter and placed it on a pinnacle. Tree had to begin where Irving left off, and raised the theatre even higher.

What were almost the last words he ever spoke in his 'beautiful theatre' were not spoken to the audience but to companions in the Royal Box. He had been filming in Hollywood where he was most unhappy. I think the studios were unhappy too. It was of course in the days of silent pictures and he was filming *Macbeth*. He insisted on speaking all the lines. They had to put up with it. Then came the time when some 'rushes' could be seen. Everybody went into the small theatre and watched those rushes in the dark.

When the lights went up they all turned to the great English actor to hear his opinion. Sir Herbert Tree was fast asleep. But to those famous last words at His Majesty's. He came back from Hollywood to find *Chu Chin Chow* running there, produced and written by a man who had played in his company for years, Oscar Asche, and with him was his lovely wife, Lily Brayton, also a member of many companies under Tree. The Chief wanted to get back into his theatre and start producing. The enormous success of *Chu Chin Chow* prevented him. Indeed his manager had invested some of Tree's money in the venture. Tree was lost without his theatre and for a long time he would not come and see the play. At length he was prevailed upon to do so. He sat in his own royal box and regarded that lush, rich, exotic production but spoke no word. It will be remembered that *Chu Chin Chow* was one of the first of the rather 'undressed plays', so far as the ladies went. This did not escape the pale but observant eye of Sir Herbert, who remarked 'I see. I see. More navel than millinery.' He watched again for a while and then sat back and turned his face to the wall. 'Scented hogwash,' he murmured, and would not be comforted.

He shed greatness around him and he founded the Royal Academy of Dramatic Art. This was first held in the theatre but the students coming and going disturbed Tree who moved the place to Gower Street. After a while another manager, wishing to gain favour in Sir Herbert's eyes said, 'I say, Sir Herbert, I've got one of your pupils in my new show.' Tree gazed at him with a look of deep pathos. 'Indeed?' he said, 'I sympathise. I've got two.'

The Carlton Hotel has gone but Her Majesty's once again bearing its original title, still stands. It is still a beautiful theatre and a most successful one. But something has gone from it which can never be replaced. It won't be missed by the moderns but it is always missed by those of us who know. For a very great man of the theatre, a very great man in himself, a man who perhaps never quite grew up, but always possessed the heart of a child, has gone from us. That child's heart kept him perpetually young and gave him his tremendous tireless energy. He never slacked, he never ceased from endeavour. Beauty was his goal and he always reached it. One went to his theatre with bated breath, one saw marvels and one came away starry-eyed and refreshed. It was the magic of Sir Herbert Tree of Her Majesty's Theatre in the Haymarket who did that to us and I am sure that his spirit, with its detached if somewhat conspiratorial air, his complete dignity without a trace of pomposity and his mirth bubbling inside, still passes down that street of London which he loved above all others because it was his home and his workshop in one—the Haymarket of London Town.

14

Still in the Haymarket

It is impossible to leave the Haymarket without paying some attention to the great theatre which bears its name and to some other haunts and characters who, at one time, were part and parcel of the daily story of that delectable part of London, that most suitable neighbour to Piccadilly. And one of the bright particular gems which still retains atmosphere, quality and tradition untarnished is the noble playhouse which calls itself Theatre Royal, Haymarket. It has in reality only a slender right to that regal title but it is such a lovely place, such a Theatre of Perfection, that nobody will quarrel about it. And for a while it was in every sense, a Theatre Royal.

Its long history has already been set forth in a book concerning it. Here there is only space for an outline and highlights. And they exist in plenty. It has such a dignified and peacefully serene air that you would not suspect it of having been the scene of so many riots and turbulent scenes in its time. Yet it has had more than its fair share of them. It is actually the second oldest of London's theatres which are still in use, only Theatre Royal, Drury Lane, is its senior. For the original Haymarket Theatre was built in 1720 by a carpenter named John Potter, who erected it on the site of an inn called 'The King's Head'. It is surprising how many theatres and music halls in London occupied space originally given over to inns and taverns. The whole building, inclusive of everything—decorations, fittings, scenery and wardrobe—cost £1,500. Mr Potter had his theatre but it was not much use to him. He had no Royal Charter or Patent and so Drury Lane prevented it being used. Also it stood in what were still almost rural and very outlying surroundings. Nothing much happened for some time. They called it 'The Little Theatre in the Hay'. Then the Duke of Montagu pulled a few strings and opened it with a French company on 20th December 1720, but it was a short visit. Prevented by Drury Lane from playing the drama it housed amateurs, acrobats and the like. Madame Violante the tight rope walker, who discovered the great Peg Woffington, was there with her act. Success came in an odd way. A dancing master from Cheshire, one Samuel Johnson, not to be confused with the great lexicographer, wrote and composed a wild, extraordinary burlesque, called *Hurlothrumbo* in which he himself appeared as a character called 'Lord Flame'. It was so unusual and probably so bad that everybody went to see it and it ran for 30 nights—a most exceptional run for those days. It was probably the forerunner of that equally extraordinary play *Young England* which caused such excitement and success more recently. *Hurlothrumbo* was produced in 1729.

Then came Henry Fielding, to become later the great novelist, and he produced bitter political satires there—starting with *The Tragedie of Tragedies; or The Life and Death of Tom Thumb the Great*. Altogether Fielding produced eight plays there and mostly they were aimed against Sir Robert Walpole, the Prime Minister. That worthy went to see one of them himself and was so incensed at what he heard that he went back stage and thrashed the actor who had uttered what he considered were libels on himself. The poor actor was only doing his duty—Walpole should have thrashed Fielding. But it is the only recorded instance of a Prime Minister 'beating up' an actor in a theatre, and it happened at the Haymarket. Walpole eventually got Fielding turned out and most indifferent productions took place. In 1734 Fielding came back. He evaded the patent of Drury Lane by selling tickets, not at the theatre but at coffee houses. He was still attacking Walpole who, in 1737 and really in self defence, introduced a new Licensing Act. That act is the basis of the theatrical licensing laws to this day. It made Fielding close down. But the public were on his side. A French company once again invaded the Haymarket. The intensely patriotic English audiences of those days, especially of the cheaper parts of the house, were not going to have true-blue Britons displaced by a lot of Frenchies. Violence was openly suggested and was indeed, promised. The authorities got nervous and overdid their precautions. They actually sent a detachment of British soldiers to protect the detested French, also Mr Justice Deveil, a Westminster magistrate, with a copy of the Riot Act in his pocket, for use if necessary. The English of those days had not only a very active dislike of but also a hearty contempt for the French whom they always defeated in battle, thanks to the Duke of Marlborough.

When the night came for the French troupe to appear, the Haymarket Theatre was packed from ceiling to floor by a noisy, milling crowd, obviously out for mischief. They whiled away the time before the curtain rose by cheers for their favourite personages, hoots for the others—very lusty in the case of Walpole—and the loud singing of patriotic songs, especially 'The Roast Beef of Old England'. Mr Justice Deveil took a hand. He rose and said that what was going on was a riot and that if it did not stop, he would call in the military and arrest the ringleaders. But the public disagreed with his views and argued the point ably. Deveil took no action then—he had started too soon. It was almost time for the show to commence. Great dignitaries now appeared in the boxes, including the French and Spanish ambassadors with their wives—and some local bigwigs—including Sir Thomas Robinson, who, as a Commissioner of Excise, was anything but popular and was loudly booed. The Ambassadors did not impress the sturdy, protesting British at all. Then those in charge made another mistake. The curtain rose and disclosed a couple of files of British Grenadiers, with fixed bayonets, and between their ranks the French players. That did it. The crowd was beside itself with rage. British Grenadiers being used to protect Frenchmen instead of killing them! This was not to be stood. There was a terrible uproar. They turned on Deveil and asked him what this insult meant? He tried to temporise. He said he had not been told anything about it. The whole audience then demanded, in tones which brooked no argument, the immediate withdrawal of the soldiery. Deveil went round to ask the Colonel, Colonel Pulteney, to withdraw his men. And during that time it is not too much to say that the lives of the wretched French players hung in the balance. One false step and nothing could have stopped tragedy. The Colonel understood the position. There were some sharp words of command, and the Grenadiers wheeled and left the stage. Instantly the mood of the mob changed. They roared with laughter. A voice shouted 'The British Army is in retreat' and another yelled, 'Send for His Grace the Duke of Marlborough!' Although there were shouts of laughter, the trouble was by no means over. The Frenchmen tried to perform their play but nothing could be heard above the continuous pandemonium. They tried to sing but that was equally useless. So they decided to dance. That move had been foreseen by the crowd. And an avalanche of dried peas flooded the stage. The Frenchmen slipped and fell over, the V.I.P.s hastily withdrew from their boxes, and were hooted by the mob. One could sense the crisis in the air. The mob began to mass together as for a rush at the stage. Deveil once more announced that he was going to read the Riot Act and that their fate would be on their own heads. But there was a man who had commonsense. He persuaded Deveil not to read the Act but to order the curtain to be rung down; otherwise he prophesied disaster and probable loss of life. Deveil agreed and gave the order. The curtain descended amidst deafening cheers from the patriots, who now dispersed in high good humour, reckoning that their victory in the Little Theatre in the Hay was as complete as that of Blenheim. When the curtain fell that night it did not rise again for some considerable time.

Various things were tried but they all failed because there was now double opposition: Covent Garden had a Royal Patent as well as Drury Lane, and was also out to crush the upstart in the Hay. Charles Macklin, a fierce, desperate man who killed a brother actor at Drury Lane—and got away with it—tried his luck. He had left Drury Lane when there was a strike of actors which he was considered to have caused. He went to the Haymarket and although he dared not perform a play he put up an entertainment. He advertised a concert, sold tickets in the coffee houses, and gave exhibitions of what he called rehearsals. The public could watch him training young and inexperienced actors. It was all pretty grim, for the would-be actors were no good at all and they never stayed the course because of Macklin's temper. But there was one amongst them who was to have a great role to play in that very same theatre, and his name was Samuel Foote. Macklin staged what he said was a rehearsal of *Othello*— because he wanted to play 'Iago' himself. The Moor was played by a Gentleman—thus anonymous on the bills—who was actually Samuel Foote. The result was disaster. Macklin shut up shop. But he had achieved something that he did not realise. He had brought upon its stage the man who was to make the Haymarket famous— that same Samuel Foote.

In 1747 Foote, who was a gentleman by birth and education, took charge. He advertised something which he called 'The Diversions of the Morning' and ballyhooed it in a style which would have done credit to the slickest modern publicity man. But he slipped up: what he did was too much like a play, so Old Drury intervened. However, nobody could defeat Foote. This brilliant if unscrupulous man, who was a master mimic, had made up his mind to rival Garrick, whom he hated, and to make his tiny playhouse into a Theatre Royal. So, he tried a new tack. He invited his friends to come and take a cup of chocolate with him, for which tickets could be obtained at George's Coffee House,

Temple Bar, and, like Macklin, he pretended to hold a rehearsal. The real attraction was however his amazing and cruel imitations of celebrities of the day. Everyone flocked to see it. Those who had not been mimicked went to see their friends' displeasure— those who had suffered from Foote's attentions went hoping to see their friends pilloried. The only person he did not dare burlesque was the great Doctor Johnson. He carried on in this way with variations in form for a long time and the whole town was afraid of him. The Little Theatre in the Hay became famous. He perpetrated a great joke. He advertised the appearance of the Great Bottle Conjuror, who, after performing, so it was said, did quite amazing feats, would get inside a quart bottle and sing a song. Now anyone might have known such a thing was impossible, but the public will always flock to see the impossible, in hopes. . . . On the night advertised the theatre was packed to suffocation, and amongst the spectators was the Duke of Cumberland himself. Needless to say the Bottle Conjuror did not materialise, and the audience was furious. Led by the Duke of Cumberland, sword in hand and purple face still further empurpled, they invaded the stage and did much damage. Foote did not care—he had made a lot of money by the spoof. He was famous but he was disliked. He was a bit of a snob too and given to inordinate boasting. In 1766 he was a guest of Lord Mexborough and amongst the company was the Duke of York. Talk turned on horse riding. Foote boasted the steed had not been foaled that he could not ride. In the stables was a very vicious animal which nobody had been able to break. They got Foote on it. He was thrown and fractured his leg, which had to be amputated. Foote bore the pain nobly and cracked jokes. The Duke of York repented of his share in the affair and asked Foote if there was anything he could do to make amends. 'Ask His Majesty to give me a Patent for the Haymarket,' said Foote, and the King did so, but with certain reservations, and for the lifetime of Foote only. But Foote now stood, in his own estimation, equal to his detested Garrick, who had been good to him and lent him money.

He went on acting with one leg in what was now Theatre Royal, Haymarket, and then sold out to George Colman, a celebrated manager. Part of the payment was an annuity, but he only lived to draw one quarter—he died at Dover, joking to the last. He had made the Haymarket Theatre famous and Royal, and it still keeps its title and although not strictly legal, nobody worries about that.

Colman did magnificent work there and the theatre rose in fame. Great players made their debut there but at a command performance fifteen people were trampled to death and many injured. There was another riot when a splendid actor named Dowton revived one of Foote's plays—for Foote wrote good plays —all about tailors. The tailors of London resented it. Dowton persisted. There were dreadful scenes when they threw tailors' shears at Dowton and had to be dispersed by the Life Guards. Colman's son succeeded his father and was always in trouble. For some time he was in prison for debt, but he ran the theatre from there. An extraordinary amateur named 'Romeo' Coates caused a sensation there in 1810. But the Haymarket prospered and in 1820 it was rebuilt next door to its original site; and that gracious theatre can be seen today, with Nash's columns fronting it. Benjamin Webster, John Baldwin Buckstone (whose ghost still haunts it), Samuel Phelps, Macready the eminent tragedian, Barry Sullivan, all made history there. In Buckstone's reign, *Our American Cousin* was produced which provided the record run—400 nights—up to that time and which created the character of 'Lord Dundreary' who set a fashion in clothes and especially whiskers. The part was played by Edward Sothern. Mr and Mrs Kendal rose to fame there, and the negro actor, Ira Q. Aldridge, played 'Othello'. In 1880, Mr and Mrs Bancroft (to become Sir Squire and Lady Bancroft) took the theatre over. They had revolutionised the English stage. They caused a revolution at the Haymarket too for Bancroft did away with the pit which led to real ructions on the opening night of their management and a truly Haymarketian riot.

Herbert Tree became its actor-manager in 1887, and from there he swooped across the road to build Her Majesty's for himself. Cyril Maude in partnership with Frederick Harrison made the Haymarket the home of English comedies with productions and acting worthy of that elegant setting. In 1926 Horace Watson became manager and his family still carries on the tradition of the theatre, which has seen so many beautiful plays and productions, and still continues to stage them. It has real atmosphere, and if coming round a corner on the stairs you met a beau in powdered wig and satin breeches, you would not be in the least surprised. The spirit of the Haymarket itself has its home in its own theatre. Long may it remain.

On the site of that original Little Theatre in the Hay there stood, for years, an excellent restaurant run by two Italians who were masters of the art. And because in London places have names which are often misleading, this restaurant in the Haymarket was called the Pall Mall. There was a bar attached to it, which was an unofficial Bohemian club of London. Strangers of course *could* use it but were not made very welcome by its regulars, all of whom were friends and most of whom were in the theatrical or journalistic professions. You would find dear old Bill Leverton who for over half a century presided over the box office at the Haymarket Theatre. He had gone there as a lad, from the telegraphic department of the Post Office. To see him outside the theatre you would never have dreamed that he was at all theatrical. He was a tall, lean, well-preserved man, fresh complexioned, clean shaven and rather sharp in the nose but with a constant smile in his blue eyes. For generations he was the outward and visible sign of the Haymarket to playgoers, and he numbered his acquaintances by the thousand. He seemed ageless, his hair, which kept its colour miraculously, was always parted in the middle and he wore to the end one of those high, stiff starched single linen collars known as 'chokers'. His attire was the formal, correct wear of the 'eighties', and matched his manners. He would sit inside his box office window, fitting exactly into his surround-

A Victorian mounted policeman

Piccadilly Circus in 1904

ings, and knowing almost every regular customer by sight and name, he would greet them as friends but never with familiarity. Had you not known him, you might have guessed that he was a prosperous country solicitor, with well filled black deed boxes. He was a great Haymarket character.

He would relax in the Pall Mall buffet and enjoy jokes. That buffet was under the management and guidance of 'Mac'—Helen Macdonald—who with her great friend Bunnie was one of the two premier barmaids of London. She was a really delightful woman, and she ran that bar to perfection. She trained many girls to be expert in their job. She knew all about everybody and never betrayed a trust. She was scrupulously honest and had a real knack of handling men. We all held her in great respect and some of us would go to see her when she retired. She still kept up her high standard and her spotlessness. She sat in her rooms, her cat on her knee and held court like a duchess. When she was at the Pall Mall—and she was there for years—nobody ever dared question her judgment or her command. She did not strike terror but she understood discipline and you always felt she was right. And so she was. Perfect order reigned. One could write a whole volume about the Pall Mall and its customers; it was a real galaxy of stars in the great days of the theatre and the real days of the West End. A very regular customer at the Pall Mall was a man named Sydney Ellison. He was one of the very best producers of musical comedy this country ever knew. A tiny man, he was always marvellously dressed and most meticulous but with a decidedly effeminate manner. He was the man who created the famous 'Tell Me Pretty Maiden' business in *Florodora* to the music of the composer Leslie Stuart. The two men, both most self-willed and difficult had a battle royal over whether it should be a duet or octet—Stuart wanted the former and Ellison the latter. Ellison won, which shows what a tough character he was. He had to go into the Army during the First World War, which he loathed. He had lived an exotic life, wore silk shirts and silk pyjamas, and khaki was not to his taste. They tried to break his

spirit but after his O.C. had discovered him walking down the
Haymarket in uniform, but with an enormous sunflower stuck in
his tunic and when he totally refused to fire a machine gun and
defied a whole battalion, they reckoned they could do without
him. He went back to work. One night, in perfect dinner jacket
and all that went with it, he was standing in the Pall Mall buffet
talking to Mac. He had with him the things he said were the best
in the world, a bunch of roses and a big bag of small chocolate
creams. 'This is heaven, Mac', he said in his lisping voice, 'look
at these lovely roses, right out of the Elysian fields, and taste these
perfectly marvellous chocolate creams, nectar and ambrosia. The
world has no greater pleasures.' He kept on like this, sipping his
drink between whiles, sniffing the roses and eating the chocolate
creams and keeping up a running commentary on both. A very
large Australian officer came in, who stood about six feet four
inches. The sight and sound of this strange little man arrested him.
He had never seen anything like this in the back blocks from which
presumably he came. He gazed and listened in astonishment and
took a deep breath. 'Double brandy please, Miss,' he said to Mac,
who served him but was not too well pleased at the form of
address. He drank it at a gulp and continued his inspection of the
little Sydney, who continued his harangue and his praise of roses
and chocolate cream. The gigantic Australian was non-plussed
but he could not take his eyes off Sydney. He had three more
double brandies. Sydney Ellison was perfectly aware of him but
cared not a whit. The Aussie then had his sixth brandy, took a
deep breath and went over to Sydney Ellison, who faced him.
'I say,' he said, 'you're one of the pansies, ain't you?' Sydney
Ellison put down his roses and his creams. He leapt high in the
air, bringing himself level with the Australian's chin. His left fist
shot out and caught the giant right on the mark. Astonished and
truly knocked out the Aussie crashed to the floor. 'There,' said
Sydney. 'You see? And *I* didn't need even *one* brandy to do that.'
'Outside, please,' said Mac and the attendants removed the Australian. Ellison quietly finished his drink, cool, calm and collected.

But on one occasion Ellison gave Mac offence. She 'barred' him from his beloved bar. He was shattered. It was like an Archangel being turned out of Paradise. He went down to a friend of his in Fleet Street who had a special 'contents bill' printed (the papers used them with every edition then) which said, 'Sydney Ellison barred from the Pall Mall'. Ellison fastened it round his neck and stood at the door of the buffet, right in the Haymarket, the cynosure of all passers by, bearing his legend on his chest and wearing the most doleful, sorrowful and heartrending expression. Mac saw him, laughed, and relented. All was happiness again. Those things don't happen in the West End today and there are not any women like Bunnie or Mac. When Mac died, it was my privilege to write the little epitaph which was to mark the fact that her ashes lay in the Garden of Rest at Golder's Green, and I was very proud to do it. But she lives on in that lessening little band who used the Pall Mall, which alas vanished some time ago to make room for business premises.

There was another character there who deserves mention. He was tall and of military air; he looked like and assuredly was a retired regular officer. He belonged to a club in what is now King Charles Street. The strange thing about him was that although everybody knew him by sight, nobody, not even Mac, knew his name. For he was never known to speak. He began his morning, so far as the world was concerned, about 12.30 p.m. by falling down the steps of his club. The porter outside would pick him up, brush him down, face him towards the Haymarket and give him a gentle push. The gentleman then proceeded, staring straight before him and disregarding the traffic entirely, into the Haymarket, across the road and straight into the Pall Mall. As soon as Mac, or her assistant, saw him, his morning draught was made ready—a double Scotch and baby Polly. He drank it at a draught, replaced the tumbler on the counter to be filled again, as before. He drank that, put down the right money and left the buffet. He went straight up the Haymarket, crossed the Circus, quite miraculously never touched by the traffic, into Warwick

Street and then into the Sceptre Chophouse—a real and delectable chophouse which in those days was well known and celebrated. A place was always kept for him. He would study the menu, point to what he wanted—and a pint of beer arrived. No word was spoken. He ate a good lunch and then had two double ports after which he went quietly to sleep. Sometimes he was still there when dinner time came, sometimes he went away and returned about seven. Still no word was spoken. He would have a good dinner, a bottle of burgundy and three ports. Then he would pay, nod to the proprietor, leave a tip, and pass out into the night. Nobody knew where he went then. He moved in a world of his own, one of complete silence. Once I saw him on top of a bus which was going up the Haymarket. It was almost at the top, where the Haymarket runs into Piccadilly, which actually begins at the Haymarket Corner. This was before the days of one-way streets. He had risen to descend the staircase and the bus swayed as it turned the corner rather sharply. He bumped against the rail, lost his balance and fell from the top into the road. People shouted and came running and the bus pulled up. But the silent gentleman arose, pushed aside those who wanted to help him, recovered his bowler hat which had come off and walked on through the crowd to the Sceptre without a word, apparently none the worse. Truly a special providence looks after those who are devoted to their cups. I don't know what became of him for I was away from Town for a considerable time. When I came back I enquired but he had not been seen for some weeks. The porter at the club vouchsafed no information. That man just vanished into another world of silence, and maybe found the shades of the Pall Mall and Sceptre there.

There has been a mention of that barber's in the Royal Opera Arcade—that genuine remnant of Georgian London which still surprises those who see it for the first time. It would cause no astonishment if Brummell himself stepped up and offered his snuff box. That barber's had very important customers. I have seen no less than six famous actor-managers in there at one time and all of them were knights. Rudyard Kipling was a customer for a long time, but one day he came in and saw, sitting in the chair he usually occupied, a man of whom he did not approve. It was Ramsay MacDonald. He never went there again.

Once the Haymarket won me a considerable victory—Piccadilly Circus tube station did it for me. We were staging an American comedy and the original American producer was coming over to supervise it. He came via Liverpool and I had to meet him at Euston. He had never been here before, and I had never seen him either, but I had no difficulty in picking him out by the description given to me. It was very late in the First World War. He was a nice looking, fresh complexioned, aquiline featured man, wearing a deerstalker, which he probably thought was a necessary article of headwear in this country, and smoking an outsized pipe of a twisted curly shape. He nodded at my greeting, shook hands and we walked to the taxi I had ready. He went straight to business losing no time in preliminary chat. 'Say,' he said, 'there's some difficulty about the effects of this play. There has to be the sound of an elevator. Now I'm told there's no such thing as an elevator in this country.' 'Oh yes, there is,' I said, 'only we call them lifts.' He brushed aside my statement and shook his head. 'My information is, and on good authority,' he said, 'no elevators.' I tried to reassure him but he would have none of it. The problem was obviously worrying him. So I told the taximan to drive first of all, before going to the hotel, to the exit from the Piccadilly tube station in Jermyn Street. 'I'll show you some elevators—or lifts—whichever you like to call them,' I said, 'I assure you you need not worry.' 'You are very kind,' he said, rather sadly, 'but my information is—no elevators at all in this realm.' We arrived at the tube station. Those were the days before escalators and lifts arose by the dozen in constant stream, discharging thousands of people into Jermyn Street. 'Take a look at those,' I said quietly. He gazed in open mouthed astonishment. He was dumbfounded. He had never seen so many elevators at one time in his whole life. He would not come away. It fascinated him. I had to pay the taxi off, take off his baggage and wait until he had looked his fill. Then he turned to me and extended his hand, 'I apologise,' he said. 'There are elevators in this realm. I was told wrong.' After that we were firm friends. I persuaded him to discard his deerstalker and, perhaps as a return of courtesy, he spoke of elevators no more, but called them lifts. Those lifts were a feature of London life and of course they came to the Haymarket when the tube opened there. Each lift had an attendant, who opened and shut the gates by hand. As the people entered he kept up a continuous cry of 'Pass right across the lift, please, and hurry along,' until his lift was full—and they could be very full. He then shut his gates and pushed across to the other side, with difficulty, shouting as he went, 'No Smoking in the Lift, please.' But nobody heeded that nor could he have enforced his order. On arriving at the top he shouted, 'This side out please,' and battled with desperate characters who tried to get in the wrong way, according to his rules. Those men had a pretty hard life, and a monotonous one. There are only a very few of them left now. But in the old days the constant ascent and descent of those lifts and the streams of people was one of the sights of London.

The Haymarket is still a street of charm and atmosphere although it has altered greatly. It presents a fine vista down which to gaze, for it is not level but slopes quite steeply down hill towards Cockspur Street and Pall Mall. At the end it is dominated by the dome which supports a globe and a ship and marks the office of Thomas Cook. The Haymarket has kept up its standard better than many streets in the West End. Its skyline is irregular in the usual London way; there are minarets, pinnacles and little towers, variations of style and date, but the gracious pillars which Nash placed there still stand outside the Haymarket Theatre and Her Majesty's still carries its dome. The Carlton Hotel, one of the best and smartest in London and the architectural twin of Her Majesty's, is swept away—its wonderful cuisine, its delightful panelled grillroom and its bar are now just memories. But the

Haymarket is still there and down it the traffic flows like a flood from that reservoir which is the centre of London, Piccadilly Circus.

15

A Beginning Which Never Ended

Much has been said and written to the detriment of King George IV, the self-styled First Gentleman of Europe. He was not a pleasant character in the main and he had a record of despicable acts to his discredit. He was dishonest in money matters, he treated his women victims shamefully, he was a liar and a boaster; but he was always proud to be an Englishman. His youth had been clouded by his royal father's dislike, and maybe old Farmer George had good reason for that. He was a disgraceful husband. Yet he loved his realm in the general way, he had ideas as to culture and above all he had a great love of London and a tremendous desire to make it noble and beautiful. For that, much can be forgiven him by a Londoner.

He held court in Carlton House, where as Prince of Wales he set up in a sort of opposition to his Father. There also he dreamed dreams, one of which was the construction of a new palace for himself, situated in the park which owes so much to him—Regent's Park—and probably sited on the summit of Primrose Hill. One cannot imagine him disregarding such an eminence. That palace never materialised and it is pleasant to conjecture what it would have been like had it done so. He might have commanded something exotic and entirely out of place like his pavilion at

Basil Hallam

Sir Herbert Beerbohm Tree as 'Svengali'

Brighton (another city which has much to thank him for) but one does not think that the architect who had charge of the scheme—John Nash—would have allowed it. He was a very successful architect, a protégé of George IV and indeed, some say, his son.

That dream of magnificence, of a thoroughfare which might have been the finest in Europe, never quite came off. But enough was done to make a new London and a very beautiful one architecturally and to leave a mark which endures in the Nash terraces facing Regent's Park—which form a section of urban beauty unequalled anywhere else and which have so far escaped complete destruction from those who always wish to demolish what a previous generation has built and who believe that modernity should take precedence over grace and loveliness. Compare the perfection of form and symmetry, of dignity and quiet unassuming splendour of those terraces with the towering plain, featureless and impersonal blocks of flats which arise today. And for those terraces, the park itself, Regent Street, Lower Regent Street and Piccadilly Circus we are indebted primarily to George IV. Georgian architecture is one of the brightest jewels in our architectural crown. The idea originally was to drive this great road straight through, from Carlton House, which stood where Waterloo Place now stands, to the new residence. But Nash found that he could not do just that. He was prevented by certain vested interests and the like. But nevertheless, he cut through old buildings of doubtful interest, through rather mean side streets, and made a grand entrance by means of what is now known as Waterloo Place and Lower Regent Street. He drove through what was known as St James's Market—its name hangs on in Market Street—which was the property of the Earl of St Albans, whose title still has a local habitation there in St Albans Place and whose family name is perpetuated in Jermyn Street.

Piccadilly lay right athwart his path. And here George IV himself took a hand. It is believed that it was his own idea for Nash to maintain a semblance of continuity and straightness by making a circus—now Piccadilly Circus—to join Lower Regent Street to Regent Street proper without a break. Nash did this and continued his stately way up Regent Street, with its beautiful curve and its elegance—now slightly spoiled from the original conception, as will be seen when that street comes under observation. So the wide, straight road was never quite accomplished and never reached its destined end. But Regent Street itself was made into a glorious thoroughfare and Piccadilly Circus—originally Regent Circus—became what it is today, the centre of the world. Had those vested interests not interfered with Nash's original idea, London might never have possessed its celebrated axis.

There is no great antiquity therefore in Waterloo Place or in Lower Regent Street, for they are, as London goes, comparatively new streets, constructed only in 1814, the year before Waterloo. But Waterloo Place, as befits its name, has become a sort of London Valhalla, for it holds statues and groups to the great ones of this land—to soldiers and sailors, to Benjamin Franklin, to Clive, to Captain Scott of Antartic memory (and that statue was sculpted by his widow), to King Edward VII, and to immortal Florence Nightingale. It is one of the well known sights of London. It is dominated by an enormous column, 124 feet high, erected to the memory of Frederick, Duke of York, second son of George III, at a cost of £25,000. It is surmounted by a statue of the Duke, in bronze, which is 14 feet high. This Duke was the soldier of the old jingle:

> 'The brave old Duke of York,
> He had ten thousand men;
> He marched them up to the top of the hill,
> And he marched them down again.
> And when they were up, they were up,
> And when they were down, they were down;
> And when they were only half way up,
> They were neither up nor down.'

Mind you, men have received statues before now for doing

even less than that. Even so, it did not seem a qualification for a column which rivals that of Nelson's.

But the Duke was a much better soldier than the rhyme suggests. He saw much active service against the troops of the newly fledged French Republic when the Terror tried to overrun Europe. He fought the French in the Low Countries and had many victories. Sometimes he was let down badly by professional but incompetent generals who were given equality of command with him and who sometimes were placed over him. When he had command he proved brilliant and also a first class fighting man. He deserves that column and better knowledge of his deeds. He had foresight and fine judgment and his men would follow him through thick and thin. It was not his fault that his column proved a favourite jumping off place for suicides in the days when the public were allowed access to it.

Some years ago it was suggested that Lower Regent Street, which stretches from Pall Mall to Piccadilly Circus, should be called Waterloo Place throughout its entirety. This was strenuously resisted by the ratepayers and shopkeepers of the neighbourhood and was abandoned. It was a very good idea. For most people, Regent Street begins on the other side of Piccadilly Circus and Lower Regent Street confuses them. But this is at heart a very conservative country, except when it comes to preserving ancient objects of historical fame or beauty.

Both Waterloo Place and Lower Regent Street contain many banks—they form what is almost the Lombard Street of the West End. Those banks are British, Dominion and foreign. There are plenty of insurance companies there too. These streets are now most respectable, dignified and successful places of business. But it was not always so. On a site at the corner of King Charles II Street, where now stands British Columbia House—there once stood a very different sort of place. This was the Continental Hotel—a by-word in London for all that was naughty, and not at all nice either. It was a place of flagrant bad behaviour. Originally it had been Warren's Hotel, much patronised by the nobility and the higher ecclesiastical dignitaries. Their influence did not last. For when it became the Continental Hotel its clientéle really lived up to the name. In Victorian and even early Edwardian days the Continent was regarded as a most immoral if not amoral place. The Continental did nothing to check this idea. It outdid any Parisian haunt in its licence and the demi-monde, the so-called Bohemians, the crooks, the blackmailers, the card sharpers, the ladies of the town of a grade just above those who were 'on the Dilly', flocked there, and drew there all the men who wanted to taste what were loosely called 'the pleasures of the town'. It was nothing but a drinking den, a gambling hell and a glorified brothel. Every form of vice was practised there. It was a wonder that the authorities put up with it for as long as they did—but the end came in 1906, when the police carried out a big raid. As a result of their captures and discoveries, the place was closed down. The wicked Continental was no more. A few months later it reopened again, as the Hotel Chatham. It was under entirely new management and as respectable as could be. But it did not succeed as a reformed character and was pulled down in 1914.

There was another place of entertainment in Lower Regent Street—of an entirely different nature from the Continental. It was at the very opposite extreme. So far from being disgraceful and licentious, it was the very zenith of Victorian rectitude and respectability. It was called 'The Gallery of Illustration'. It formed part of a mansion which Nash is said to have built for his own home, and on the same site was the Raleigh Club. Part of the site is now occupied by Dorland House. In this curiously named establishment a Mr and Mrs German Reed gave what were known as 'Drawing Room Entertainments'. They claimed and with complete justification that in their entertainments 'nothing was said or done thereat which would have brought a blush to the cheeks of a young person'. That was a matter of great importance in those now seemingly distant days, for the young person, the teenager, was a very different kind of being from the teenager of today, who probably does not know what a blush is, anyway. But the Victorian young person had a very different upbringing and education. She was taught to be refined, to have delicacy, to behave herself and above all, to be a lady. She was guarded from the wickedness of the world and such things as innocence and chastity were of high value.

Yet, despite their immense respectability, which can be described as monumental, those German Reed Entertainments were never dull or fusty. They were clean and they derived their entertainment value from wit, from clever performance and from good light music and honest fun. Many of the most distinguished performers and personages in the world of the theatre, literature and music, had their origin there. Both Mr and Mrs German Reed were people of quality and background. It is a pity they are not better remembered. He was born in Bristol in 1817. He was an actor and a musician, better known in the latter than in the former capacity. And during his theatrical career he was also a church organist and a conductor of more than average merit. Indeed, he had conducted at the old Opera House in the Haymarket and was Musical Director there from 1838 until 1851—and no higher musical post than that was to be found in London. He married Miss Priscilla Horton in 1844.

She was famous. She came of most respectable parents, who were apparently well off, for she had the best musical training money could buy. Her singing master, Sir George Smart, thought so much of her beautiful contralto voice that he got her a job in the chorus at Covent Garden. There she gained useful experience. Next, she took her chance as a 'straight' actress. In 1833 two enterprising men, Abbott and Egerton, were running the Victoria Theatre, now the Old Vic, and were having an uphill fight, despite the assistance they received from Sheridan Knowles and Miss Mitford, two leading dramatists. Miss Horton went to the Victoria Theatre with her sister. She had only small parts at first but it was chronicled that 'her acting in them was always marked with the strictest propriety and good taste'—signs of things to come. But Abbott and Egerton met with misfortune and closed.

Miss Horton had to find work elsewhere and did so, although at a small salary. She made a success at the now vanished old Strand Theatre—playing 'April' in a play called *Tears and Sunshine*. An admirer was moved to drop into poetry, like Silas Wegg, only into original verse. He wrote:

> 'Oh Miss
> Pris
> Cilla Horton
> I have thought on
> You and April.'

Not very good poetry maybe but doubtless very gratifying to a young actress. But William Charles Macready, the eminent and most respectable tragedian, was her real discoverer. He engaged her when he took over the management of Covent Garden Theatre. She pleased him because of her beauty—she was very fair—her undoubted talent and also because she never indulged in the 'temperaments' from which he suffered in respect of his other actresses. He wasn't so bad at them himself, either. He staged a very lovely production of *The Tempest* and Miss Horton triumphed as 'Ariel'. Her name was made. He looked after her in every way and she showed her good sense by treating him with the reverence which he considered his just due. She rose in fame and when Macready left Covent Garden he took Miss Horton with him to Drury Lane as his leading lady. And at Drury Lane she had many triumphs, the greatest being in *Acis and Galatea*. There was never a breath of scandal against her in a most censorious age. She was a good linguist, wrote verses and composed songs, was quite a good painter of portraits and a wonderful mimic. In private life she was the quietest and most unassuming of people—there was nothing of the flamboyancy of the 'pro' about her. She rose to very great heights in her profession but always maintained the most terrific respectability. No wonder that she and her husband—also a monument of respectability and gentility

—scored a success with their own brand of entertainment, when they left the ordinary stage.

Mr and Mrs German Reed took the Gallery of Illustration in 1855 and started their unique entertainment. It says much for their joint respectability that although she was still following her stage career at that time it made no difference to the success. Staid, conventional Victorians, who regarded the theatre as a sinful place and actors and actresses as moral outcasts beyond the pale, flocked to the Gallery of Illustration. The entertainments were a success from the very first night. Yet what they saw were plays, operettas and entertainments at the piano. There were costumes and make up, just as in a real theatre—but somehow it was all respectable and different. The word 'Illustration' applied not only to the productions and solo entertainments but to the characters, each of whom was mentioned on the programmes— price 6d. and including a book of words—as 'Illustration'. One such character, played by Corney Grain (the supreme entertainer at the piano of his day) as 'Sir Plumly Partridge, an Elderly Baronet and Injustice of the Peace'. The music was supplied by a piano and a harmonium. Here is the lyric of a little duet for two lovers from one of the shows. His name was 'Tom', hers 'Georgie':

> Tom. 'If I were to whisper in you ear
>   What do you think I'd say?
>   Just come close and you shall hear
>   But don't tell anyone, pray.
>   You're my life, my future wife,
>   My love what e'er befall,
>   But don't tell anyone, no, not anyone,
>   Don't tell anyone at all.
>
> Georgie. If you suppose that I shall say,
>   Words of a similar kind,
>   Turn your face the opposite way,
>   And don't tell anyone, mind.
>   Till life depart, I'm your sweetheart,

My love I'll ne'er recall.
But don't tell anyone, please, not anyone,
Don't tell anyone at all.'

There are worse lyrics than that today. Corney Grain was a tower of strength and a really magnificent entertainer, who sent everyone away happy. He eventually became a partner. 'The Gallery of Illustration' had eminent composers and librettists working for it and indeed it helped many people to fame. Brough, Parry, Burnand, Clay, Cellier, Macfarren and Arthur Law figured on its programmes. Sir F.C. Burnand wrote a comic opera for the German Reeds, in the German Reed style and persuaded a young composer to write a score for it. That young man's name was Arthur Sullivan. The operetta, called *The Contrabandista* was not a great success but it gave young Mr Sullivan a taste for writing for the stage, and he first met W. S. Gilbert at a German Reed show. They were introduced by Frederick Clay and Gilbert, of course, could not resist a joke. He knew nothing about music and had read something in an encyclopaedia which to him seemed nonsense, so he decided to try its effect on a real musician. He said, 'I'm very glad to have the pleasure of meeting you, Mr Sullivan, for you can decide the argument which has arisen between Fred Clay and myself. I maintain that if a composer has a musical theme to express, he can express it as simply on the simple tetrachord of Mercury in which, as I need not tell you, there are no diatonic intervals at all, as upon the much more complicated dis-diapason, with the four tetrachords and the redundant note, which embraces in its perfect consonance all the simple, double and inverted chords'. Sullivan was considerably taken aback and asked for the question to be repeated. Gilbert did so, word for word. Sullivan then said he would like time to think it over before replying. Gilbert never got his answer. That was their first meeting. So the German Reed Entertainment might claim to be the godfather of Gilbert and Sullivan. Both had worked for the German Reeds. Those entertainments moved from Lower Regent

Street to St George's Hall, right at the other end of Regent Street, in 1878 and flourished there for years. But to Lower Regent Street crowds of Victorians of all classes and conditions flocked, in their carriages and on foot. There is still entertainment to be found in Lower Regent Street, at the Plaza Cinema, on the corner of Jermyn Street, where history of a kind was made when it opened, for its usherettes wore trousers—which would not have pleased the patrons of The Gallery of Illustrations. The Gallery of Illustration shared its site with the Raleigh Club. There was plenty of room in that magnificent Nash mansion, which had a courtyard before it in which history was made. For in 1925 a steel house was erected there, built to show the merits of this kind of construction. It was elaborately furnished and fitted with every possible modern convenience. During the short time it stood there it was visited and inspected by thousands of people and the whole thing was organised, with great success by the *Evening News*.

There is little of historical interest to be seen in Waterloo Place and Lower Regent Street, except the statuary. But there are big commercial undertakings in handsome buildings, one extremely good restaurant at least, a cinema, shipping offices, travel agencies and even a large place given over to the British Railways to glorify the railway systems and to give service to the public. You need a good deal of time on your hands and a large amount of grim tenacity of purpose if you attempt to deal there. The rebuilding of Lower Regent Street made Piccadilly Circus into a square and not a circus, as it had been originally.

Lower Regent Street and Waterloo Place were never fashionable thoroughfares and they are essentially male in quality. Commerce moved in as they were built. When the Continental Hotel was swept away, the last vestige of 'gay life' departed. The 'ladies of the town' never frequented Lower Regent Street as they did its neighbours. Smart, well-to-do men went to the Raleigh Club but they were not likely customers for the Daughters of Joy. There is the majestic and austere Athenaeum Club, like a Grecian temple, at the corner of Pall Mall and Waterloo Place, which is a landmark of London. But it is still a place of contrasts. It begins in what remains of the spacious splendour of the Georgian days, which cling about Waterloo Place, where there are still lawns, shrubs and trees wherein blackbirds sing, and where the Duke of York's Steps, made of granite from the island of Herne, near Guernsey form an approach into St James's Park, which was opened by order of King William IV to celebrate his coronation. As you proceed up hill towards Piccadilly, it becomes modern and very businesslike. Nowhere here does the past call strongly. But turn when you reach Piccadilly Circus and look down the vista which lies before you. It is as fine a view as London can show. Framed in the tall buildings which bring it into focus is that rearing ducal column at the top of its steps, and fringed with trees. And behind it is a wide skyscape, pierced with towers and minarets, the towers of the Houses of Parliament, and the spires of that quarter of London which is the seat of Government, Whitehall, from whence at one time a fifth of the globe was controlled; Whitehall, the centre of sovereignty and—by a purely British contrast—the place where a King of England lost his head.

16

London's Theatre Street

Those streets which flow into Piccadilly Circus are like rivers, bringing a human stream into the central lake and also draining it away again. Humanity flows into Piccadilly Circus along them and then flows out to proceed on its way. One of these thoroughfares is called Shaftesbury Avenue and it is a very young street indeed. It is rather a sad monument to a neglected opportunity for noble town planning which was not understood and so was wasted. That is a very British situation, for so often the best intentions in that direction go wrong. But one must admit that later years showed some improvement. Shaftesbury Avenue links Bloomsbury with Piccadilly Circus. It rises, if we may keep the river simile, at New Oxford Street, it runs along to Cambridge Circus, where it swirls like a whirlpool and then flows directly to its destination—the Third Magnetic Pole.

There is little that is striking or imposing about it, although its Piccadilly delta is better than its source and upper reaches. They too have changed out of all knowledge in recent times and modernity has displaced Victorianism, yet with that Victorian tenacity a bit of it still hangs on. Nevertheless, its creation washed away mean streets and slums which were a disgrace to the West End of a great capital city. The freedom to build it was obtained

through an act of Parliament brought about by a very great
Englishman indeed, from whom Shaftesbury Avenue gets its
name. That man was Antony Ashley Cooper, seventh Earl of
Shaftesbury. How many of the millions of people who pass up and
down that Avenue, who flock into the theatres which deck it,
know why the street is so called or know anything about the man
whose name it immortalises—if he needed such a thing. It could
have been an avenue as noble as the man whose name it bears—
but it missed it. Shaftesbury Avenue is a strange jumble of all sorts of
things, but Antony Ashley Cooper wrought his country and his
fellow men lasting good. Once again the name of a great Englishman goes right down into the soil of London. He has another
memorial, which we shall meet later.

He was born in London, in Grosvenor Square, in 1801. He died
in 1885, full of years and honours, vigorous in mind right up to
the last. His life had spanned a very great period of English history,
a period of vast expansion, naval and military glory, industrial
supremacy, great and ever growing wealth, the spread of Empire
and of reform. It was in that sphere that the greatness of Antony
Ashley Cooper manifested itself. He lived in a time of very great
men, but he was a giant amongst giants, yet a man of gentleness
and simplicity. He fought many battles and he won them. But
his battles were fought to preserve life, not to destroy it, to make
it better and not to maim and deface it. That, of course, is why
they are not so well remembered. His whole life was devoted to
the 'underdog', the poor, the needy and especially to little
children, whom he loved. He was their dauntless unswerving
champion.

That may well have been because he himself had a most
unhappy childhood which made him quick to see and speedy to
relieve unhappiness in others. Soon after his birth, his father
inherited the title and the family estates. He was a hard, stern man,
very self-contained and aloof, who neglected his tenantry and paid
scant attention to his wife and family. It was anything but a happy
home. When Antony was seven years old he was sent to a school

in Chiswick, which proved even sterner, harder and more austere than his home. It is a moot point which place he hated the more.

But when at home, he came under the influence of an old servant, one Maria Mills, who instilled into his bright young mind her own ideas of right living and morality, based on the evangelical model. This became the way he followed all his life.

He went to Harrow and liked it there. But whilst at school, he saw a pauper's funeral, in all the grim stark squalor and disregard of all decent humanity which marked such things. It made a deep impression on his mind, which was never eradicated and awoke in him a desire to help the poor, to give them a measure of happiness and a decent chance in life. From such chance encounters do great happenings spring. He did brilliantly at Oxford and entered Parliament in 1826, when the Duke of Wellington was Prime Minister. He might have attained the highest offices but Parliament did not mean to him a path for personal advancement and fame. It meant a place in which he could be loyal to his friends and wherein he believed he could effect reforms and help those who needed help so sadly. In 1828, however, he was a Commissioner of the India Board of Control.

All that he wanted was to bring hope, help and happiness to those in need of those things. Of noble birth himself, he was not *of* the people, but he was always *for* the people, their loving benefactor and sympathetic friend. He knew, to his cost, what unhappiness meant, he had suffered and he wanted to prevent suffering in others, especially in the case of little children.

There is no space here to set out the vastness of his labours, the long list of reforms which he brought about. He fought for reform from his earliest manhood. Amongst the most important which he achieved were the Licensing Acts and the Factory Act, and one which regulated the employment of women and children in coal mines. The women and children were treated like beasts of burden. Little mites, sometimes only four years old, were made to toil in the dark depths of the mines, harnessed to trucks, crawling on all fours like animals. Antony Ashley Cooper stopped all that. He put an end to the tyranny exercised by chimney sweeps on their unfortunate young boy apprentices. These poor children were made to climb the chimneys and sweep them by hand, blinded and choked by soot and dust. Sometimes they got wedged in the smoke stacks and perished there. Charles Kingsley drew a picture of them in *The Water Babies*. The Earl of Shaftesbury gained those children their freedom. He became interested too in slum clearance and better housing. He got The Lodging House Act passed and Charles Dickens, himself a great reformer, said it was the best bit of legislation which ever came before Parliament.

The establishment of the Peabody Buildings and other schemes of the same kind—great advancements in their day—were due to his influence. He practised what he preached. On his Dorset estate he had a model village, where the cottages were indeed models of comfort and perfection and for which he charged his tenants, as rental, one shilling per week. He championed what were then called the Ragged Schools in which very poor children got a chance of education. In 1848 he told the House of Commons that by means of those schools, 10,000 children had been given a chance in life. He became chairman of that movement and held the post for 39 years, during which period 300,000 children who would otherwise have been illiterate, got a sound education. He had a mind and care for them when they left school too. He founded the Shoe Blacks Brigade which gave employment to over 300 of them and enabled them to earn a decent living. In their little round hats and their red jackets, they were a feature of London life. Many men who had been educated at Ragged Schools rose to positions of eminence and trust. And reforms in the way of treating juvenile offenders owed much to the Earl of Shaftesbury. He guarded young lives.

Public health and sanitation came into his scope too. He was Chairman of the Central Body of Public Health and helped to defeat the scourge of cholera. Florence Nightingale went so far as to say that he saved the British Army in the Crimea. Many honours were offered to him but he refused them all save the Garter and that ancient and high Order of Chivalry never had a worthier Knight. A deeply religious man, in his evangelical way, he worked for Christianity, and was indeed a true follower of Christ. He was Chairman of the British and Foreign Bible Society for many years, and also of the Society for the Conversion of the Jews. He showed deep practical interest in the London City Mission for the Poor and also in The Young Men's Christian Association.

The people whom he befriended loved him and trusted him. It is certain that by example and precept he prevented many serious riots and possible bloodshed in the industrial disputes in 1848. Like Wesley, he may even have prevented a revolution.

What was he like, this good man of good works? He was tall, handsome, with regular features and he moved with grace. He had a fine voice and was a splendid orator. He was a patrician whose heart was with the people. He always had the courage of his convictions. He opposed the idea of making Queen Victoria Empress of India. That he lost. But he helped in the establishment of the Crystal Palace for the recreation of the people.

His work goes on today, some of it unseen and unrecognised, but there still remain the Shaftesbury Homes and the *Arethusa* training ship to testify to his achievements.

His work in respect of slum clearance let in sun, light and air into what had been places of sordid grime and disease. He called attention to this need in 1851, and as a result two Acts were passed—Lord Shaftesbury's Act and the Labouring Classes Act. They empowered local authorities to deal with disgraceful housing conditions. And in succeeding years they were implemented and strengthened. It was because of them that the old Metropolitan Board of Works, in 1886, was able to demolish bad slums in the West End and replace them by a new and broad thoroughfare, which they called Shaftesbury Avenue. Down the years that avenue has altered in appearance and character and is now the main theatre street of London. And even in that there is a link with the

Earl. For he originated a movement to give religious services on
Sundays in theatres and music halls. The House of Lords attacked
him but, as usual, he won.

Shaftesbury Avenue stands as a memorial to this great man
and so does the most popular statue in London which we shall
meet very soon. Amongst other things Shaftesbury Avenue
with its fine English name, is a boundary of Soho, now looked
upon as the crime centre of London and for years the foreign
quarter. It is so still but the tremendous influx of aliens, of all
races and colours, has long since burst its narrow boundaries and
spread far and wide. It has been in existence for only seventy-four
years, and was almost the last work undertaken by the old
Metropolitan Board of Works, before that body surrendered to
the London County Council. It is a pity that the construction of
the Avenue was not delayed a little longer, for whatever opinion
many people may hold of the L.C.C. there is little doubt that
they would have made a far better job of this new artery of
London and made it much on the same scale as Kingsway and
Aldwych. They would have seen to it that it was constructed in
accordance with the importance of its locality, and given London
a grand vista to Piccadilly Circus, equal to anything in the world.
All the old Board of Works did was to drive through the mean
and shabby district and to throw into one, two streets which
already existed—King's Street and Dudley Street. They left
many of the old undesirable buildings standing, especially on the
south side. In course of time they came down and others went up
of a better quality, but it was a very slow job and should have
been done at once, and the avenue made wider.

It contains nothing of historical interest, but right at the start
there is a theatre—as befits London's Theatre Street—the Prince's
Theatre built and opened in 1911 by those two remarkable men
Fred and Walter Melville, who also owned the Lyceum and some
suburban places as well. They were a perfectly astounding pair
and Dickens would have adored them. Although tightly bound
by blood and business interests, they would quarrel fiercely and

often not speak to each other for a year on end, although they both occupied the same office, a very shabby Victorian room. They would converse entirely through their faithful and long suffering manager, Bert Hammond, who sat between them. Each heard what the other said but took no notice of it until it was repeated to him by Mr Hammond. The quarrel would not end until somebody from outside attacked one or the other of them and then they came together with a click and fell upon the foe. But shortly afterwards, hostilities would break out again. They were both very rich men; Fred Melville left £314,228 and Walter left £205,861. They died within a year of each other, both at the age of 62. To look at them in life, you would not have thought they had a copper between them. Mr Fred's suits were odd in the right meaning of the word—not only were they aged but hardly ever, except on gala occasions, did he appear in a complete suit. As a rule, jacket, vest and trousers were of different vintage and colour. His hat had a hole in it and he said it was good for ventilation. I have seen him wearing a bootlace as a tie and there was almost always a tear in the left-hand top corner of his shirt— near the collar. His boots were bought for hard wear and not for elegance. I once saw Mr Walter taking the air on Hampstead Heath one bright sunshiny morning in October. He had on a straw hat, many, many seasons old and tinted by the weather, a blue coat so shiny with age and wear that it reflected the rays of the sun like a mirror—a waistcoat the original colour of which defied detection, grey flannel trousers now green with long service. He had on a pair of brown boots which had been blacked over. On his right hand was a very old and dirty white woollen glove, on his left was a sock.

For some time the Princes was not a very lucky theatre—but whoever lost money there, it was never the Melvilles. Nowadays it is a popular playhouse and a very good one. But the Melvilles were real theatre—they even wrote their own plays and pantomime, produced them and if need be played in them too.

On the north side of Cambridge Circus there is not much of

note. The old buildings were only cleared away quite recently—and huge blocks of flats and offices have arisen. But there is the Saville Theatre, a very handsome and excellent playhouse, opened in 1931 and although successful too young yet to have any tradition. It was damaged by enemy action in the Second World War but withstood the shock and soon got going again. A little behind the actual Avenue but near enough to be considered ancillary to it, is the fine old church of St Giles, in the churchyard of which is the grave of Penderell, the man who saved the life of King Charles II after the disaster of Worcester fight, by hiding him in the oak tree. The gravestone is suitably inscribed.

Almost next door to the Saville is what used to be the offices of the firm of Feldman, the great music publishers. It is still in the same line of business for it belongs nowadays to Francis, Day and Hunter, the senior and world famous firm of music publishers. But Bert Feldman built Feldman House as he had founded the business. He was also a colourful and curious character, a real eccentric. Enormously rich, he hardly ever spent a penny on himself. He never married but lived with his sister in an enormous house where they only occupied two or three rooms. The lawn in the garden was Bert's pride and joy and nobody was ever allowed to walk on it. Every week, as part of the housekeeping, he took home to his sister, who was as eccentric as he was, a five pound bag of silver. Hundreds of these bags, unopened were found all over the house when he died. He had supper every night, with his sister, at a celebrated fish restaurant in the Tottenham Court Road, which had scores of branches. The proprietor's name was Sam Isaacs and his slogan, blazoned over the country was 'This is the Plaice'. Bert Feldman never spent more than 10d. on supper for himself and his sister together. The block of offices he built, quite an enormous place, was far too big for his wants, big as his business was. It had scores and scores of rooms and in every one was an occupant who was supposed to be working at something or another. I once asked him why he had so many people on his staff. 'Well', he said, 'if you've got a lot of rooms you must have somebody in them. Empty rooms are no good to anyone.'

He did let off whole floors—one to the famous theatrical firm of Grossmith and Laurillard. When they broke up, Julian Wylie the pantomime king, took the whole floor. He was a wonderful man, a great character and a real king of pantomime. He himself had the heart of a child and he brought happiness to countless thousands of children. He and Bert Feldman were friends and there was no hard and fast agreement. For seven years Feldman never demanded any rent. Julian said nothing about it. At last Feldman woke up to this and sent in a demand. Wylie replied he was not going to pay anything; he had now established squatter's rights. That flabbergasted Feldman. There were most protracted negotiations which Wylie conducted with his tongue in his cheek. It was eventually settled, in his favour, and he paid much less than had been demanded. Feldman learnt his lesson. He had agreements with everybody after that.

The building is still there. It had a large resplendent entrance hall—where music was sold at a counter and on settees you could always find songwriters waiting in hopes of selling Bert Feldman a new song. Off the hall was a very large rehearsal room around the walls of which were enormous pictures of music hall stars who sang Feldman's songs. A large and ornate staircase led up to the first floor, where Feldman's own offices were situated. It was heavily carpeted, but above that there was only lino and the splendour waned. His own private office was meretricious to a degree—a shocking imitation of Empire style with a truly awful painted ceiling. He thought it was wonderful and did an amazing amount of business there. He was large and florid, with very keen, twinkling eyes and a very big moustache. He would perhaps meet you on the stairs and stop dead, surveying you with wonder. 'Where've you been?' he would demand. 'To China? I never see anything of you—you never come and see me. What's the matter? Come in soon and have a cup of tea.' You had perforce to accept the invitation. You would be kept waiting and then shown into his private room, where he would regard you with deep suspicion. 'What d'you want,' he would demand, 'Come to borrow money have you?' You would remind him of his invitation and he would be a bit stand-offish—but you got your tea and an amusing chat.

Pianos were always being played in scores of the rooms—all different tunes—men orchestrated music, prepared band parts, did all sorts of things—or nothing at all. It was all the same to Bert Feldman. He did an enormous show in Blackpool every year; to plug his songs he had a huge concert hall and theatre there. He had showrooms too where song pluggers sang and played new 'numbers' all the time. In those days sheet music was popular and had not been ousted by gramophone records. He published thousands of song hits, all more enduring than what are called 'The Top Ten' today. I am told that some of those last for quite a couple of days before being supplanted. But he has a right to a place in this book because one of the songs he published was *Tipperary*. He bought it cheap, it hung fire and then the first world war made it a classic. He made immense sums and to his credit he saw to it that the original author had his share too. For Feldman and his firm, for all their oddity and sharpness, had a heart. I had offices there myself for a long time. The Second World War broke out and all places of amusement closed down. I, in common with all the other tenants, received a note from Feldman's saying that we were not to trouble about paying rent during such a crisis. If things got better, then the matter could be discussed, but in the meantime—carry on as best one could—and not to worry. Shaftesbury Avenue wrested the title of London's Theatre Street from the Strand, which famous street had held it for years. At one time there were eight theatres in it, a famous Theatre of Varieties, which often was used as a theatre, as indeed, it is today, a small cinema and another music hall which gave way to a restaurant. In Cambridge Circus, but belonging to Shaftesbury Avenue stood, and still stands, that Theatre of Varieties which became a remarkable theatre—The Palace.

It was built and opened by Richard D'Oyly Carte on 31st January 1891, and entitled The Royal English Opera House. That of course was fatal, for to call a theatre an English Opera House is certain destruction as has so often been proved. Carte had made a fortune out of the Gilbert and Sullivan Operas and he was going to make another out of real opera, so he thought. He did not realise that although the British public responds warmly to comic opera, it is chary of opera itself. Carte opened the theatre with an opera called *Ivanhoe* composed by Sir Arthur Sullivan. It failed quite miserably although it pleased Queen Victoria. Nothing succeeded. The great Augustus Harris of Drury Lane took it over. Failure was his fate too, but he altered the name to the Palace. Shares in the undertaking were offered in bundles at knock down prices. Then came the man who saved the day. He was Charles Morton, the man with the touch of gold. He had invented Music Hall itself at the Canterbury across the river and had saved many other places, such as the Alhambra and the Tivoli in the Strand. He saved the Palace. He called it a Theatre of Varieties—not a Variety Theatre or Music Hall, you will observe. Ladies could not go to such vulgar places, but they could and did go to the Theatre of Varieties—that was different. Morton made it the smartest Theatre of Varieties in the world. He had a motto 'One Quality Only—the Best', and lived up to it. He looked like a solid country solicitor or banker, not a bit like the manager of a music hall. He pervaded the place, first to come and last to go. With 'bills' of amazing talent he made it a great success. He worked there almost up to his death, at the age of eighty-five. He nominated his successor, a young man named Alfred Butt, and Butt showed genius. He kept up the quality and constantly produced novelties. Pavlova the Peerless was seen there for the first time—Maud Allen danced in scanty clothes and bare legs to the music of Mendelssohn's 'Spring Song' and in even scantier and exotic raiment she was 'Salome', complete with the head of John the Baptist. Was this art or a stunt? There was great contro-versy but all London flocked to see. Butt invented the Palace

Girls—the first dancing troupe to be associated with an individual theatre. They became the rage. Every star came to the Palace, and then, in 1914, when the taste for revue was rampant, Butt produced his first Palace revue—*The Passing Show*. It began a series of such productions which have never been equalled or surpassed—*Bric-a-Brac, Vanity Fair, Airs and Graces* and *Hullo America*, the last in 1918. Famous names were in the casts: Gertie Millar, Nelson Keys, Arthur Playfair, Billy Merson, Stanley Lupino, and it was in *The Passing Show* that Basil Hallam sang 'Gilbert the Filbert' (the Pride of Piccadilly) composed by Hermann Finck, the Palace conductor. Elsie Janis was there too, one of the greatest stars ever to cross the Atlantic, and her amazing mother came too. Elsie, whose mother announced that she was the Virgin of Vaudeville, was a wonderful performer. She could do it all, and her impersonations—done with a minimum of effort and merely screwing up the hair and fixing it with one hairpin—she had a little line of them on the stage before her—were so real that she drove the celebrated Gaby Deslys screaming from a box. I can see her now, a slim figure in midnight blue, dancing and singing 'GiveMe the Moonlight' in *HulloAmerica* whilst an audience largely of men on leave from France went mad with delight. Datas, the Memory Man, was of the Palace, so was Margaret Cooper at the piano, and Barclay Gammon. *The Follies*, who will never be equalled, first burst on London there. When Sir Alfred Butt, knighted and later made a baronet for war services, sold the Palace, there were films, which did little good, and then musical plays. There were great ones amongst those—Clayton and Waller presented *No, No, Nanette* there amongst other big successes of theirs. That belongs to Shaftesbury Avenue. C. B. Cochran did a lot of shows, but amongst them the famous Marx Brothers flopped. Some of his revues were of course outstanding, and much of the music came from our own Vivian Ellis. That amazing couple, Cicely Courtneidge and Jack Hulbert, had a run of success here in the Second World War, and Ivor Novello staged his last musical play—the last in which he himself appeared—at the

Palace. Presented by Tom Arnold, it was *King's Rhapsody* and was one of Ivor's best. It also contained his best acting performance. But alas, during the run that genius of the British Theatre died—almost in harness—only a few hours after appearing on the Palace stage. His very last play belonged to Shaftesbury Avenue too—*Gay's the Word* at the Saville. Ivor was very much of Shaftesbury Avenue—he had successes at the Queen's, the Globe, the Apollo and the Lyric too.

Time was when the Palace Theatre was an outstanding landmark in London's theatre street. You might or might not like its Victorian terra cotta but you had to admit its dignity, and in the old days it was a blaze of flowers. Every one of its innumerable windows had window boxes gay with blooms. Great flower baskets hung from the portico and the box office was a bower. This floral domain was ruled over by an amazing little Frenchman named Clement-Leroy. The fact that the Palace was a place of entertainment and a busy one meant nothing to him. He saw it only as a background for his floral art. He would water the flowers along the top of the box office oblivious of the fact that he drenched the customers. During my management of the Palace there was a most important board meeting. I went into the room about an hour before it was due to start, to see all was well—and was frozen dumb with horror. M. Leroy had decided that this was the day he must change some of the window boxes, so he had piled them all in the sacred Boardroom and had earth all over the lovely carpet. I stormed and raged and made him shift the lot (only just in time) and turned on an army of cleaners. Leroy was most annoyed—what was a board meeting to him?—his boxes had to be changed. It took him some days to recover and forgive me. The Palace always glittered with lights and was brilliant with fresh paint. That was in keeping with the West End of London which seems to me, and to others of my generation a shabbier place today and certainly less dignified. But inside the Palace retains its atmosphere.

Opposite the Palace nowadays is a bomb site. One presumes in the near future shops and offices will arise there. But it was once the site of the Shaftesbury Theatre. This was built and opened in 1888 by Miss Wallis, a leading actress herself. It was never one of London's lucky theatres. It had a run of failures until that great actor E. S. Willard brought some degree of success there with plays by Henry Arthur Jones, such as *The Middleman*. *Cavalleria Rusticana* had its first London production there in 1891. A very early musical comedy called *Morocco Bound*—it was really musical farce—had some success in 1893. On the first night a 'skirt dance' by Letty Lind 'stopped the show'. Lewis Waller, needless to say brought success there in 1897 in a stage version of that best seller *The Sorrows of Satan* by Marie Corelli (does anyone read her now?). But £15,000 was lost over another production called *The Little Genius*. But success came full measure and brimming over when a completely unknown American company brought in a despised American musical play—on borrowed fares—which they produced on 1st April 1898. That company and its play leapt to fame overnight, for it was *The Belle of New York*, and when lovely and talented Edna May bade us 'Follow On', we did so in shoals. The play lives on, one of the loveliest scores of all time. It ran for 697 performances, up to then the Shaftesbury's longest run and not equalled or exceeded until 1909 when Robert Courtneidge produced *The Arcadians*—a thing of beauty in every way—which ran for 809 performances and which will never be forgotten, for 'The Pipes of Pan' and others of its songs are firmly embedded in the national repertoire. Sweet-voiced Florence Smithson, dashing Harry Welchman, the two contrasted comics Dan Rolyat and Alfred Lester—'I've gotter motter', was an Arcadian song—that ideal leading lady Phyllis Dare and a young recruit named Cicely Courtneidge were all in the amazing cast, and when the curtain rose on *Arcadia*, which had been forgotten by Father Time, London gasped at its beauty. Some of the girls in the Courtneidge musical productions at the Shaftesbury rivalled those of the Gaiety for glamour—the memory lingers over May Etheredge, Sheila Hayes, May Kinder and many more—nor must one forget the combined talent and beauty of Cicely Debenham and Iris Hoey. An important milestone at the Shaftesbury was the production of the first 'all black show' which London had seen, in 1903. It was called *In Dahomey* and had two remarkable coloured comedians in Williams and Walker. The Shaftesbury Avenue fortunes improved as time went on but that jinx was always waiting and a German bomb destroyed it completely in the Blitz.

The shops of Shaftesbury Avenue and the residential flats flow along both sides. They are neither arresting nor have they famous names; it is a welter of all kinds and conditions—with perhaps costumiers for ladies in the ascendant—but no stores with famous names. Shaftesbury Avenue is always being modernised. Quite recently a large section, next door to the Palace, came down and modernity arose, with a luxury cinema in the basement, called the Columbia. There is, however, an old established and excellent firm of English haberdasher's, Colletts, on the corner of Wardour Street which keeps its quality high. Then on the right-hand side, just off the Avenue in Soho, is St Anne's church, once the great centre of London's church music—its concerts and oratorios being frequently attended by Queen Mary—but now a bombed shell. Its churchyard has been made quite a pleasant spot for those who want a little rest whilst still living. That churchyard contains a monument which is probably unique in London, for it is to a king, Theodore of Corsica, who died bankrupt in London and was buried by a tailor to whom he owed money. Then we come to the theatres again, which, apart from the destroyed Shaftesbury, hug the right-hand side going towards Piccadilly in this street. Here are the twins, the Queen's and the Globe, which share the same party wall. The Globe was the second to open, on 27th December 1907 and Sir Seymour Hicks, built it and gave it his name. It did not do very well for some reason as the Hicks, and the name was changed to the Globe. It has been for many years a most successful playhouse, housing all sorts of plays and all the best names, a quite delightful and intimate theatre useful for any kind of show. For some time it was the London headquarters of Charles Frohman, the great American impresario, who installed a lift which was unlucky for him, for he was stuck in it for the best part of a day on one occasion. He had asked nobody's permission to construct this lift and the owners lodged a suit against him. It was whilst coming to London, in the First World War, to defend this action, that he was torpedoed on the *Lusitania* and went down into the great wastes of the Atlantic with a smile on his dauntless face and a quotation from his favourite play, *Peter Pan*, on his lips—'To die will be a very big adventure'. The Globe has been a lucky theatre for years and is at present the headquarters of the H. M. Tennent firm of producers, one of the most important in the country.

The Queen's does not now resemble its twin as much as it did. Once the Globe and Queen's, externally, were almost identical, but the Second World War altered that. It opened on 8th October 1907 with a curious manager named J. E. Vedrenne in charge and a play called *The Sugar Bowl*. That did not succeed and indeed success was a long time coming to this charming theatre, named after Queen Mary and with a big picture of her in its white and green vestibule. Big names tried but nothing would bring the people in sufficient numbers. Then a dance craze hit London and everybody went mad about the tango. An enterprising management started Tango Teas at the Queens; you paid 2/6d., sat where you liked, saw a fashion show, and watched experts dance the tango, joining in if you so desired. Everybody flocked to the Queen's, But an odd couple of Hebrew gentlemen in the ready-made clothes business, whose names were 'Potash and Perlmutter', put this theatre on the map in 1914 and it never looked back. Owen Nares was an actor-manager there in 1919, and later such plays as *The Apple Cart*, *The Barretts of Wimpole Street*, *Dear Octopus* and *Rebecca*, packed the place. Still some ill-luck waited and during the run of *Rebecca* a German bomb hit the Queen's on the night of 24th September 1940. It was the first London theatre to become a casualty. It has been rebuilt in most modern style and success goes on. But the Globe remains the complete example of the elegant Edwardian Theatre.

Proceeding towards Piccadilly Circus, you cross Rupert Street. On the corner was once the Prince Rupert Tavern, whilst on the first floor was Fitz's Bar, run by a clever actor known as Aubrey Fitzgerald and one of the places which visitors to London wanted to see on account of its 'artistic' clientele. It has gone now and a wine merchant's is there. Then come two more theatres: the Apollo, opened in 1901 by Henry Lowenfeld, which has been consistently successful and which was for years the headquarters of that divinely inspired and still unrivalled super 'Pierrot' show, 'The Follies' headed by the genius H. G. Pelissier; and next door, surrounded by offices largely given over to theatrical enterprises, is the Lyric Theatre, another Shaftesbury Avenue playhouse of note which was opened on 17th December 1888. Its history is long and colourful and perhaps its greatest landmark was the production of that memorable play, *The Sign of the Cross*—with its author, Wilson Barrett, superb actor, as 'Marcus Superbus' and its message of Christianity which drew myriads to see it. It was this theatre which was managed by Mr Pitt, the gentleman who lost the bag of gold in Piccadilly. He had a flat and a roof garden above it and played the harmonium in and out of season. But he had his dislikes. One day I found him making up the salaries for his artists on the stairs outside his office. On asking why he was doing this extraordinary thing, he told me there was a mouse inside. I went in, defeated the mouse and Mr Pitt re-entered his office, but with some trepidation.

On the corner of Shaftesbury Avenue and Gt Windmill Street used to stand the Avenue Buffet, which was run by a gentleman of the ancient faith who also owned racehorses and who spent his life dashing from cash register to cash register to see that his staff had not 'done him'. But the food was good. I went down there to lunch one day whilst producing a play at the Queen's. R. C. McCleery, the scenic artist—and nobody could paint trees and foliage as could 'Mac'—said he would accompany me. He

was a bit late, however, and I had started. ' What are you having?'
he asked. 'Irish stew and apple pudding to follow, Mac,' I said,
'both excellent here.' Mac hailed the waiter. 'I'll have the same as
my friend,' he said, 'Irish stew and apple pudding. But I'm in a
hurry. Bring 'em both together on the same plate and I'll eat 'em
that way. It'll save time.' And he did. Above the Avenue was the
old home of the Eccentric Club where we revelled until the small
hours in those days of long ago—in loyalty to the bird who was
our badge and symbol—the owl. Just further along was a Lyons
Corner House which during the Second World War became
'Rainbow Corner', the gathering spot for American Forces in
town. There was also the Monico, which really belongs to
Piccadilly Circus—and anyway only its front wall remains now
—but we shall meet it later.

The other or southern side of Shaftesbury Avenue is rather
without feature until one comes to the very end—almost at
Piccadilly Circus. And there stands what is perhaps the most
important and characteristic place in Shaftesbury Avenue. That is
the Trocadero Restaurant. It is hardly possible that there is a
Londoner or a visitor to London who has not at least seen and
heard about 'The Troc', as it is popularly called. It made history.
On its site or part of its site stood a small music hall known as
the Trocadero run by Albert Chevalier and a famous agent
known as Hugh J. Didcott. It was in this hall that old Charles
Coborn first sang *Two Lovely Black Eyes*. But astute, and not so
black eyes were on the spot, belonging to the directors of the
firm of J. Lyons and Co. Ltd. They had envisaged a great new
restaurant, the like of which London had never seen, run on novel
lines and right in the centre of things, practically in Piccadilly
Circus. Their dream came true when they opened the Trocadero
Restaurant in 1896, one year before the Diamond Jubilee of
Queen Victoria. London was at its mightiest and its wealthiest
and yet it lacked a restaurant where one could dine with elegance
and ease. The men had their clubs, but there was still little else
but coffeeshops, indifferent eatinghouses, the old-fashioned chop-

houses or the meals in pubs. Lyons foresaw the need and filled it. London gasped at this new palace of gastronomy—with its handsome exterior and interior, its magnificently decorated rooms, its sweeping staircases and twinkling chandeliers, its frescoes of the Knights of King Arthur. It approved the waiters—not in dirty stained old evening clothes and 'dicky' fronts but resplendent attire, with gold braided collars and well trimmed side whiskers. The customers gasped at the scope and variety of the menu, and at the most reasonable prices, the quick silent service in luxurious surroundings and a wine list which provided superior drinking to the popular beer or spirits. Lyons had hit off the spirit of the age to perfection. Ladies could and did dine there unaccompanied by a gentleman and suffer no shame. Once, though, a rather worried but obliging management covered a lady in with screens because she insisted on smoking. Elsewhere she would have been expelled.

The Trocadero always had excellent orchestras which played good music. Later C. B. Cochran himself was to provide a supper show. It had a Long Bar which rivalled that of the Criterion. It became a rendezvous—'meet you at the Troc'—and it had thousands who dined and supped there regularly. It became and it remains a family house, for the quality has been kept up. And here it still stands, at the end of Shaftesbury Avenue to show the world what living was like in the days when that thoroughfare was built, when income tax was 8d. in the pound and considered ruinous; a place of Victorian and Edwardian atmosphere and surroundings and of service and quality, which has moved with the times but kept its reputation unsullied. Famous people have dined there—still dine there—for the Troc is one of the great centres of London. It would indeed be a grievous day if we ever had to sing 'Goodbye Trocadero'.

17

Regent Street and the London Ladies

Regent Street is the joint dream of a king and an architect, who envisaged what was to be one of the finest thoroughfares in the whole world, but which never quite materialised. The intention was to link Carlton House, the residence of the Prince Regent, afterwards George IV, with a new mansion he proposed to build in Regent's Park. But when the Regent became King he left Carlton House, which was pulled down in 1828—although bits of it survive, in the true London fashion. The Ionic columns at the front of the National Gallery came from Carlton House. The Regent's Park Palace was, of course, never built at all. But Nash lavished beautiful mansions around the Park, and he erected Carlton House Terrace where the old princely residence had stood. Had that road been built as was originally intended, it would have been a wonderful vista. But it had to take a sweep around the end of Piccadilly. What was accomplished had—and still retains—a nobility of its own and a kingliness which its royal sponsor never attained himself. It is a young street as London goes and its birthpangs were not easy. It was actually begun in 1814, when the Prince Regent, as George IV was then, himself got the plans through Parliament. Both street and park were to bear his title of Regent. He himself approved those plans and gave the word to 'Go'. Four architects were involved—with Nash in command—and many believe that Nash was a natural son of the Regent as I have said. The other three men were Soane, Repton, and Decimus Burton. The estimated cost was £300,000, a vast sum in those days. But the Napoleonic War was raging and that held up the construction. War impeded Regent Street again when in the fullness of time it was reconstructed. That was the First World War. So George IV saw its beginning and its first edition and George V saw the new Regent Street completed. Three monarchs had reigned in the interim, William IV, Victoria and Edward VII. It was first completed in 1820 and in 1927, one hundred and seven years later, King George V and Queen Mary rode down the Regent Street we know today to the acclamations of the multitude.

Regent Street north of Piccadilly Circus was originally stopped by lack of funds in July 1816, but Lower Regent Street was proceeded with. However Napoleon was beaten in 1815 and peace brought new hopes and prosperity, so the work eventually went on and was completed in 1820. And what was there before Regent Street? Well, of course, once it was open country. Woodcock were shot where the County Fire Office now stands. That was in the reign of Charles II, when London was a small city indeed. The few houses which stood about were looked upon as country residences. What is now Oxford Street, then just the road to Oxford, ran between hedges. There was a meadow from which bubbled a spring, the memory of which is preserved in Conduit Street. And where you now find Golden Square was a tract of ground past which travellers hurried and in horror. It had been a plague pit into which the dead of London were shot in loads during the Great Plague. For many years it was believed that the earth still held the dreaded infection and two generations passed before any building arose on it at all.

As all roadmakers must do, Nash had to adapt existing thoroughfares which lay about and across his site, and he utilised quite a lot of the course of one of them when making Regent

Street. This was a pretty old pathway or roadway or lane, whichever you like to call it, and it had a variety of names, being known
at various times as Suggen Lane, Shug Lane and Shrug Lane. It
ended up in 1770 as Titchfield Street and finally vanished when
Shaftesbury Avenue was made. Between Shrug Lane and Windmill Street was a triangular piece of land which had been built
on in Restoration times. It was crossed by Queen Street, which
joined Windmill Street to Sherwood Street, which in turn ran
from Shrug Lane to Brewer Street. This little colony was
described as 'pretty, neat, clean and quiet, with good houses, well
inhabited'. Its location is now Denman Street. Sherwood Street,
which still remains, was called after a local squire, but underwent
certain changes of name, being variously known as Sheriff Street
and Sherrard Street. Shrug Lane, which seems to have been a
pretty poor sort of place, merged into Marybone Street and ran
as far as Brewer Street. What remains of it today forms Glasshouse Street. But a part of it to the north—for it wound around—
called Swallow Street (and indeed Swallow Street is the real
ancestor of Regent Street) crossed the site mapped out by Nash
and bordered on Piccadilly. In 1650 it had been called Swallow
Close, named after its owner, one Thomas Swallow who has thus
left his mark on London. It became Swallow Street about 1671
and then it ran from Piccadilly to Oxford Street. Its upper or
northern part was called Great Swallow Street, and that was the
basis of Regent Street. Its lower part was known as Little Swallow
Street—and as Swallow Street it still remains, off Piccadilly. To
the west of Great Swallow Street lay a tract called the Great
Common Field. The whole of the centre section of Nash's Regent
Street follows the old line of Swallow Street, which appears to
have been a dismal sort of place, muddy, full of ruts and potholes
with a low class livery stable in it which was a resort for footpads
and highwaymen. From such a lowly beginning did Regent
Street arise and one may be grateful to Nash and his royal
patron for sweeping away such slums.

When Nash at last got well under way and his street was taking

Gertie Millar

Vesta Tilley
'Algy—the Piccadilly Johnny with the little glass eye.'

shape he came in for much obstruction, actual and verbal. He built in brick but he covered the brick with plaster. For many years the fashion had been for plain brick. Naturally such an innovation had its determined opponents. There are still many who prefer plain brick, especially when mellowed by time; Queen Anne and early Georgian houses show how gracious it can be. But Nash believed in plaster and he slapped it on. This gave rise to what would now be called wisecracks, one of which appeared in the *Quarterly Review* of June 1826:

'Augustus at Rome was for buildings renown'd,
And of marble he left what of bricks he had found.
But is not our Nash, too, a very great master?
He finds us all brick and he leaves us all plaster.'

Not that Nash cared two straws about that. But he met determined opposition and defeat over what he considered was to be the crowning glory of his lovely Regent Street, at its Piccadilly end, which he called the Quadrant. He lined the curve of the street at that end with a great colonnade of cast iron columns—actually they were made of a composition of his own invention—which were 16 feet 2 inches in height, exclusive of the plinths. The pillars supported a balustraded roof which joined the frontage of the buildings. His idea was to provide a nice promenade for the householders on the ceiling, as it were, a delightful covered way for pedestrians in the street, protecting them from rain and wind, and the architect thought everyone would be delighted, especially the shop keepers who could thus provide shelter for those gazing in their windows. It was a popular form of building abroad and not unknown here either for there had been the famous Piazza at Covent Garden. But the inhabitants of that part of Regent Street covered by the Quadrant would not have it at all. When told that such things were common in foreign cities, that only increased their dislike. The public were essentially English in the early 19th century and foreign ideas were taboo. They maintained that this Quadrant made the ground and first floors gloomy and prevented ventilation; they said that doubtful characters would lurk amongst the shadows of the pillars to the detriment of all concerned. Nash's suggestion of a glass roof and proper super-vision to remove the doubtful characters, if any, did not go down well at all. What did go down was the Quadrant. The public won and Nash had to surrender after a fight. To remove the Quadrant required an Act of Parliament. One was passed to that purpose in 1848 and down came the pillars, the whole 270 of them. With their granite plinths they were sold by auction. Railway companies snapped them up to embellish new stations and they realised in all £2900, but the total cost of their demolition was £3900—which those who had objected to the Quadrant had to pay—so their victory cost them dear in increased rates. And so a street feature which was unique was swept away by sturdy London conservatism—although a semblance of what it might have looked like is still provided by the County Fire Office at the bottom of Regent Street and the arches of the Ritz in Piccadilly. Not all those Nash pillars left London and they may still be seen. The proprietors of Theatre Royal, Drury Lane bought some of them and they stand along one side of that great theatre yet, forming a colonnade of majestic proportions, protecting the people who in the old days used to wait there for the pit and gallery doors to open, giving a covered way to the players going to the stage door and also forming a canopy for the Royal Entrance. Those pillars are part of Nash's Regent Street Quadrant.

They were a source of anxiety to those responsible for Drury Lane during the Second World War, and especially to me. I was then Chief Air Raid Warden of the vast building. A salvage drive was at its height and despite my earnest plea, the authorities took away the old railings which protect the walls and which were embrasured every now and again for the sentry boxes which had stood there in the brave days when Old Drury had a guard mounted every night like the Bank of England. Underneath their paint those railings were little but rust; they had been there since 1812 and were roughly 130 years old. But they took them away.

My chief anxiety was, however, that they would discover that the columns were not stone but composite metal. Misled by the granite plinths they never interfered with them, although a good ringing blow would have disclosed the secret. So part of the Quadrant of Regent Street, the Royal Road, remains at Theatre Royal.

It is interesting to note that the destruction of the Quadrant took only twelve days.

When Regent Street was ready and glowing with magnificence, it was not the success which had been expected. It had been reckoned that tenants would swarm to occupy this noble street. But that was far from being the case. The tradespeople refrained from moving in and opening up. That was of course the inherent British dislike for anything new—one of the strange paradoxes of a race which always itches to destroy the old and then regards the new with grave suspicion. A nation which opened up the world had always been backward and unreceptive to anything new within its own borders. That was proved more recently by Kingsway and Aldwych and anyone who has tried to open a new theatre in London knows to his cost the reluctance of the public to respond. So the ground rents had to be reduced and everything offered at a much lower rate than had been anticipated. The leases are with the Crown. However, at last Regent Street caught on and became what it is today. The value of property rose and rose. When some of the original leases expired their value had risen from £50,000 to £450,000, and the value continues to rise. Some smaller firms have retired to side streets but the big and mighty of Regent Street hold on.

There have been many changes in the shops and stores of course. Fifty or sixty years ago, between New Burlington Street and Conduit Street, with an entrance therein, stood Lewis and Allenby's, a famous firm of drapers and milliners. In the same block was the firm of Messrs James Holmes and Co, who dealt in shawls. In their emporium you could buy a Cashmere shawl costing three hundred guineas, or an equally costly and lovely shawl from China. Where that celebrated firm of men's outfitters, Austin Reed, now stands, was once the shop of Johnson and Co, milliners and hatters to Her Majesty Queen Victoria and the final arbiters of hat fashions.

Regent Street became the most fashionable shopping street in London and remains so today. It is essentially given over to the ladies although men hold grimly to a foothold here and there. It was never a place of residence to any extent. Trade and commerce had it from the start. As becomes Crown property its shops show a display of Royal Appointments which I do not think is equalled anywhere else. The display of heraldry is positively mediaeval. In Regent Street are the premises of Messrs Garrard & Co Ltd, the Court Jewellers; Robinson and Cleaver, the famous linen house; Liberty's, whose fabrics—Liberty silks and satins—indeed everything, set a stamp over the whole world, and the standard is still maintained. That is a wonderful shop. There is a carpet department there and when you go into it Regent Street has vanished—you are in Samarkand. When Regent Street was rebuilt in the 1920's Liberty's conformed to the new style on the main street frontage, but at the side in Gt. Marlborough Street they caused the glories of Tudor days to rise again. There are those who wish that all Regent Street had been like that. There are too many firms to mention but Jay's still keep the flag flying on the Oxford Circus corner as they did in Victorian and Edwardian days, when a musical comedy thinly veiled under the title of *The Girl from Kay's* gave much delight. Regent Street has bewildering variety, for there is Hamley's, probably the finest toyshop in the world and a seeming paradise to children who gasp with amazement and become rigid with excitement on beholding it for the first time. They soon get moving, however, as I can vouch for as a grandfather. Regent Street, a royal street, reflects that in the service it gives, as you will find to a marked degree in every shop. I have no doubt that it exists in the ladies' shops for I do not penetrate there, but I can vouch for the shops which look after men. Austin Reed's give you personal service. When I got married, forty-eight years ago, I bought all my things there, and they looked upon it as their own wedding. Not a collar stud was forgotten. Going there again a few months ago I found the same spirit. And there is a tailor's—Hector Powe. Many men are scared of tailors and find the measuring and the fitting irksome and embarrassing. But from the moment you enter the Regent Street premises of Messrs Powe they take charge of you gently and without your being aware of it. You are wafted along, guided and handed over to an expert who knows all about clothes, who is not anonymous but who has his name on his table. You are given a minimum of trouble, you feel at home, eager and helpful men get enthusiastic about your choice—and probably head you off bad ideas—and at the end comes a suit which is real Regent Street.

Regent Street has never been famous in the entertainment world. Quite nearby is the London Palladium, standing on a site which was once Henglers—a miraculous circus, and in Regent Street there has been one cinema, the New Gallery, which is still a cinema but run by a religious denomination.

Despite the dominance of the ladies there are famous restaurants in Regent Street. Verry's is still there, modernised but of the same quality as when it seemed a bit of Paris slipped into London, and there are the Giants, the Café Royal and Oddenino's, known to so many as Oddy's. Much has been written about both places, which are as high in standard today as ever. The Café Royal has almost a literature of its own, there is no need to expound on it here. But there was a customer there who should not go unrecorded in this humble volume. His name was Jim Carney and he was the undefeated light weight champion of the world. He fought his battles under the old prize ring rules—a round did not end until one of the contestants was on the ground and practically nothing was barred. He fought with the 'raw 'uns' (bare fists) or the skin gloves (ordinary gloves with the fingers cut away at the knuckles). An amazing man of a bygone era, he was a link with the days of the Regency. He could neither read nor write and for years

I did his correspondence for him. But although illiterate he could always pick out a letter he wanted from a whole pile of them. He was very fond of what he called the 'Kaffy Ryle' and would sit there for hours amongst his friends—and he had many in the sporting world—listening to the conversation. He did not speak much himself and his method of expression was, to say the least, obscure. He would say, 'Well, there was me and 'im and that other bloke—you know 'im—what owns 'em (he meant a race-horse owner) we wos altogether and the other chap come up and there we was on the buffett at Liverpool Street and I see the other fellow as well, but he got away before I could reach 'im. So he said it was all right and I didn't see no 'arm in it, so there we were.' He was quite sure you understood all this. It was clear enough to him. At the 'Kaffy Ryle' he would consume quantities of port wine which he was convinced was a teetotal drink and nobody had ever seen him the worse for liquor.

He was a Birmingham boy and his first fight was there, when his father matched him against a lad from another mill at 10/- a side. Most of the hands from both mills took the afternoon off to see the scrap. Jim nearly killed the other boy in the second round, and got a good hiding from his father for making all the men miss half a day's work to see so little fighting. It was his first taste of how hollow a victory could be. Once he fought a man who died as a result of the battle. Jim had to lie low for a bit. But he told us there were no hard feelings—he went and saw his victim and 'bid him goodbye'. His hands seemed very small but they were like lumps of granite. When talking of his fights he would hit himself terrific blows in the face to illustrate what he meant—an ordinary man would have been knocked out but it made no difference to Jim. Nobody ever heard of a fight being stopped because of a cut eye in his day. Those old-timers pickled their faces in brine until their skins had the consistency of leather. He won all his fights and he finally retired. He became a 'minder' to a sporting character of no great repute named Abingdon Baird, known as 'the Squire', who at one time had Mrs Langtry under his protection. To hear

Jim's stories of those days made one's senses reel. He always kept in training. He walked round Richmond Park twice every day and made long country excursions to friends who gave him eggs, to which he was most addicted. He always had a mutton chop (cooked) in his pocket and a twist of salt and pepper in case he should get hungry, which he always did. He did debt collecting where debtors proved very difficult. He had his own methods which were ingenious and striking and he always got the cash. He was rather more violent than persuasive.

When he found some of his speed leaving him, he retired from the ring, an unbeaten champion with hundreds of grim, gory fights behind him. He found relaxation at race meetings and his hosts of admirers would always 'mark his card'. A very warm friend and patron was Lord Lonsdale, whose Belt Jim held. When King Edward VII went racing, there were just two people outside the approved circles with whom he shook hands—old 'Kate' the famous seller of race cards and Jim Carney. So long as Jim stuck to his information he did pretty well, but flushed with victory he would have a plunge on the last race. He would find one to beat the winner and in his own words, 'I turned rahnd and took six to four off a Sheeny'. That horse in the last race always lost and with it went most of Jim's winnings. He was loud in his lamentations and it was his firm and vehemently expressed decision that, 'There didn't orter be no last race.' To this he held tenaciously. It was no good trying to persuade him that there had to be a last race—he didn't believe it. The one before the last had done him proud; the last race had slaughtered him. No sort of proof of the necessity of finality was any good. According to Jim, last races should be banned for ever.

When he was in his late forties, the lightweight championship of the world went to America and stayed there for some time. They took old Jim off the shelf, dusted him and gave him a coat of paint as it were—he was in excellent condition—and sent him over to regain the Belt for England. Jim hated America, its food and all Yankees, except the men he fought. Those he regarded as his friends. He and his opponent met on a barge moored in the Hudson River. The battle lasted for ninety three rounds. Jim soon found he was fighting his opponent's seconds as well as his man. One of them tried to screw his ear off, another prodded him with a revolver. In the ninety-third round the American went down and showed no intention of getting up again. The crowd broke into the ring and tried to interfere and get it made a draw. Jim appealed to the boxing authorities and got the title—and the Belt. He came home in triumph, and never fought again. Many years afterwards that doughty American 'pug' came to London and we gave the two old warriors a dinner at the 'Kaffy Ryle'. It was quite wonderful. They went over that fight round by round, almost blow for blow, and they got so sentimental that they almost wept on each other's shoulders. Jim would show you his gloves—of course he called them his 'turtles'—and his Belt: those were the things in the world which mattered most. He was a giant in his day. Yet he was a small man, but up to his end, quick and active. He did not so much walk as trot on his toes. His face was square and devoid of expression, his eyes seemed half closed yet glittered under the lids. He was no punch-drunk fighter but, within his illiteracy, keenly intelligent and a good judge of character. He might have been carved out of oak. He had a smile which was a joy to see. He was always very clean and well shaven and wore a neat lounge suit—he had quite a wardrobe—and, incredible as it may seem, he always wore a bowler hat. When astonished it was his habit to seize the brim on both sides, lift it from his head and say, 'Oblige me.' I never heard him use foul language. He divided mankind into three classes—'them wot owned 'em'— racehorse owners; 'toffs'—the smart gentry who were wont to patronise him—and 'gents'. Those were the people he liked and respected. I am proud he put me in that category. He had a poor opinion of the modern fighter of later years—certainly of those who were post-1914. When asked about them, he just spat on the floor. But he had one exception to that rule—Jimmy Wilde.

He died during the Second World War—a very old man,

nobody quite knew how old, not even himself. A man of violence, he was really a gentle soul. There are no such men today—
and he was always to be seen in Regent Street. Only he always
called it Regency Street.

Nevertheless Regent Street belongs to the ladies. That great
man of the theatre the late Sir George Dance, the Napoleon of
touring companies and a very rich man, stated the fact clearly in
the immensely successful musical comedy which he wrote,
entitled *A Chinese Honeymoon*. It ran for 1075 performances from
its first production in 1901. In it Dance wrote a song called *The
A La Girl*—to be 'A La' something was very smart in those days.
Dance surveyed the girls of all nations and when he came to
England, this is what he said:

> 'Oh, the A La Girl is an English girl,
> With lots of A La Talk,
> And when she goes down Regent Street,
> She has an A La walk.
> She's an A La twinkle in her eye,
> She wears an A La curl,
> And she cuts a dash,
> With an A La Mash,
> Does the A La English Girl.'

For the sake of those who are not conversant with dead slang, a
Mash was the same as a K'Nut—or a Lad of the Village—a man
about town. Marie Dainton, a very great artiste, sang that song.

Mash was short for 'Masher' and there were lots in Regent
Street on account of the ladies to be found there.

For about 140 years the ladies have owned Regent Street. That
is only fair because men seized Piccadilly. But Swan and Edgar's,
facing into Piccadilly Circus and having frontage in both Piccadilly and Regent Street accentuated the female note. All sorts of
ladies have passed along that noble street. The Georgian ladies,
high waisted, classical lines and much befeathered, would step out
of their ornate carriages—coaches is the better word—driven by a

liveried coachman and with liveried footmen standing behind, carrying long rods to beat off hangers-on and footpads. And the Victorian ladies, who underwent such changes of style and figure during that long reign, also drove in carriages, not perhaps quite so showily magnificent as in Georgian times but still with resplendent liveries in early Victorian days, with coachmen and footmen and much the same routine. Ladies in great sweeping skirts, standing around them like balloons, crinolined and covered, with shawls over their shoulders and little round bonnets or poke bonnets on their heads; then with less full skirts and much larger bonnets, all very ornate and covered in frills and furbelows and with layers of petticoats. Legs must never be seen, ankles must not be displayed, but sometimes as the lady stepped down there was a glimpse of a striped stocking and the footman hastily averted his eyes. And the later Victorian ladies—crinolined again and wasp waisted, tight-laced to a degree but still most ornate, demure and circumspect. Not a trace of make-up anywhere, but full of dignity and poise. They thronged Regent Street and as they walked towards the shops from their carriages, all sorts of itinerant salesmen tried to catch their attention, especially those selling puppies and little dogs—to be driven off by the footmen and the uniformed men outside the shop doors. Regent Street knew them. And then the late Victorian and the Edwardian ladies, when perhaps femininity reached it highest point—their shopping Mecca was Regent Street.

They were, of course, the slaves of fashion as women have always been and always will be—that is the great difference between the two sexes. But in Edwardian days, although every woman followed the fashion, she adapted it to her own personality and physique. They kept within the framework but they exploited their own personality, they never all dressed alike. Their waists were movable, their sleeves were long or short, tight or full, balloon or even skimpy. There was a time when sleeves had huge balloons just below the wrist, another time when they were skin tight, decked with buttons and ended in a point just below the knuckles. But although they did not all dress alike they conformed. They never wore a tight skirt in a full skirted period or a loose sleeve when tight ones were in vogue. Their dresses might—and did—go through revolutionary periods but they remained essentially feminine. They had 'figures' of which they were proud and they made the most of them. Emaciation was not a sign of beauty then—but they did not want to be fat. Curves were attractive to men, and they knew it. If Nature had omitted these in their structure, their style of dress allowed for gentle assistance. In other words they padded. For men liked what was called 'a fine woman', so they did not bother much about diets. In those days they had not achieved equality or a vote. They were not anxious about either, in the main. For marriage was their profession; their menfolk looked after them and were inclined to regard them as superior beings, to whom homage was to be paid. The women encouraged this. At public dinners the toast drunk with the most enthusiasm was 'the Ladies'—and almost always the words, 'God Bless Them', were added. Women then believed in the power of mystery, and how right they were. Their legs were secrets, their clothes were not too revealing but enticing. Even when a Directoire style came into vogue and a leg could be glimpsed through a slashed skirt, only a few and ultra-smart women attempted it. Many wore the style, which was most becoming, but eschewed the slash. The fashion was introduced from a musical comedy at Daly's Theatre —the stage set the fashions then—called *Les Merveilleuses*. It did not succeed, largely because the English could not pronounce the name and were not going to look fools by trying to say it. Even when changed to 'the Lady Dandies' it came to nothing much. But it did set the fashion. I remember that my wife—we were engaged then—had a Directoire dress. It was of tobacco brown, with no belt, and had a little coat or bolero, I suppose, with black revers—and the buttons were black too. It was quite charming. But the skirt, needless to say, had no slash.

At one time there was an attempt to introduce what was called a 'harem skirt'—which died a sudden death—men called it the 'harem-skarem' and derided this attempt at female trousers. The women took the hint. Furs were largely worn, but the most exclusive and popular of them were sables and ermine. Mink had not yet come into its own. Fur stoles replaced the one-time fashionable shawls and girls wore little fur tippets round their necks, fastened with the actual head of the little beast who had owned the fur in the first place. In the winter women carried muffs, and that was a charming fashion. They varied too, large and small, round and oblong, all sorts of materials but mostly fur and often of astrakhan, but it depended largely on the main set of furs. These were supported round the neck by cords and sometimes by muff chains, made of metal, gold or silver (or imitation thereof) and very delightful to see. In the summer, when furs were not worn, they were replaced by feather boas—long strips of feathers of all sorts—which were worn according to fashion, sometimes round the neck, sometimes over the shoulders but most fashionably half way down the back and supported by the elbows. That must have been quite a knack. Capes were largely worn and were very fascinating. Few women wore any make-up; it was considered 'fast' and if you were 'fast' then you could not be a lady, and if you were not a lady you were outside the conventional pale—a lost soul. Women guarded and cherished their complexions. To have a good complexion was a gift from the gods—to have a bad one was to be heavily handicapped in the matrimonial stakes. Complexions were guarded like treasure as indeed they were. Some women wore veils—those veils came and went in vogue. They must have been very inconvenient, for they fitted over the hat, and over the face, and were somehow anchored beneath the chin. A lady wishing to have a cup of tea had to roll up that veil and then reset it. Some of the veils were plain, some ornate with velvet blobs on them. It must have impeded the vision. But no woman complained.

There was hardly any dyed hair. It was also considered 'fast' and the sign of prostitution. Marie Corelli was once sued for libel by a lady who ran a hotel in the loveliest part of the country and who found herself described in a Corelli novel as a woman with dyed hair. The lady won—she got a farthing damages. She might have got more but the dyed hair was most apparent. Novelists do not run such risks today.

Women's hair was still their crowning glory and they took the greatest care of it. There was no such thing as bobbing, shingling or the extraordinary coiffures which make the more elderly of us gasp today, nor were there the blonde or white forelocks which became fashionable. The more hair a woman had the more delighted she was. If she could sit on it without bending her head back, that was a great credit to her. The rich ladies who drove up in carriages to the Regent Street shops had ladies' maids who 'did' their hair, and male hairdressers came for special occasions such as balls and Court functions. But the more humble ladies of the middle class, who also thronged Regent Street and its shops, did their own hair. So they saved hours and hours of their time and pounds of their money by evading such things as permanent waves which seem to belie their permanency—nor was there any cutting, snipping and bristly necks. Friends would 'do each other's hair' and take pleasure in it. There were discussions about a style and many were tried and surveyed in the mirror. For women liked individuality, not mass production effects. Hair might be worn piled high on the head or done low on the neck. The lady bowed to the main rule of fashion but suited herself in detail. But it was always 'done up', not left long and dangling like that of a school-girl, as one sometimes sees today—not that the style is unbecoming. The first real landmark in a woman's life was when her skirts went down to her ankles and her hair went 'up'. Fringes came and went. Queen Alexandra, who always wore one, had set a fashion there. A certain amount of false hair was worn and there were things called 'foundations' over which the hair was piled and which acted as support and also as a fixing place for hat pins. But most of these were made from the lady's own hair—she saved the combings in a little bag which hung from the mirror of her dressing table and hairdressers made them up. 'Ladies' Combings Made Up', was the sign—and it was all they got from most women. Little false curls were made of that hair too and artfully pinned in. Fixing long hair meant the use of innumerable hairpins. These were of all sorts, some of wire with little squiggles in each leg, some quite stiff. Hairpins were always falling out and the pavements were littered with them. Men rejoiced in them— they made admirable pipe cleaners. Every woman prayed for naturally curly hair but few of the prayers were answered. So she had to do her best. She washed her own hair just as she dressed it herself. And at night she put it into curlers. Such things still exist but not in the variety of the days of Regent Street's Edwardian glory. And the ladies used curling irons. Like scissors with rounded blades, were these instruments. They were heated either in a candle or over a little methylated lamp on the dressing table. Some even had wavy sides as an extra inducement. There was always a slight smell of singed hair in almost every woman's bedroom or dressing room.

On top of the magnificent head of hair went the hat. That was the keystone of the whole turnout. The hat was of pre-eminent importance. There is no space to describe the numerous changes in ladies' headgear during the life of Regent Street. The Victorian ladies would, of course, throng to that shop of Lewis and Allenby, from which 'the dear Queen' got her millinery. But times changed as hats with them. There were toques, pork pies, bonnets of all kinds; young women did not wear bonnets but matrons did— quite imposing affairs—very ornate and with long ribbons to tie under the chin. That 'dear Queen' Victoria—who deserved her title—wore one at her Diamond Jubilee during which she passed along Regent Street maybe for the last time. It was a black bonnet ornamented with jet and silver, trimmed with white acacia and ostrich feathers, and it held her only gesture to her exalted rank —a diamond aigrette. Bonnets are not much heard about today but some of the older theatres—which are so conservative—used to print on the programme, as regards the seats in the Upper

Circle, 'Bonnets allowed'. The prevailing Edwardian fashion in hats was size. Some of them were stupendous. There was 'picture hats'—of a Gainsborough touch—and there were creations which were truly amazing. The groundwork was either cloth or straw but it was the trimming which mattered. They had flowers, veritable gardens and herbaceous borders, fruit in great piles, feathers and plumes and birds. They had, of course, to be fastened with the hatpins already referred to, long sharp pieces of steel like thin knitting needles, some with plain knobs, some with coloured and some with little jewelled hilts like swords. They had to be used because no hat fitted the head. And the great question which vexed every woman's mind was whether her hat was on straight. But the most charming of all was the Merry Widow hat. One wore one's best when visiting Regent Street. Gloves could be long or short, elbow or wrist length. Smart shoes had Louis heels which were considered high. And there was one type of fur coat which could be seen in Regent Street and its wearer envied by less lucky ladies—and that was one made of sealskin. Such coats were handed down the generations.

Women wore a tremendous amount of underclothing as compared with today. They wore many petticoats, fringed with lace which formed an enchanting foam around their ankles, their corsets were formidable affairs, whalebone covered in silk or other material and laced up the back. These things were never openly displayed in shop windows with the complete lack of reticence of today, but such as were shown were folded up to disguise their real form but to show their quality and lace trimming. Suspenders were not worn; the romantic garter still enclosed the knee, or encircled the silk clad leg just above it. Belts of all sorts were worn and changed in shape according to fashion. They carried handbags but not the species like shopping baskets or carpenter's baskets of the present time. Handbags were of many materials but reasonable in size. They contained much the same litter as now, also a little packet of 'Papier Poudre' for powdering the nose—but not in public—and sometimes a little jar of what was called 'lip salve'—the colour of which actually stayed on the lips. There were no such things as compacts, although there might be a powder puff of swansdown and a little box of powder. No woman ever 'did her face' in public. Skirts were long and swept the ground—most unhygienic, but women handled them with grace.

The sight of an Edwardian lady, stepping out of her brougham, her victoria or landau outside a Regent Street shop was a spectacle which cannot be seen today. The plush liveries had gone but the footman and coachman were there, in hats with cockades, blue coats, striped waistcoats, buckskin breeches and black top-boots with turned down brown tops. The lady swept across the pavement like a queen, like a procession of one, for she knew how to move and carry herself. She had balance and poise, she had elegance and she was one hundred per cent feminine. She paid no attention to the world around, to the envious glances of the less favoured sisters but she proceeded like a ship in full sail, a gracious galleon into the harbour of the favoured emporium. And later came the limousine, the motor, but it never had the same vivid elegance of the carriage and pair.

When night fell and the gas lights glittered, if you happened to be passing the Café Royal or Oddy's, you would see a carriage draw up and the footman leap down to open the door. From it would step the Edwardian lady, complete in grande tenue. Diamonds glittered in her hair and she moved as if on air. Escorted by her cavalier, in white tie, top hat and tails, maybe with evening cloak and gold knobbed stick—she was Night in Regent Street personified.

18

Goodbye Regent Street

There are one or two more things which must be said about Regent Street before the chronicle closes. Amongst its famous shops is Fuller's the confectioners. If you escorted a lady you always gave her Fuller's chocolates in their distinctive white wrapping with the autograph of the firm in red. Fuller's carries on, although now, I believe, in amalgamation. There was another shop which stamped the feminine quality of the street. It stood high upon the left-hand side, going from Piccadilly. The right-hand side has always been considered the better side, though it is doubtful if there is much in that. The ladies of the town stuck to that side and studiously ignored the other, probably because there were such places as Oddy's and the Café Royal there. But this particular shop was notable. It belonged to a firm which sold special dressing for the hair. In the window, with their backs to the passers-by—and their faces quite invisible from any angle— sat a line of ladies displaying their long hair. And what hair it was, it reached down to the floor! There were all shades there, black, brown, tawny, golden, auburn and real red. It attracted men and women alike. The women gazed at the hair in awe and reverence and not a little envy. The men tried to see the faces which that hair framed. One man told me that he actually did so, and was most disappointed—but I am not so sure about it myself. That hair was a glory of Regent Street womanhood and the faces were a secret which Regent Street kept. Life in those Regent Street shops was not a bed of roses for the workers. The hours were long, the rules of service rigid and there was a dignitary called a Shop Walker who ruled with a rod of iron. Shops kept open much later then than now and the windows were not lit up all night. But Regent Street provided the pioneers of early closing. As early as 1843 Swan and Edgar, Redmaynes and Hitchcock and Williams closed at 7 p.m. Other shops kept open much later. In 1844 a meeting was held at the old Exeter Hall by the Metropolitan Drapers' Association to protest at the late hour at which so many shops closed.

Owing to the restlessness of this world, Regent Street was not allowed to enjoy that beauty and serenity which Nash had conferred on it for very long. Destruction actually began in 1897 when the Hanover Chapel which stood on the west side of Regent Street, near Oxford Circus, was demolished. The building which arose was to set the fashion for a new street. That reconstruction went on right through the 1900's up to the First World War, and indeed there were times when Regent Street looked like a battlefield in Flanders. It was still going on in 1922 when Liberty's new buildings were erected, and completed in 1925. In 1927, when King George V and Queen Mary drove down the length of the newly constructed Regent Street, splendour and modernity were there but the old gentle gracious sweep that Nash gave it had gone. It still curved of course, but the heightened buildings seemed to dwarf the elegance and make it much more commonplace, and also to take its old character from it. Here was a magnificent street in a modern city, but something very like it could be found in any capital city anywhere else in the world, whereas the Regent Street of Nash had been unique.

Life flowed along it in the First World War and it was packed with uniforms. It saw the unrest and frustration of the inter-war period, when cloche hats, short skirts and the display of knees, many of which would have been much better hidden, replaced the old and elegant individuality of Edwardian times. It saw the traffic get like a torrent and the internal combustion engine replace the horse. It saw old firms go and new ones arise, and the Age of Equality replace the Age of Degrees. Yet it was still Regent Street and still regal.

I recall a summer's morning in the year 1937 when my wife, my daughter and myself arrived in Regent Street at a very early hour indeed. We had come to see the Coronation of King George VI and we had seats in a window of Swan and Edgar's on the Regent Street side. It was not a bright morning, but dull and inclined to rain, but crowds were there even as early as 7.30 and many had been there all night. We came by our car to as near a point as allowed and then walked the short distance. A friend of mine in the C.I.D. had been in constant telephonic touch with us, telling us about the gathering crowds and when we should start to get through in comfort. We did that all right. We all wore our best and I had my morning coat and shining topper. I had seen two previous Coronations—King Edward VII and King George V. I had seen the Diamond Jubilee of Queen Victoria and her funeral, also that of Edward VII and George V and I had seen the latter's Silver Jubilee. But neither my wife nor my daughter had seen a coronation before, so we did it in style. I had a lot of money in those days—I wish I had it now. We had magnificent seats and Swan and Edgar's did us proud. Breakfasts were served from 8.30 to 10.30 and there was a deliciously served buffet luncheon from 11.30. The most expensive dish, Scotch salmon, cost 2/9d. and a variety of cocktails cost only 1/- each. We had a bottle of Pol Roger in honour of the day and I broke my non-alcoholic rule for His Majesty. Well fed and completely comfortable we saw the pageant of England pass by. I did not think it came up to the previous Coronations and it was far short of the tremendous magnificence of the Diamond Jubilee. But it was all right and it delighted my womenfolk. Mr Baldwin, the Prime Minister got a special cheer, the Navy as usual drew the big acclaim and there was all the pomp and circumstance of steel and scarlet which Elgar put into music so nobly. There was a tremendous cheer for Queen Mary, who was so beloved and who looked so regal. And with that cheer went a nation's sympathy for this great lady who had suffered so much. And there was a great and warm welcome for the new King and his delightful wife as he passed by, a little stiff and upright in his crown and finery. There came from him a feeling, even then, that this was going to be a good and a great monarch. He seemed to radiate reliability; that day was his and his people rejoiced with full hearts and cheering voices as another King George passed along Regent Street which his ancestor, the fourth of his name, had created.

I look at Regent Street today and wonder what some of the Edwardians, who were my contemporaries but who have passed on, would think if they could see it. The street itself they would approve although they would miss the authentic creative note. But what of the life that passes by? That never ending stream of motor vehicles making it almost impossible to cross the road, making it indeed difficult to travel the length even when riding in one. What would they think of the attire of the passers by— the lack of elegance in so many cases, especially among the young—the oddity of appearance and hair style, the odd, foreign looking young men with sidewhiskers and mops of long hair, and the boosting of American goods in windows which once displayed what was British and best? We are told all is prosperous and that we have never had it so good. Some of us—the older ones—rather wonder. Old fashioned and stubborn, we prefer the Regent Street we knew.

19

The Third Magnetic Pole Itself:
Piccadilly Circus

And so we come to Piccadilly Circus, the centre of London, maybe the heart of the world—maybe the most famous spot on the globe. For everybody knows Piccadilly Circus. Young in years in its present form, a most modern place when set against the thousands of years of England's history, its central figure, its rallying point, the Statue of Eros, has become the symbol of London. Small replicas of Eros are what the vast majority of visitors carry away with them to remind them of London town; they buy also replicas of the Tower Bridge, the Tower, Nelson's Monument, but to nothing like the extent that they buy Eros. He is what Mr Cole Porter would call 'The Top'. But he is no ancient monument such as abound in London, he is a very new boy indeed, younger than the writer. Yet he has caught the imagination of the world. He is probably the most photographed statue on earth. Nobody knows why. It is a trite saying—and not very true—that all the world loves a lover; so maybe all the world loves Eros because he is the God of Love.

Piccadilly Circus was completed in about 1820 and it was originally called Regent Circus. Who had lived around here before that?

There was quite a network of streets and fields. There was a gravel pit not far away and of course the famous windmill which

gave Windmill Street its name. Mr Robert Baker, the tailor who
gave the world the name of Piccadilly, owned a lot of the land.
There were three taverns, The Crown, The Horns and The
Feathers. Shrug Lane, already mentioned, crossed it and where it
met Piccadilly was a small close called 'Round Ringill' or
'Rundell'. This seems to have been incorporated into the garden
of a house in which Lady Hutton resided, the first distinguished
resident the Circus ever had. But the Pulteney family owned
most of the land thereabouts and had been in possession for some
time. Their name is enshrined in Great and Little Pulteney Streets.
They went up in the world and became noble and the land they
acquired—and kept on acquiring—constantly rose in value. One
of them, Thomas Pulteney, had held St James's Farm nearby, of
100 acres, in the reign of Elizabeth at a yearly rental of £7.16.0d.
On his property he exhibited a notice saying that it would be
'death to anyone who should presume to open what he had
enclosed'. That sheds a light upon how some of the property was
acquired by the ancient and gentle method known as enclosing.
Later Sir William Pulteney developed some of the land, for when
Sherwood Street was being built he laid out Brewer Street, which
had a brewery in it.

There arose a network of streets, many of which were swept
away when Shaftesbury Avenue was built and many of which were
demolished during the constant rebuildings of Regent Street and
its surroundings. Many old buildings went down in dust when the
Regent Palace hotel arose—between 1912 and 1915. More went
when the fabulous Edward Laurillard built the Piccadilly Theatre
—which is not in Piccadilly or even in Piccadilly Circus—in 1928.
But some of the old names and places survive even yet. Golden
Square is still there but Windmill Fields have gone, for that is now
the site of the Piccadilly Theatre. An old map shows a large pond
on the very spot but let nobody suppose that handsome theatre is
in any way damp. There were Great and Little Gelding Close, a
busy gravel pit, the old plague pit referred to previously and
Golden Square was then Golding Close. It was developed under a

licence from Charles II in 1673 by John Emeline, who made bricks there. There was Silver Street now swallowed by Beak Street. When Denman Street actually came into being is obscure —it is called Queen Street on a map in 1682. It may have got its name from Lord Chief Justice Denman, the doughty champion of poor Queen Caroline of Brunswick, the ill-treated spouse of George IV—for there was a public house on the corner called the Queen's Head which may have been dedicated to the luckless royal lady too. There is still Glasshouse Street, Warwick Street, Air Street and Kingly Street, although at times they had other names. Sherwood Street is almost entirely occupied by the Regent Palace Hotel, but there still remains Snow's Chop House, now entirely modernised, but once a fine example of the old fashioned chop house with oaken pews and cubicles. It had been there for many, many years. In its chophouse days it was a most democratic place where the gentry sat shoulder to shoulder with the working classes and regaled themselves on good old English fare. The great speciality of the house was a huge dried haddock of the finest quality, surmounted by two poached eggs. That cost tenpence and was enough for a family. The old building of Snow's collapsed in 1905 but it was rebuilt and today is a most excellent pub and restaurant. And on the site of the Regent Palace stood another old hostelry—the Brighton—much resorted to by young men about town with money to spend and female companions on whom to spend it. In Warwick Street was The Sceptre Tavern, one of the best eating places in the West End, supplying good genuine English fare cooked in the best English manner, and when the two come together as they did at the Sceptre, nothing can be better. It was run by the same family for generations. Thackeray was there, so was Dickens, and so was that famous silent 'drunk' already mentioned.

Not far away was Foubert's famous riding school and military acadamy, established by Major Foubert, a French refugee in 1681. His name survives in Foubert's Place, which lies only a short distance from the Circus itself.

And who lived round about where the Regent Palace and the Piccadilly Theatre now stand? In Golden Square was Harry St John, Lord Bolingbroke—politician, essayist and hardened Jacobite; William Pitt, father of the Earl of Chatham, the Great Commoner, lived there too, and so did William Windham, another statesman. Angelica Kaufman, who was a painter and decorator, was another resident, so was John Hunter, a famous surgeon and William Plimer a miniaturist of note. To keep the balance even there were also the Brothers Perreau, who were hanged for forgery. And Dickens immortalised Golden Square in *Nicholas Nickleby*. Many musicians lodged in Golden Square and there was a small hotel there which they affected. Pachmann, the great pianist was often there and so, in his young days, was Fritz Kreisler the master violinist, who has many tales to tell about it. Pachmann loved Golden Square and Piccadilly but the best story about him belongs to Birmingham. He was on a tour and a special matinee was booked in Birmingham at very short notice. To his delight it was at once sold out. The finest exponent of Chopin was no fool financially and he rubbed his hands. His manager was Harold Holt, one of the finest musical impresarii this country ever had. Pachmann was eccentric to a degree and his clothes were old, shabby and dirty; you could not make him change. But he told Holt that afternoon to go on and thank the public and to say that he would play an extra piece (we will call it the Nocturne in F minor) and also to say that as he had not played it for some time he would have the music before him. Mr Holt, very dapper, debonair and well dressed went on and bowed. He addressed the audience—many of whom of course were elderly ladies of the very greatest respectability. 'Ladies and gentlemen,' he said, 'the maestro is so delighted with the wonderful support which you have accorded him this afternoon that contrary to his usual custom he will play an extra piece (applause). He will play the Nocturne in F minor (loud applause) but he asks me to say that as he has not played this for some time he will have recourse to the score, just in case—and for this he begs your indulgence.' He bowed and went off to loud applause. Then old Pachmann shuffled on, in his dreadful old clothes and the trousers which he had worn without creasing for at least twenty-five years. Cheers greeted him but he gazed at the audience stolidly. Then, on getting silence —he spoke. 'You see dat man?' he enquired, 'He iss my manager —why, I do not know. His name is Harold Holt—why I do not know. He is very rich, he is well educated, he goes to both Oxford and Cambridge—why I do not know. And another thing I do not know. That he should ask for your indulgence for me—that I do not know! I am Pachmann. I am the greatest bianist in de world. I am the greatest man in the world—more. I am greater than God . . . (and the audience froze into astonished silence) . . . and I will tell you why. God cannot play de biano'— and he sat down and began. That was typical of Pachmann who liked living in that little Golden Square hotel with a fortune in the form of coloured diamonds hidden in the lining of his dreadful old hat.

His Grace the Duke of Grafton set up house in Brewer Street for a young lady friend of his named Nancy Parsons and in Shrug Lane, whilst it was still so called, there was Chatelain, a famous engraver, who ate himself to death by too many lobsters consumed in conjunction with 100 sticks of asparagus. In Gt. Windmill Street itself, Emma Hart—to become Lady Hamilton, Nelson's inamorata, lived with an early lover, Sir Harry Featherstonehaugh who treated her badly. Nelson was not around in those days but there is a link with him nevertheless, for he kept his coffin—the Aboukir coffin—in an undertaker's shop in Brewer Street.

The aspect of all the streets has altered nowadays and for the better. In the early days of this century no lady would have dared walk down Glasshouse Street alone. It was a very rough place and the resort of itinerant musicians and nigger minstrels of the public house door variety. They performed in the street for the delight of the staff of the Café Royal and the Gambrinus, whose living quarters looked out on to Glasshouse Street and who threw them coppers. But irate shopkeepers fetched coppers of another kind and had them moved on. Many of the old buildings swept away were plagued with rats. A neighbouring silversmith had a dog which was a renowned ratter. When sufficient rats had been trapped, they brought them up into Glasshouse Street and let them loose. The dog never let one escape alive. Van drivers and people of all minds crowded to see the 'sport'.

Piccadilly Circus has entirely changed in my lifetime and now the last corner of the older circus is to be pulled down and modernised. It has almost gone as these lines are written. It is the corner where Shaftesbury Avenue flows into the Circus and had become so familiar to us that the idea of a change shocked us all. There is, also as I write, violent opposition to the proposed new buildings which include a tower and a vast advertising site, although advertising has been a feature of the Circus for years. But there is no saving the Monico, the famous hotel which occupied so much of the space. Only a few fragments of outer wall still stand and one can see the marks of the old staircases and dining rooms and still some of the faded decoration. The Monico was a very cosmopolitan place. You could meet everybody there if you so chose. You could dine, lunch or sup in an atmosphere of complete respectability; but in and around it were crooks, con men, racecourse gangs and tough characters of all sorts. It was all right if they knew you. And if you were broke you could always borrow ten bob in the Monico bar. But in the restaurant the food, wines and service were beyond reproach and it was extremely well run and orderly.

There was a nice touch of sentiment about the old place too, for it was the scene of a very celebrated if somewhat unusual wedding breakfast. The day was 3rd October 1893. A young couple had just been married—almost a runaway wedding at the Brentford Register Office. He was a very handsome and forceful young man of great charm and she was a sweetly pretty girl, wearing a navy blue dress, and navy blue straw hat trimmed with white wings. They drove away from the Register Office in a rickety old hansom and then determined to make for the centre of things—for Piccadilly Circus. They paid off the hansom and boarded a horse bus—the old knifeboard type—and so came to the Third Magnetic Pole, whose pull they had felt. They entered the Café Monico and had their wedding breakfast all by themselves. No guests, no speeches, just the two of them. They had Irish stew and a bottle of Burgundy. The young man's name was Seymour Hicks and his bride was Ellaline Terriss. They were destined for a long and happy married life—they celebrated their Golden Wedding—and both were destined for fame in their profession. The very beautiful silver haired gracious lady who is now Lady Hicks still graces this world. She mourns her husband —she finds pleasure in her daughter, her grandson and her friends —but she will, I know, regret the passing of the Monico.

Before the Monico was built there was a forgotten little place of entertainment on the site called the International Hall. In it performed a troupe of nigger minstrels who needed no burnt cork, because they were all coloured men. They were led by the Bohee Brothers, who were very great artists indeed. James Bohee was about the best banjoist the world ever knew—he made the banjo into a society craze and taught the Prince of Wales (King Edward VII) how to play it. His brother George did the singing and had a magnificent tenor voice, full of feeling and expression. His most famous song, which swept the world, was 'A Boy's Best Friend is His Mother'.

That vanishing corner of Piccadilly was never one of architectural beauty or even distinction but it was a bit of London we Londoners treasured. For years past it has been covered with advertising signs which filled the night with flickering colour and meretricious gaiety. At one time it was called 'The Scotsman's Cinema'. The canny Scot could watch the constant changes and a sixpence never banged. One is aware that advertising signs at such a wonderful spot bring in vast revenue. This is a blatant, loud shrieking age. Publicity pops up everywhere—it dominates one of the two sources of the marvel of television, it keeps the news-

papers and periodicals going and defaces beauty spots and land-
scapes. I have dealt in publicity and know something about it. I
know the value of a site and I cannot help thinking nevertheless
that it is a pity one of our most valuable tourist attractions should
be merely an advertising hoarding. No doubt the brilliant lights
delight the young people. Keep the lights but use them for a
better cause. There has been a suggestion, still under debate, that
Piccadilly Circus should be a great funfair and holiday centre.
But we might make a real effort to save a precious spot. Piccadilly
Circus has never had a really famous person live in it but it has
added perhaps just one event to the history of its country, for on
the corner where Shaftesbury Avenue runs into the Circus stands
the London Pavilion, Piccadilly Circus's own music hall. It is a
cinema today and the original music hall was rebuilt years ago.
But the London Pavilion is famous. It began a short distance away
from its present site, over a stable yard of the Black Horse Inn in
Titchborne Street. The mourning trappings used in the funeral of
the Duke of Wellington were kept there. Then two men, named
Loibl and Sonnenhammer took it over and made it a kind of free
and easy music hall. You brought a drink voucher which admitted
you free to the show, you had your drink, watched the entertainment and, the landlords hoped, had many more drinks as well.
You could also eat. There were galleries along three sides of the
hall and in one of them was the so-called scientific collection of
Dr Kahn, a collection of waxwork horrors which would not be
tolerated today. It may be some lingering form of auto-suggestion
from those things which is the cause of so many horrific films now
being shown at the London Pavilion Cinema. But the place made
money and stars rose there. And from that rather dingy, beer-
stained, spirit-smelling and smoky spot, history was made. In
1878, a writer of music hall songs, a most precarious occupation
in those days, read a story in an evening paper which gave him
inspiration for a song. His name was G. W. Hunt. He went home,
and he wrote the song during the night. Next morning, at the
almost unheard of hour of eight a.m.—unheard of by the man on

whom he called, who was the Great Macdermott, a famous music hall star—Hunt called on his chosen singer. He woke Macdermott up and told him he had a song for him, but the star threw a boot at his head. Hunt persisted and eventually made the artist listen to his song. 'You must sing it tonight, at the Pavilion,' he said. And Macdermott agreed. The night came and the song was ready. Macdermott, a huge man with sweeping whiskers and a powerful voice, sang that song with all the force and vehemence at his command. Starting right at the back of the stage he made a dramatic stride forward after each line and sang: 'We don't want to fight, but, by jingo, if we do, We've got the ships, we've got the men, we've got the money too.' The audience roared its approval, of the singer and the sentiment. He had to sing it over and over again. People rushed outside and called in friends from pubs. That song was all over London by midnight and was setting the country ablaze before the night following. It was electric. It hit the right note at the right moment. Russian aggression was threatening Turkey, weak and ill-ruled; England stood by and did nothing although aware of the peril. The Government shilly-shallied. That song was a kind of Marseillaise. It was shouted and howled everywhere. The Foreign Secretary sneaked down to the shabby Pavilion to hear it. The great French newspaper *Le Figaro* printed it in a special edition. The people clamoured that the Russians should not have Constantinople, and the Government changed its policy. The British Fleet moved in, the Russians climbed down and they did not get Constantinople—indeed they have not got it yet. It was a song from Piccadilly Circus which altered the destiny of Europe—probably the only historic event to which the Circus can lay claim. It put the word 'jingo' into our language, and as a result, Turkey presented this country with Cyprus. And G. W. Hunt, who conceived the whole thing? Oh, he got £5.

Albert Chevalier the great coster vocalist made his variety debut at the London Pavilion—and there was another romance there. One day, Mr Loibl, one of the partners who controlled it, was handed a note from a celebrated agent. Something seemed to have an effect on him and he said that the woman who brought it might come in. And in she came. She was a tiny little creature, almost in rags, obviously desperately poor and more than half starved. She looked at him with a mute appeal for help and mercy in her eyes. Something about her impressed him. 'All right, my dear,' he said, 'I happen to want an extra turn. You can appear tonight. Get yourself ready.' She had few preparations to make except to dash home and see if her baby was safe. She had had nothing to eat all day, but she stood ready for her 'turn'. She was announced—and she went on. She showed such vim, such vitality, such attack, such enormous talent that the customers forgot their steaks, chops and even their beer and stood up to see her better, so small was she. And at the end they clamoured for more. She had to sing and dance again and again, there was such enthusiasm for this amazingly vital little creature. The great George Leybourne (Champagne Charlie himself) was the next turn, but that little woman 'stopped the show' and at the end, when she could do no more, the great Lion Comique came on and held her up in his arms for all to see and acclaim. It was complete triumph. Upstairs in the manager's office she was praised, given a contract and a glass of champagne. 'By the way', said Loibl to her, 'you might have a look at the note your agent gave you to bring to me.' She took it and she read it. This is what it said, 'Dear Loibl, don't trouble to see the bearer. I have merely sent her up to get rid of her. She is troublesome.' The girl who had scored the triumph fainted away. Loibl had taken that chance and a great star was born—Jenny Hill, the Vital Spark, who rose to fame and fortune.

Loibl rebuilt the shabby little hall and it moved right into the Circus. It was rebuilt again in 1885 and that is the building one sees today. For how long, one wonders? Later in its career C. B. Cochran did a marvellous series of revues, which were the true essence of Piccadilly Circus. One of the London Pavilion partners, Sonnenhammer, broke away from the concern but he did not go far. He founded Scott's, the splendid restaurant which still stands today, with its little minarets and towers and Victorian embellishments, and still purveys the best of everything, still has a feeling for the spacious and more elegant days. Nowhere does a lobster and a bottle of cool Sauterne taste better than at Scott's.

Underneath the London Pavilion was a beer cellar, which announced its presence by a large shining red spade trade mark— Spatenbrau. There you could get the best glass of lager in London, there you could get the dunkel lager—the München-Löwenbräu —just as one drank it in Germany. There is a good bar still there. But it is no longer the Spaten. Across the road, at the top of the Haymarket, was another landmark. Here you could get a light meal and a drink free from any annoyance or the importunity of prostitutes, who thronged the Circus. It was called Appenrodt's and was a famous delicatessen shop. It was cheap and it was superlatively good. It offered an amazing number of dishes of all kinds, its salads were a speciality, its Russian salad the very crème de la crème. You could stand at the counter or sit at a table. There were Continental delicacies of all kinds, sausages in bewildering variety, wonderful salami, splendid lager and coffee it was a privilege to drink. For half a crown you were as replete as an old time Alderman at a Lord Mayor's Banquet. When the first war came an English firm took over and of course it was never the same. The snack and coffee bars which today bestrew the West End could not have lived with Appenrodt's.

One great rock of stability still stands in the Circus to keep alive the older days and that is the Criterion Restaurant. It has been completely modernised inside but the exterior is the same as when it arose in 1873 at a cost of £80,000. It was run by Spiers and Pond who were great caterers at that time. It was a big success; to lunch in Piccadilly Circus was something, and amidst luxurious surroundings and distinguished company, too. For everybody went to the 'Cri' and you could always see a large sprinkling of stage folk there. That was unusual in those days when the people of the theatre, the sons and daughters of illusion, wisely kept themselves to themselves and did not mix. Still, it did no harm to be glimpsed occasionally lunching at the 'Cri'. West End, suburbs and provinces all converged upon it. It flourishes today. But one of the outstanding features has gone. That was the Criterion Long Bar. The Trocadero had a Long Bar but that was as nothing to the Long Bar at the Cri. It was the most famous bar in London and indeed a microcosm of London itself. It was all marble with pillars supporting arches down each side and it had a kind of mosaic roof. The bar ran the entire length and there were plenty of tables. You would not find many people there until lunch time—remember that bars opened early then, but there was a good brisk trade at lunch. There was an array of barmaids and memory seems to insist that they were all dark and fuzzy-haired. There were scores of waiters with white aprons.

All the world went to the Long Bar—but not its wife. No ladies were admitted. In the evening it was thronged with men of all sorts and conditions in the democracy of drinking. Here were big men from the City, men of the arts as well as of commerce, men in all walks of life—crooks, thieves, forgers, swindlers, rubbing shoulders with men with enormous bank balances. There were jockeys and racing men, professional backers, bookmakers and touts. There were men of distinction and men who had the distinction of being well known to the police. Soldiers, sailors, tinkers, tailors, all used the Cri Long Bar.

Nobody who was sober and who behaved was refused. There were never any disturbances or fights. If sometimes some voices were raised, the waiters and the barmaids saw that peace was kept. Maybe one saw a rather bulky gentleman in a plain blue suit edge a bit nearer, and one realised he was the law out of uniform but on duty. Sometimes a rather furtive eyed man would come in, order a drink, see one of these rather stolid gentry, and be gone before he was served. It got very rowdy on Boat Race Nights but that was expected and so it did on Derby Night. Cup Finals had not reached their immense importance in the palmy days of the Long Bar. There was always a sprinkling of provincials with whom smartly dressed crooks would get into conversation, and always a sprinkling of rather callow youths 'up West' to See Life. You saw life in the Criterion Long Bar. Next to the Empire Promenade it was the most likely place in which to run into an old friend from abroad. The barmaids were omniscient. They knew all the regulars. If you left a message for a friend he always got it. It was a place of complete male democracy, where there was solid drinking but little drunkenness, and the stuff sold was the best. It was cheap; a Scotch cost you threepence and a splash of soda was free. If you wanted a box of matches, they gave you one. Bitter was twopence, but there was not much call for that. Everything from champagne to cider, from burgundy to beer, from port to peppermint was drunk there. I remember an old habitué who was there every evening. He was tall and portly with beautifully brushed silver hair and a complexion wonderfully matured. The salient feature was the nose which out Welling-toned Wellington. His drink never varied. It was always what he called Ginger Gin. And as it went down his throat I swear sparks came out of that nose. There are no longer such places as the Long Bar. Perhaps it is for the better, perhaps for the worse. Nowadays they all go home and watch 'the telly', or push into milk and coffee bars and consume American food. The Long Bar at the Cri was as British as the British Empire. Both have gone now.

The Criterion Theatre still stands, for which those who love the Circus may be grateful. When it opened in 1874 it was the only underground theatre in London. It had originally been a wine cellar. It did not succeed at first but then a man named Charles Wyndham came on the scenes and he by his genius and judgment made this small place one of the smartest theatres in London. He had a policy, which is invaluable in a theatre. He ran it at first as a home for light and slightly risqué farce—as risqué was then understood—of the type popularised at the Palais Royal in Paris. But he and his leading lady—Mary Moore, who later married him—raised the Criterion to a very high standard indeed. The best plays, the finest comedies and the best of acting were there. Wyndham pervaded the whole place; he never missed a single thing. And he and Mary Moore, who besides being a great actress was a splendid business woman, founded a little empire of their own, the Criterion, the New and Wyndhams Theatres. Those theatres still remain in the family—for in command today is Sir Bronson Albery (son of Lady Wyndham by her first marriage) a theatre manager of supreme quality and integrity, and his son, Donald Albery. Long may that family, which sprang from the Cri in Piccadilly Circus, flourish for the good of the living theatre. I have a very tender memory of a play I saw there many years ago now, when I was a boy in fact, called *Rosemary*. It was produced there in 1896—written by Louis N. Parker and Murray Carrington. I was taken to see it as a birthday treat but I am sure my people wanted to see it too and this was a good excuse for an extra theatre visit. It was, of course, costume and sentiment but it was as sweet and wholesome as the herb whose name it bore. I can remember the dainty charm of Mary Moore and the gracious dignity and mellow voice of Wyndham today, and I can even recall some of the dialogue.

Wyndham's favourite part was that of 'David Garrick' in the play of that name. He became identified with it and was always reviving it. He loved to sit under the portrait of Garrick in the Garrick Club. A great joker and wit of the period, one Charles Brookfield, took advantage of this. Wyndham was playing Garrick at the Criterion and was, one lunch time, sitting in his favourite spot beneath the picture. Mr Brookfield made it his business to pass by. As he greeted Wyndham, he gave a start and stopped. He stared at the actor and he stared at the portrait, and he muttered, 'Strange, strange.' 'What is strange, Charles?' asked Wyndham. 'Your amazing likeness to Garrick,' said the joker. 'Do you think so?' said Wyndham, really delighted. 'Yes, yes,' said Brookfield,'So like him by day—and so unlike him at night.' —and passed on. Sir Charles Wyndham was a much more handsome man than Garrick and a great pillar of the theatre and Piccadilly Circus.

Swan and Edgar's dominated the Circus then as it does now. You could not miss it. It was the great trysting place of London —'meet you outside Swan and Edgars' was the appointment made by millions, and millions went inside too, as they do today. There was nothing else in the Circus of much distinction before its re-building; several railways' booking and parcel offices there were destroyed by enemy action in the First World War.

The coming of the tube railways made a great difference—the Bakerloo arrived in 1905 and the Great Northern and Piccadilly in 1906. So now one went to the Circus underground as well as on top. I remember Piccadilly when the horse buses crowded it— or so we thought—and all the traffic was horse drawn, and I remember the clatter of the hooves, the tinkle of the hansoms as they bowled swiftly and smoothly along. I remember the victorias, the landaus, the broughams, the dog carts and the phaetons, the great horse drawn vans and the brewers' drays, with such horses as one can still see used by Messrs Whitbreads. The brewers' men were giants. They had Herculean strength and carried barrels as we might carry a bottle. They had leather aprons, and knitted brewers' caps on their heads. They have vanished altogether. I watched the onrush of mechanism, the beginnings of the motor cars, the electric broughams, and then the taxis and I watched the horses go. To cross Piccadilly Circus today is a feat and the safest way is underground, but in my youth, although it teemed with life and traffic, nobody got run over. Piccadilly Circus was always busy, day and night. Always one felt its lure and always one put on one's best clothes when going up West—which to most people meant Leicester Square and Piccadilly Circus. On warm summer nights it had a charm of its own for every building had its window boxes. On wet nights it shone and glistened like polished onyx. But the lure was greatest at night. From six o'clock it really came alive as the Magnetic Pole drew all sorts of people to it. The prostitutes—the ladies on the Dilly—seldom used the southern side, but they were crowded on the pavements as far as the London Pavilion. There they turned and retraced their steps back across Leicester Square again. There were plenty of policemen and they seemed much larger and indeed were much larger than the officers of today and, to us who were younger, they seemed older. Many wore beards. It was a common sight to see two of them taking a drunk or a lawbreaker off to the station in Vine Street, with a tail of riff-raff following on. But there was no coshing and no flick knives and nobody got their faces kicked in.

Boat Race Night in Piccadilly Circus was traditional. Everyone went mad. They shouted, they danced, they did all sorts of things. Queer, improvised round dances grew and grew until hundreds were capering. Young men in evening dress felt impelled to ride on the roof of hansom cabs and shout all the while. Very few of the revellers had ever been to Oxford or Cambridge even as a visitor or tourist but there was a leavening of revelling undergraduates. This was tradition. Their fathers and grandfathers had done this and they must follow on. The ladies of the town did a fine trade; so did the pubs, who removed everything breakable off the bars and tables. Boat Race Night was one of London's great holiday nights, but today the Boat Race does not arouse the same enthusiasm. The police, heavily reinforced, were very forbearing. They understood. You had to behave very badly to get run in. The commonest cause was to knock off a 'bobby's' helmet. That did it. You were up before the beak in the morning. Yet I know some men who still treasure those helmets as trophies.

Probably the greatest night Piccadilly Circus ever saw was that on which the news came of the Relief of Mafeking. That broke quite late in the evening. It was announced in the theatres, restaurants and music halls, and London went mad. The West End converged on Piccadilly Circus. Such scenes will never come again. This was victory at a time when it was needed. Its fall would not have affected the course of the Boer War two hoots but it had held on—it had, in its truly British way, never dreamt of surrendering. To say pandemonium broke loose is to understate. All reserve vanished like a theatre curtain ascending, people embraced, everybody seemed to be old friends bent on celebrating. They sang, they danced, they made high holiday. Street vendors appeared as if by magic, everybody had a Union Jack, everybody had a tickler and many had squirts. To the uninitiated a tickler was a peacock feather, peddled at one penny, with which you tickled everybody within reach. A squirt spoke for itself. Fortunately squirts soon got empty and could not be refilled. Nobody will ever see such scenes again, for the nation has changed now and different temperaments prevail. I saw Piccadilly Circus at the outbreak of the First World War, on Armistice Day, 1918, and on both the peace days in the last war, but that was nothing to Mafeking Night. It just cannot be described. Imagine a host of men and women of all kinds, classes and costumes, all mixed together in a vast mob and all letting themselves go without any attempt at reserve. Traffic gave it up and made diversions. Members of the Forces were carried shoulder high— even some policemen were so treated. I was a lucky lad to see it.

Perhaps my most vivid memory of it is a small procession of men trying to force their way through the crowd and being cheered to the echo. They all carried broomsticks and on the end of the sticks were loaves of bread. Hastily written labels proclaimed this as 'Food for Mafeking'. No wonder the verb 'to Maffick' became general.

Night-life in Piccadilly in the Edwardian days went through stages. The real crowding began shortly after six and reached its height as people proceeded to the theatres and music halls around half past seven and eight. At eight or thereabouts it would slacken off although the pavements were thronged with all sorts and conditions of men and women and there were crowds going in and out of the pubs. And then at about eleven, it became a whirlpool, as the crowds emerged from their entertainments. Viewed from above it was like a disturbed ant hill. Vehicles of all kinds, people of all kinds, hurrying and scurrying but not with the blind haste of today for there was more leisure. At about half past one Piccadilly Circus became fairly quiet.

In the midst of it all stood the Guardian Angel, the Spirit of the

place, the statue of Eros. Today he symbolises London. He is a
newcomer. He only arrived on the 29th June 1893, and he was
unveiled by His Grace the Duke of Westminster. There was not a
lot of fuss about it. The statue is the work of Alfred Gilbert.
Nobody paid much attention to him and most of them were not
quite clear as to who he was—some foreign god, they reckoned,
and the general impression was that he might be Mercury. Greek
mythology was not the Cockneys' strong point. Nor were they
interested as to why he was put there—the authorities were always
shoving up these statues. If it was to a king or a general they could
recognise them, but this chap with a bow and arrow—and the
arrow wasn't there—well, who cared? There he stood, a gentle
fountain playing round his feet, but few if any took the trouble to
read the inscription which surrounded the statue itself and
gleamed through the silver water. It says 'Erected by Public
Subscription to Antony Ashley Cooper, Seventh Earl of Shaftesbury. During a public life of half a century he devoted the
influence of his station, the strong sympathies of his heart and the
great powers of his mind to honouring God by serving his fellow
men, an example to his order, a blessing to this people and a name
to be by them ever gratefully remembered'.

It is as simple and noble as the man himself. But who reads it, I
wonder? When Eros first arose he did so from a bed of flowers and
perfume, for at his base sat the flower girls of London, their
baskets full of posies, so fresh, so lovely and so cheap. You could
buy anything from a buttonhole to a bouquet and the 'girl' who
served you would freshen her wares from the Eros fountain itself.
You ran no risk in those days of being run over as you crossed to
the island. The world 'girl' was figurative. Mostly they were
motherly souls, with fresh, brown faces, for they spent their lives
in the open air. They wore a variety of hats or bonnets, voluminous skirts, boots which were mostly disasters—and always an
elaborate shawl. They were one of the sights of London and more
people looked at them and bought their wares than looked at
Eros.

Then London decided to go underground, as far as Piccadilly Circus was concerned. The tube railways made a great station, with shops, and all sorts of things right under the circus, under Eros himself. The flower girls were evicted and went with wrath and sorrow. And Eros himself was taken down because of the mining operations beneath him. That happened about 1925. At once London missed him. They demanded him back, they never knew how much they loved him until he had gone. And return he did, to be crowned King of all London's statues, to be the epitome of London itself. He now stood on top of the world and he stands there today. He was protected during the Second World War and he is protected now when fun and games are likely in the Circus for young men have an ambition to climb up on top of him and that is not allowed. It is *lèse-majesté*. And there he stands today surrounded by a maelstrom of traffic. He pays no attention to that. He is perhaps wondering what target his discharged arrow has transfixed. He should know by this time. It has transfixed the heart of the world. For from all corners of the earth they come, all races, creeds and colours, to visit Piccadilly Circus. They gaze and they wonder. Men and women, youths and girls, in all sorts of attire sit around the base of Eros, and watch the traffic revolve, feeling the world go round. They are supremely happy. They stay there for hours. I have asked them why they do it and it is always the same reply. 'This is the centre of all things, you know. We can hear the heart of the world throb.' The phraseology is different but the sentiment the same, and it comes in all languages. They stand in the Circus at all points of vantage and take pictures of Eros. Day and night, the cameras click and flash. They go reluctantly—and turn to take one last look—one last picture. They surge up from the underground, and their faces are blank, but when they emerge into Piccadilly Circus something lights up inside and a smile comes—the magic works. They all look round at Eros. This place is magic.

Piccadilly Circus changes, has changed, is changing now, will change again. But perhaps the magic which lay in the soul of that great man whom Eros commemorates may keep the power and the imagery and the attraction which Eros radiates always alive and perhaps, who knows—even if we say Goodbye Piccadilly— we may never say Goodbye Piccadilly Circus—or Goodbye Eros—the symbol of London town. For despite warring generations London has a habit of enduring and going on.

Coventry Street, 30th March 1960.

Index

INDEX

Dens, 229
Denman, Lord Chief Justice, 321
Denman St, 288, 321
Derby Day, 50-1, Plan 150
Desaguliers, R. E., Lieutenant, 197
Dèvant, David, 81
Deveil, Mr Justice, 243-4
Devonshire, Duke of, 29, 30; Dukes of, travel together, 33
Devonshire, Georgiana, Duchess of, 30, 226; canvasses, 31
Devonshire House, 30, 121; last of, 162; new, 163; gates, 163, 204
Diamond Jubilee, 232, 284
Dickens, Charles, 52, 77, 270, 311
Dickson, Dorothy, 185
Didcott, Hugh J., 284
Dilly, Ladies of the, 22, 90, 94, 125, 144, 171, 174, 182, 189, 323
Directoire style, 299
D'Israeli, 66
Diversions of the Morning, 245
Dodsley, 59
Dogcart, 99, 323
Doghouse Close, 218
Dorland House, 260
Dorset, Duke of, 226
Dover, Earl of, 28
Dover St, 28
Dowton, actor, 247
Drawing Room Entertainments, 260-1; changes, 124
Dress, 92, 105, 129, 171, 248; clergymen, 131; clubmen, 128; coachmen, 99; party, 117; evening, 133
Drinking, 136, 229-30; good, 321
Drivers, 123
Drury Lane, 262; theatre, 183
Dudley, Countess of, 55
Dudley St, 272
Duels, 194, 200
Duke St, 47
Dunbar, Lord, 208
Duncombe, the Ladies, 73
Dundreary, Lord, whiskers, 92, 247
Dunkirk, 177

Early closing, 306
East India Company, 48
Eccentric Club, 284

Eden, Sir Anthony, 131, 186
Edward VII, 102, 111, 169, 287; likes and dislikes, 112; racing, 295
Edward VIII, 169, 170
Edward St, 218
Edwardes, George, 136
Edwardian type, 135
Egremont, Earl of, 37
Egyptian Hall, 77, 79, 119; end, 84; magic, 80
Elgar, 308
Elizabeth I, 225
Ellis, Vivian, 278
Ellison, Sydney, 249; and the Aussie, 250; offends, 251; contents bill, 251
Emeline, John, 321
Emery, Winnifred, 216
Empire Promenade, 321
Enclose, 320
Engineers' Club, 217
Entertaining, 106
Entertainment, 76
Eros, 12-13, 326; inscription, 326; returns, 327; slaves of, 18; as symbol, 309
Escort, 108
Establishment, 113, 158
Etheredge, May, 280
Etiquette, 106
Evasion of Military Service, 150
Evelyn, 26, 29; records, 225
Everett, Edward, 79
Exeter Hall, 306

Faces coloured, 188
Factory Act, 269
Fanum House, 217
Farce risqué, 321
Farquhar, George, 227
Fascists, 162
Fashions, 165, 298; fur, 300
Favours, 28
Feathers, 302
Feathers, The, 320
Featherstonehaugh, Sir Harry, 313
Feldman, Bert, 274-5; suspends rent, 276; music publisher, 274; publishes *Tipperary*, 276
Female figures, 299
Fête, 202

333

INDEX

INDEX

Tipperary, 142
Titchborne St, 316
Titchfield St, 24, 288
Titiens, 232
Tivoli, 277
Tonson, Jacob, 59
Toppers, 130
Tower besieged, 192
Trade, 43
Tradition, 36
Trafalgar Square, 225
Traffic, 118; congestion, 98; lights, 164
Transport, 224
Tree, Sir Herbert Beerbohm, 132, 216, 223; actor-manager, 248; character, 234-5; and the horse, 236; in Berlin, 237; at rehearsals, 237; at hairdressers, 237; illusion principle, 232; banquets, 233; as actor, 234; sympathises, 239
Trocadero Long Bar, 320; Restaurant, 284; transformed by J. Lyons and Co, 285
Trousers, women in, 151
Tube railways, 174, 327
Tupper, Martin, on John Hatchard, 70
Tyburn, 191

Ugliness, Age of, 165
Umbrellas, 132
Underclothing, 303
Unemployment, 166
Unicorn, The, 227
Uniforms, 175-6
Unknown soldier, 251-2

Vanbrugh, Sir John, 230
Vanbrugh theatre burnt down, 231
Varieties, Theatre of, 276
Vedrenne, J. E., 282
Veils, 300
Verry's Restaurant, 293
Vestas matches, 134
Vestris and wife, 231
Victoria, Queen, 50, 80, 93, 169, 287
Victoria Theatre (Old Vic), 261
Victorian era, end of, 109, 111
Victorias, 323
Victory in Europe, 187; in sight, 146
Village, model, 270

Vine Street Police Station, 153, 324
Violante, Madame, 242
Vista, 266
Volunteers, 200

Waitresses, 157
Waller Lewis, 193, 216, 280
Wallis, Miss, 280
Wallis, Bertram, 223
Walking sticks, 132
Walpole, Horace, 32
Walpole, Sir Robert, 242-3
Walsingham House Hotel, 119
War 1914, 142-3; 1939, 173; again, 172; Declaration, 144; trench, 148
Warcup, Edward, 226
Ward, Roland, 84
Wardour St, 218
Wartime, 147
Warden, Chief (author), 179, 183
Wardens, 174
Warren's Hotel, 259
Warwick, Lady, 73
Warwick St, 252, 321
Warwork, women's, 151
Watch chains, 134
Waterloo Place, 257-9, 265
Waterloo Tavern, 226
Watier chef, his club, 37
Watson, Horace, 248
Waxworks, 316
Wealth, 113
Webster, Benjamin, 247
Welchman, Harry, 280
Wellesley, Lady Charlotte, 201
Wellesley, Sir Henry, 201
Wellington, Duke of, 41, 170, 201, 269; Museum, 41
Wentworth, Thomas, 28
West End Hotel, 211, 221-2
Westbrook, Harriet, 195
Westminster, Duke of, 326
Westminster Election, 30
Weston, Garfield, 56
Westward expansion, 24
Whiskers, 92, 105, 124
White feather, 149
White Horse, The, 227; cellars, 119
Whitcombe St, 207, 209
Whitehall, 29, 225, 266

343